Galveston
and the Great West

Number Sixty-Nine:
The Centennial Series
of the Association of Former Students,
Texas A&M University

Galveston
and the
Great
West

Earle B. Young

Texas A&M University Press
College Station

All photos appearing in this book are courtesy
of the Rosenberg Library, Galveston, Texas

The paper used in this book meets the minimum requirements
of the American National Standard for Permanence
of Paper for Printed Library Materials, Z39.48-1984.
Binding materials have been chosen for durability.

Library of Congress Cataloging-in-Publication Data

Young, Earle B., 1929–

    Galveston and the great West / Earle B. Young.

        p.   cm. — (Centennial series of the Association of Former
Students, Texas A&M University ; no. 69)

    Includes bibliographical references (p.   ) and index.

    ISBN 0-89096-773-3 (cloth)

    1. Galveston (Tex.)–History. 2. Galveston (Tex.)–Economic
conditions. 3. Transportation–Texas–Galveston–History. I. Title.
II. Series.

F394.G2Y68   1997

976.4'139–dc21   97-19543

                                                      CIP

To my dearest wife,

Gaynelle.

*Without her caring love, the contentment
required to complete this task
would have been impossible.*

Contents

Illustrations

Preface

This is a book about an idea and its implementation. The port city that Galveston came to be by 1900 was the result of the flow of ideas in the years immediately after the Civil War. Then followed thirty-five years of implementation, when the ideas of dreamers and thinkers were turned into concrete results by practical men. It was engineers, bankers, politicians, civic leaders, attorneys, craftsmen, mechanics, and laborers who finally shaped a world-class harbor capable of handling the largest ships afloat.

This is also a study of origins. At several points it is necessary to stop the chronological narrative and look at some other influences upon Galveston's history. A better understanding should result from these short deviations. Of course, nothing is more interesting than rediscovering someone who had been virtually lost to history, such as Caleb G. Forshey and Judge Robert G. Street, who played important roles in Galveston's history.

At one time it seemed that it was going to take thirty-five years to tell the story. However, having already retired from one profession, I saw that there was not that much remaining time to practice a second career and found ways to hurry things.

After mulling around in general Galveston history for a time, I ran across this subject of "deep water." Unable to find the in-depth information on the subject that would have satisfied my curiosity, I soon found myself doing the research that eventually led to this book. I just hope I have been able to make the subject as interesting and compelling to the reader as it was to me.

As the research progressed I discovered the work of Professor William H. Goetzmann, whose books focused on the roles that scientists and engineers have played in American and world history. These books suggested to me what I wanted to do in telling Galveston's story—focus on the role that engineers played. However, the story was bigger than that, and it was necessary to include many others who helped bring about deep water.

My previous experiences in life also led me to write this book. I served in the Army Corps of Engineers as a second lieutenant, after graduating from the Engineer office candidate school. Then I spent my working career in an engineering environment at the Johnson Space Center, where I was a budget officer. My curiosity about the subject of deep water increased considerably when I began to find certain parallels between the management of a federally funded engineering project in the nineteenth century and a federally funded space program in the twentieth century.

This book is an example of what one historian has called "aspect" books, that is, it deals with only one aspect—albeit a very important one—of Galveston's history. Readers might also want to read a general history such as Charles W. Hayes's *Galveston: A History of the Island and the City*, David G. McComb's *Galveston: A History*, or Gary Cartwright's *Galveston: A History of the Island*. Earl Wesley Fornell's *The Galveston Era: The Texas Crescent on the Eve of Secession* and Margaret Swett Henson's *Samuel May Williams: Early Texas Entrepreneur* are excellent for the history prior to the Civil War. James P. Baugham has written two books about the shipping lines operating out of Galveston, *Charles Morgan and the Development of Southern Transportation* and *The Mallorys of Mystic. The Road to Spindletop* by John Stricklin Spratt covers the history of Texas between 1875 and 1901.

I wish to acknowledge the contribution to the concept of this book made by three earlier works: Bernard Axelrod's "Galveston: Denver's Deep Water Port"; Robert H. Peebles's "The Galveston Harbor Controversy of the Gilded Age"; and Ruth Evelyn Kelly's "'Twixt Failure and Success: The Port of Galveston in the Nineteenth Century" (master's thesis, University of Houston, 1975).

As a first-timer learning to make use of their excellent archives, I received a lot of assistance from the staff of Rosenberg Library in Galveston. Without the expertise of Casey Greene, then archivist and now head of special collections at Rosenberg, frustration and discouragement may have set in early. Eventually, with the help of Casey, archivists Margaret Schlankey and Shelly Kelly, assistant archivist Anna Peebler, and archivist clerk Julia Dunn, I became a trained researcher.

I am also grateful to a large number of library staff members at the University of Houston–Clear Lake, the University of Houston–Central Campus, the Barker and Perry-Casteneda Libraries at the University of Texas, Texas A&M University, the Corps of Engineers, and other university and public libraries located throughout the West. At Denver, the Colorado Historical Society and the public library staffs were very helpful. The cheerful assistance of these librarians made my task much easier.

Galveston
and the Great West

Chapter 1

Richardson Points the Way—West

Galveston was in its heyday in the 1890s. It was one of the nation's leading ports and the outlet to the world's oceans for the vast area between the Mississippi River and the Rocky Mountains and was connected to the nation's interior by a network of railroads. In the process of reaching this point, two of the tycoons of the "Gilded Age," Jay Gould and Collis P. Huntington, had been in and out of the city seeking to establish facilities for their continent-spanning, land-sea transportation systems.

This is the history of the creation of that port and its railroad connections—a story that begins with the damage and population decline inflicted by the Civil War. It is another success story of that era when the Industrial Revolution came to the United States and the steam engine came to Texas, an era when great cities were built, modern American corporate capitalism was created, and many private fortunes were accumulated. It was a period that will always be remembered for its dynamism, and Galveston was a full participant. Before the war Galveston's geographical position had worked to make it the leading port on the Texas gulf coast, followed by Indianola. The population of Texas was concentrated along the Brazos and Colorado Rivers, and the cotton they produced was transported by small paddlewheel steamers to the ports. A canal from the Brazos River to West Galveston Bay, the predecessor of the Intracoastal Canal, served the planters in that region. Other paddlewheelers plied between Galveston and Houston serving the growers along Buffalo Bayou and the San Jacinto River, while others navigated the Trinity River as far as possible. Technology began to push the paddlewheelers aside in the late 1850s after the Galveston, Houston and Henderson Railroad was built from Galveston to Houston. There it was able to connect with the Buffalo Bayou, Brazos and Colorado line building westward, and the Houston and Texas Central building to the north. Progress on these roads was stopped by the war, and the destinations of San Antonio and Dallas were reached when peace resumed.

This is the history of that era after the war, between 1865 and 1900, when Galveston was transformed from a small port with an obstructed harbor into a transportation center for the western United States. It is a story about railroads, ships, and deep water channels, but more than anything, it is a story about people—men who were dreamers and planners, men who were builders, men who were achievers of both public and private goals. During that era, many of the nation's richest and most powerful, its top engineering talents, and its top corporate executives came to Galveston to see this transformation, seeking to fit this rising port into their plans. The Island City was becoming a gulf terminal for systems flowing north to south, and a focal point in those land-sea systems linking east and west.

After the war a convergence of circumstances made Galveston's opportunity for growth and development very good. First, Galveston's location on the western Gulf of Mexico and its superior natural harbor put it in a position to capitalize on other events taking place. Second, the West was filling up with people, aided by railroads transporting settlers to the new territories, often to settle on land that had been granted to the railroads. The railroads were also available to move the products of the settlers of the western plains. Galveston's position on the gulf gave it a natural cost advantage over the rail routes to the Atlantic ports hundreds of miles farther away.[1]

Thus, geography, demography, and technology combined to favor Galveston's commercial development, and the city seized upon these circumstances to spur its growth as a major seaport by 1900. But it was not as simple as lying on the railroad tracks and being run over by an oncoming train. Galveston did lie in the path of progress, but the situation required an understanding of the changing economic geography of the West following the Civil War, and both the desire and ability to capitalize on the opportunity at hand.

Geography and demography (that is, population trends) had been affecting the growth of America since the landings at Jamestown and Plymouth Rock. Technology, however, was a more recent player. First, canals and the railroads made their appearance in the northeastern states. During the Civil War the Union Army used the railroads and the telegraph to enhance the mobility and effectiveness of its troops. Ironclad warships were also used. Once the war ended, technology was poised to change the face of an entire continent.

"Technology" is used here in the broadest possible sense. David McComb, in the preface to *Galveston: A History,* states: "Although no historian has yet advanced a thoroughgoing technological interpretation of history, there is power in the suggestion that technology is the dynamic element in human development. Anthropologists have long assumed this, and so did Walter Prescott Webb in his study of western America, *The Great Plains.* When motivated people use the resources of their environment with their knowledge of how to do things, change occurs. Change is history, and technology is an important dynamic element."[2]

One historian who has attempted a theory of technology is Thomas De Gregori. A reviewer paraphrased De Gregori's concept in this manner: "Technology to De Gregori is a problem-solving process. As such, technology is primarily ideational. It is the use of ideas to transform the material world into tools and techniques to control man's relationship with and facilitate his adjustment to his environment. Technology is not alien to life. In fact, it is the process which has allowed man to adapt to potentially lethal changes in his surroundings."[3]

At the core of this book is that adaptation to environment that technology made possible at Galveston, and the interplay between technology and the political processes of a democratic society. Galveston was made possible by the advances in the science of hydraulics, as applied to the Gulf of Mexico and Galveston Bay and its outlets in this case, and in the technology of jetty construction that occurred during the period from 1865 to 1900. These advances made possible a twenty-five-foot-deep channel through the Outer Bar blocking the entrance to Bolivar Pass, the Galveston Channel, and Galveston Bay. When the technological solutions to problems such as that at Galveston Harbor became expensive beyond the means of a locality, then financial support from higher levels of government was sought, and state, regional, or national politics became intertwined with technology. Consequently, at times this book will focus on engineering designs and at other times it will focus on the intricacies of the legislative process. The deep water committee had to master both. Finally only a superb lobbying effort, supported by all the western states, enabled the Island City eventually to accomplish its goal.

In this period of rapid advances in all of the sciences and technologies, Galveston was not left untouched as the face of the United States was quickly changed. The port would eventually handle as many as four million bales of cotton in a season, and the city was integrated into nationwide railroad, telephone, and telegraph networks. All of this happened only sixty years after Michel Menard purchased a league and a *labor* of land on the eastern end of an isolated barrier island off the Texas coast and founded the city. In the preface to his book, *The Galveston Era,* historian Earl Wesley Fornell stated that Galveston, and the pre–Civil War Texas coast, must be studied in terms of the drive for expansion of cotton production, around which political, economic, and social power was concentrated.[4] While cotton remained the heart of the economy, drastic political and social change occurred in the postwar era. Galveston took advantage of the expansion of the railroads to extend its reach into the wheat-growing areas of the newly settled Plains states and reduce its dependence upon King Cotton. In the first year following the war, Galveston was focused only upon resuming its prewar role as "Charleston–West." But even that was not as simple as before. The populace was now dealing with military occupation, worrying about the coming Reconstruction, and attempting to create a new labor system that would replace slavery.

Physical damage to Galveston was another factor the people had to face. Since the Union occupation of the island had lasted only from October, 1862, until it was lifted by the Battle of Galveston on the morning of January 1, 1863, not all of the destruction was caused by the enemy. One account described events this way:

> For four years this city has been little else than a military camp, and whether right or wrong, legal or otherwise, nearly all of the property here has been under the control of the military authorities, and has been

used at pleasure for the benefit of the troops, and unfortunately too often destroyed without even materially benefitting them or anyone else. Fine residences have been torn to pieces merely for fuel during the whole war, and that too while there has been an abundance of wood at the head of the bay, and plenty of small schooners, and some steamers, either belonging to the Government, or under the control of the military commanders, by which the troops would have easily been supplied with all of the wood necessary. . . . It is sickening to look over this ruined city, and see the numerous examples of reckless destruction on all hands, it is the more mortifying to the patriot to reflect that all this wasteful desolation has been the works of our own troops.[5]

In addition, the matter of amnesty was quickly becoming a concern, as those not pardoned by the president for their wartime participation could be banned from many activities. For example, General John Bankhead Magruder, the Confederate commander at the Battle of Galveston, was reported to have canceled his plans to return to his home in Virginia after seeing the amnesty proclamation by President Andrew Johnson. "From present appearances the exception from amnesty of so many of most distinguished men will lead to their voluntary exile," wrote Willard Richardson, the publisher of the *Galveston Daily News.*[6]

Half of the city's prewar population of four thousand had moved away, mostly to Houston, resulting in untended property and an almost complete halt to the city's commerce. All of the city's large commission merchants moved to Houston, from where many of them could conduct blockade-running activities safe from the threat of the Union ships that continually blocked the outer entrances to Galveston harbor. In spite of the state of destruction, however, members of the business community began returning shortly after the cessation of hostilities. A British steamer arrived from Brazos Santiago, at the mouth of the Rio Grande, on June 26, 1865, carrying Thomas H. McMahan, Frank H. Merriman, Moritz Kopperl, and George Sealy to begin restoring commercial activity in the city.[7]

As early as August 27, 1865, Richardson wrote optimistically about the number of businessmen choosing to settle in Galveston, attributing this not only to "Galveston's position as the only good shipping point of the State," but also to its geographical features, which he described as conducive to robust health, a necessary requirement for making money. He also pointed to the good physical condition of Galveston's railroad to Houston, the Galveston, Houston and Henderson, partly attributable to the leadership of its president, James Moreau Brown. The company had also just completed a $100,000 drawbridge over Buffalo Bayou in Houston that, in a few days, would enable the road to connect with the Houston and Texas Central. While recognizing that "the huge privations and sufferings of Galveston during the war, endured with so much dignified patience, have created a respect and sympathy for the place throughout the entire state," Richardson had no time to wallow in the past. He predicted that "Galveston bids fair to arise speedily from the ashes of war" and "would again soon exhibit that blend of enterprise and social life that the blockade had kept in such a long state of suspension."[8]

Within the first year following Appomattox, the *Daily News* could report that the port was booming, with ships from Liverpool, LeHavre, Bremen, Vera Cruz, Rio, Havana, Boston, New York, Baltimore, and New Orleans bringing full cargoes of every variety and taking the produce of the state. Two national banks were formed and were operating. One, the National Bank of Texas, was modeled after the liberal banks of New York City, and the other, the First National Bank, was operating in the fashion of the conservative banks of New Orleans, which, according to the *Daily News,* had held back the growth of that city. But Galveston was progressing and not clinging to the peculiar institutions and customs of the South, which were "dissipated like a morning vapor" as the result of an unsuccessful war. A new era and a new order of things was bringing new ways.[9]

In fact, it was hardly more than a year after Appomattox that Richardson published an editorial in the *Daily News* entitled "Galveston and the Great West," which was probably one of the most important ever run by that newspaper. It opened by calling the readers' attention to the fact that "few of our people have yet contemplated the vast prospective importance of that immense region of our country lying far in the West along the eastern slope of the Rocky Mountains." After describing the settlement that had taken place, he stated:

> *It may look extravagant to hold up Galveston as destined, at some future day, to be the sea-port of half a continent, yet all the premises and existing facts lead precisely to that conclusion. . . . There is scarcely a*

harbor of any importance at the North on which the government had not expended far more money than will be required to make the port of Galveston the best on the whole Gulf, as it is the most convenient of access for nearly the whole extensive, varied and productive region west of the Mississippi.[10]

Richardson went on to describe the economic development, including railroad building, that had taken place in the vicinity of Denver and stated that "if railroads are becoming important as connecting links between different points of those territories, we may well suppose that the question of railroads between those territories and their nearest sea-port cannot, or should not be long permitted to remain unagitated."[11]

Thus, Richardson set forth the ideas that would become the mainstays of Galveston's transportation development plans for the next thirty-five years—a deep water channel into Galveston's harbor and railroad connections between the port and major points in the area west of the Mississippi River. It is not known how the ideas were received at the time, or how much excitement they generated. However, until the twin goals were achieved, the *Galveston Daily News* first under the management of Richardson and later under Colonel Alfred H. Belo would continue to stress their importance to the city. Galveston would look away from its past as "Charleston-West," a port subservient to King Cotton and the area in which it was produced. Gradually, the ideas took hold and plans were formed. Through the years, a variety of people—cotton merchants, lawyers, bankers, former army officers, and those currently on duty with the Army Corps of Engineers—would step into important roles to make plans become realities. In those thirty-five years between 1865 and 1900 Galveston became a major seaport with a twenty-five-foot-deep entrance channel created by the twin jetties, and with railroad connections stretching around an arc from St. Louis and Chicago to Denver to California's port cities.

Chapter 2

The Struggle for National Attention

At the end of the Civil War the Inner Bar, extending from Fort Point at the eastern tip of the island across the entrance of the channel on the north side of the island, had accumulated sand until it allowed a depth of only nine feet. This shallow depth was causing all of the larger ships crossing the Outer Bar into Bolivar Channel (the area between Fort Point and Bolivar Peninsula) to unload their cargoes onto lighter ships for movement to either the wharves on the north side of the island or up Galveston Bay and Buffalo Bayou to Houston. One of the first to take any action regarding the problem was Major Albert M. Lea, a Confederate Army engineer on the staff of General John Bankhead Magruder during the Battle of Galveston, who took up residence on the island following the war. In 1866 Lea had two interviews with General Horatio G. Wright, the commander of the military district, who already had experience with harbor improvement on the Atlantic coast. General Wright urged that surveys be made of the deteriorating condition in order that remedies could be devised. Lea recommended to the city government that General Wright be sought as a consultant on the problem, but Wright left the city before any action was taken. Lea therefore took it upon himself to make some explorations in anticipation that he might be called upon for advice. At the same time Major Lea also became involved in efforts to attract attention to Galveston as a railway center, and a paper on that subject was read at the Tyler Railroad Convention on September 11, 1866. Galveston's importance as a port, of course, was stressed, but standing in the way of all future hopes was the problem of the Inner Bar and its blockage of Galveston Harbor.[1] Galveston's interest in a harbor improvement project resulted in prompt action. On January 6, 1867, Major C. H. Boyd, in charge of a board of survey appointed by the U.S. Coast Survey, arrived in the city to begin his work. In addition, the city engineering department hired Tipton Walker, another Confederate Army engineer who also had worked for the Galveston, Houston and Henderson Railroad (GH&H) prior to the War, to assist in the survey. By the end of January, Boyd had completed enough of the task to send a report to the Army Engineers in Washington in order for them to plan an improvement and estimate the cost of it. Boyd and Tipton concurred that the increase of sand on the bar had been caused by alterations in the shorelines of both Galveston Island and Pelican Spit, widening the channel but decreasing its depth.[2]

Following Major Boyd's report that only nine and one-half feet was on the Inner Bar at mean low tide, the chief of Army Engineers, General Andrew A. Humphreys on March 22, 1867, ordered Major Miles D. McAlester, the engineer at New Orleans, "to make a survey of Galveston harbor with the view of forming plans for its preservation and improvement." In his letter General Humphreys remarked, "Galveston harbor is the best on our whole coast from the Mississippi to the Rio Grande, and it is of the highest commercial interest of the nation that the capacity of this harbor should be maintained if possible." Lieutenant W. S. Stanton was sent to Galveston to make the study of the situation, but his work was interrupted by the severe yellow fever epidemic of 1867. He returned to the city on January 8, 1868, and completed his written report to Major McAlester on June 28, 1868.[3]

Stanton had offered three possible solutions for the erosion taking place. His first plan was to build a jetty resting on Pelican Island and Pelican Spit, intersecting Bolivar Channel, with the view of deflecting a greater volume of water through Galveston Channel and deepening and preserving it by increasing the abrading effort of the current. This plan would cost an estimated $1.3 million, and was dismissed by Major McAlester as ineffective and too costly. His second plan was to dam San Luis Pass, increasing the volume of water through Galveston Channel and increasing the abrading power of the current. McAlester called this plan legitimate and judicious but found the estimated cost of $330,000 beyond means. The third alternative, which could be accomplished for $10,952, consisted of dredging a twelve-foot-deep channel through the Inner Bar. This was recommended by Major McAlester to the chief engineer as "the most judicious and efficacious plan." However, the wheels in Washington turned very slowly. First, an appropriation for work at Galveston had to compete with many other projects to be included in the recommendations of the Chief of Engineers to Congress. Then there was another long competition in Congress as members from all the states vied to have projects in their districts incorporated into the rivers and harbors bill. Consequently, it was not until July 11, 1870, that Congress would appropriate $25,000 for the dredging at Galveston.[4]

The Dredging Alternative

By that time much had already occurred. Well before the recommendation made by Major McAlester, who was transferred out of New Orleans in November, 1868, E. B. Bishop, whose dredge had recently completed deepening the channel at the mouth of the Mississippi River to eighteen feet, made it known to the city council and businessmen of Galveston in December, 1867, that he was available for work. In fact, he offered to clear channels through both the Outer and Inner Bars and stated that there would be no cost to the city if he failed.[5] The city responded to Bishop's inquiry, and on March 3, 1868, Robert P. Rayne, an associate of Bishop, visited Galveston. Rayne, along with Mayor Isaac Williams; Aldermen Nahor B. Yard and Isaac Moses; Captains Charles Fowler and Rufus Jameson; the city surveyor, Abraham Hoxie; Henry J. Labatt, editor of the *Dispatch*; and some citizens, made an examination of the harbor. At this time the least depth found over the Inner Bar was still nine and one-half feet at low tide and the distance across it perhaps one hundred yards. Rayne expressed the view that Bishop's "Improved Patent Dredger" could easily remove the obstruction. He was afraid, however, that the channel would fill again and require periodic dredging unless protected by a breakwater. On the other hand, Captain Fowler, an experienced seaman, was of the opinion that a breakwater extending some three hundred yards northeast from the east end of the island, would prevent further formation and also increase the ebb flow over the bar. This flow would gradually cut a channel through the bar without the aid of dredging.[6]

The Galveston Chamber of Commerce met on March 24, 1868, to review an agreement signed by the owners and agents of vessels using the port, expressing their willingness to pay a toll fee not to exceed one-half of lightering charges on all ships drawing more than nine feet if the water over the Inner Bar were deepened. They also urged the city council and the military authorities (Texas was still under military rule) to take action. Caleb G. Forshey presented a letter from Bishop stating that his company would deepen the channel to thirteen feet and receive as their only compensation one-half of lightering charges as long as his services were required to keep the channel open, or until some other agency took over. The chamber passed a resolution accepting the proposition and urging other chambers to seek general agreement to the rates. When the city council met on April 20, the terms offered by Bishop had changed to maintaining a channel depth of twelve feet for a cost of $180,000 the first year and $90,000 per year for the next five years. The proposal was referred to the harbor improvement committee for examination. Mayor Isaac Williams also informed the council that Lieutenant Stanton had just finished the survey of the harbor already mentioned and was ready to make his recommendations. Captain Fowler, who had advanced his ideas on deepening the channel by means of a jetty without any dredging, also asked the harbor improvement committee to consider that alternative. As it turned out, the entire year of 1868 passed without any action being taken.[7]

In spite of the inaction, the matter was not dead. Captain Fowler presented his ideas again in a written report to the chamber of commerce at its meeting on January 25, 1869. Fowler explained his reasons for the formulation of the bar and presented his plan for a breakwater of wooden piles extending about twelve hundred yards from the east end of the island. By protecting Galveston Channel from the flood tides, the ebb tides in the channel would have the force to carry the sand out of the mouth of the channel and it would no longer be dropped on the Inner Bar. He estimated that a breakwater of three rows of wooden piles could be built for $75,000. A spirited debate followed on matters of feasibility, cost, and the protection of the piles from the teredo worm. Captain M. W. Darton; Captain Zack Sabel, a pilot; Henry St. Cyr; and Captain Robert H. Hawley, a wharf builder, essentially agreed with Fowler's plan. Tipton Walker disagreed with the cost, however, and others thought it might be necessary to have two breakwaters. The method of financing—subscriptions, bonds, a tax— also drew a number of divergent opinions. The matter was tabled, to be further discussed at the next meeting.[8]

Aware that the problem of the harbor improvement was still being discussed without any action having been taken yet, Bishop submitted another proposal to the chamber of commerce, again guaranteeing his results or it would cost the city nothing. He claimed that with his new dredge he would first cut the depth of the Inner Bar to that of the Outer Bar, then he would cut both to a depth of eighteen to twenty feet. At the time of Bishop's letter, March 3, 1869, any involvement of the Army Engineers in the dredging at Galveston was in the planning stage, awaiting a congressional appropriation. The letter revealed, however, that competition had already developed between the government and private industry over both the control of and the means for harbor improvement projects. According to Bishop, "A set of designing men—gov't officers and West Pointers—set themselves to work, built the Assayon [sic][9] (a machine to screw up the mud), approximating to my plan as near as possible, to evade my patent. The machine has done but little good, if any—broke six or eight times, costing the Government at least $300,000 with, perhaps, no good. I am, however, prosecuting for infringement of patent."[10] This competition between the Army Engineers and private contractors would continue throughout the period of the development of the harbor at Galveston. Bishop would continue to seek the dredging work at Galveston for the next seventeen years, until dredging was abandoned as a means for providing a deep water harbor and another private contractor would challenge the dominance of the Army Engineers on the design and construction of jetties.

In April, Bishop provided the chamber of commerce with a copy of a letter to him from Captain John Roy of New Orleans, who had manufactured the dredge to Bishop's specifications. Captain Roy tested the dredge himself to see if it would meet the performance that he had guaranteed—twenty-five revolutions per minute. He was well pleased and provided Bishop with the impressions that he had written down on the day of the test: "I believe it to be much superior to what I thought of it. From the compactness of the mud I believe that it cannot be washed or pumped out, but do believe that the conical screws are just the thing to do the work. If so, Bishop has got a fortune. It can take a cut off from one to two feet deep and go about one mile an hour with ease, and say twenty feet wide."[11]

The Board of Harbor Improvement Established

The Galveston City Council on June 25, 1869, voted unanimously to accept the recommendation of its special committee on harbor improvement to establish a board for the purpose of improving the channel over the Inner Bar. The ordinance provided that the work would be financed by bonds to be issued as the work progressed and that the project would be supervised by a board of harbor improvement, consisting of the mayor, two aldermen, a representative of the Wharf Company, and a private citizen. The following week Mayor James A. McKee named Judge Edward T. Austin and B. Rush Plumly as the two aldermen on the board. John Sealy was named the representative of the Wharf Company and Henry Rosenberg was selected as the private citizen. At their first meeting Rosenberg was elected president of the board and Charles Fowler was named construction superintendent.[12]

On July 19 Rosenberg reported to the city council that the board had surveyed the harbor, evaluated the problem, and reached its conclusions. Using Captain Zack Sabel's soundings, the board had decided the old channel was the best place for the new one since it would be much shorter. They estimated the distance from the twelve-foot depth on one side of the Inner Bar to the twelve-foot depth on the other side at approximately six hundred feet. They proposed "to adopt the scouring process, by employing a propeller, and attaching a drag which they now have in process of construction." In order to make the deepening of the channel permanent, it was decided that "it will be necessary to confine the waters of the Bay to the channel by a piling on the eastern end of the island." This would prevent the water from washing away the point of the island and prevent the channel waters from spreading out and losing their force, he explained. The board requested $7,000 for the first month's operation of the drag and $8,000 to begin the purchase of piles. The council approved the request and authorized the mayor to issue $15,000 in bonds.[13]

Apparently no consideration was given to the Bishop proposal, but he was in New Orleans and not around to protest. Colonel A. C. McKeen of Galveston attended the city council meeting and offered a proposal to do the job with a machine designed by a man named Byrne. Like Bishop, McKeen also proposed a money-back guarantee. Said McKeen, "Believing that the Byrne apparatus is the surest and most economical plan ever presented, and with the inventor himself interested with me, and having the working of his machine, I confidently believe that it will be the best interest of the city to adopt this plan." When rejected, McKeen, unlike Bishop, was around to protest. The invective against the members of the board of harbor improvement was so strong that the *Daily News* found it necessary to defend them against those attacking "for no other reason than because the Council and the Board turned a deaf ear to propositions in which the greatest cavilers were most interested, and because the measures agreed upon are in direct conflict with pet projects of the complaining parties." The accusation of having successfully managed their own affairs seemed a strange one to place against men performing a public service on the improvement board at no salary. Added the *Daily News,* "None of these gentlemen, so far as any information is before their fellow-citizens, have any selfish ends to subserve; they have no tugboats to dispose of, nor are they interested in any patent mud digger."[14]

The Pile Jetty Begun

Fowler moved out promptly and by September 6 board president Rosenberg was reporting to the city council that Superintendent Fowler had commenced with the piling on the point and had "run out some hundred and twenty odd feet, with three rows of piles, twenty inches apart, each row breaking joints." In addition, the old channel had filled about eighteen inches and a new channel had opened from eighteen inches to two feet deeper than when the work commenced. This Fowler saw as confirming the anticipated results. Two months later Fowler was reporting that seven hundred piles had been driven from the point toward Bolivar Channel. The Inner Bar was continuing to improve, and he forecasted the depth on it would be twelve to thirteen feet in three months when the piling would extend a thousand feet from the point of the island.[15]

At the same time, on November 19, the board reported on the sales of the first bonds and requested city council to issue another $15,000 package.[16] The announcement of the additional bonds was accompanied by a strong appeal from the board of harbor improvement for continued support by the citizens in view of the fact that, as Captain Fowler had reported, so much progress had already been made. The board added its own assurance that "we will deepen the inner bar so that any vessel which crosses the outer bar can come up to our wharves, and that we will demonstrate a state of facts which will entitle and obtain for us the aid of the Congress of the United States, to complete the work and to do all that money and science can do for any harbor."[17]

Captain Fowler's report was quickly followed by an endorsement from a group of pilots—Zack Sabel, Rufus Jameson, J. B. Sabel, Louis Best, and J. C. Walter—confirming his statement that the depth on the Inner Bar had increased by more than a foot and that several steamers drawing ten feet five inches had crossed the bar in the last two weeks. In their opinion, another five hundred to eight hundred feet of piling would produce a depth of twelve feet.[18]

Seeking National Attention

As 1869 came to a close, the effort to improve the harbor by deepening the channel over the Inner Bar was successfully under way, and confidence was running very high that the problem would soon be solved. At the same time the citizens of Galveston began a parallel activity to bring the improvement of the harbor to the attention of the nation. It was an activity that would have far-reaching consequences. In May of that year a Southern Commercial Convention was held in New Orleans for the purpose of defining and promoting economic goals important to the South. Several Galvestonians were among the delegation that represented Texas at the convention: Caleb G. Forshey, James Sorley, Judge John Dean, and Thomas H. McMahan. Other members were D. Morris, Colonel William M. Harrison, T. B. Goyne, John Speake, and N. B. Patten of Jefferson; Colonel William H. Parsons of Houston; Colonel W. T. Scott of Marshall; J. W. Moore of Corpus Christi; and C. S. Hurley of Brenham.

At the convention Forshey was named chairman of a special committee on gulf bars, harbors, and channels (other than the Mississippi

River, the subject of a standing committee). Also named to the committee were Williamson Smith, Louisiana; Dr. C. K. Marshall, Mississippi; Professor Albert Stein, Alabama; and the Honorable E. C. Anderson, Georgia. In a lengthy report to the convention, the committee surveyed all of the harbors along the gulf coast, evaluated their economic importance, and recommended several for improvement supported by funds from the federal government. Mobile Bay in Alabama; Atchafalaya Bay in Louisiana; and Sabine Pass, Galveston, Pass Cavallo, Aransas Pass, Corpus Christi Bay, and the mouth of the Brazos River in Texas were deemed worthy of attention by the committee. Galveston, however, was singled out as demanding the most immediate and the most ample assistance from the federal government. The report cited the critical timing of improvement of the Inner Bar controlling access to Galveston Harbor, and it also cited the Outer Bar controlling the entrance to Bolivar Pass and Galveston Bay as needing attention. The deepening of both bars to fifteen or twenty feet would enable the largest vessels to reach the wharves at Galveston, said the committee. Forshey did his work well, for the report went on to describe Galveston's overriding importance to that area of the United States west of the Mississippi River and how Galveston served as the natural outlet via railroads for those regions that could not find transportation by way of the Mississippi. The committee report urged the convention to memorialize—that is, petition—Congress to appropriate funds to support the recommended improvements.[19]

The History of Commercial Conventions

Although it was Galveston's first participation in such a gathering, the convention at New Orleans was only one of a series. Because of the important role these conventions would play in Galveston's economic development, a review of the history of these meetings is worthwhile. The origin of the meetings goes back to 1837 when delegates from South Carolina and Georgia met to discuss their economic concerns. Fourteen of the conventions would be held between 1837 and 1857, excluding the last two in 1858 and 1859, which were caught up in the political issues preceding the Civil War. Four of the conventions were held between 1837 and 1839, two between 1845 and 1849, and eight between 1852 and 1857 at locations throughout the South. Direct trade with Europe was the overriding issue over the twenty years, and gradually more subjects of economic concern to southern businessmen and planters were added to the agenda. A broad range of internal improvements including river transportation, canals, and railroads were added to the agenda very early, and more and more southern states began to participate. Following the Mexican War, the matter of a railroad to the Pacific Ocean over the southern route, the Southern Pacific, became a leading subject at each meeting.

In what has been described as the most significant convention of all, the 1854 meeting in Charleston attracted 1,857 delegates from thirteen states. A resolution was passed that a Pacific railroad be built by the southern states in cooperation, without the aid of the national government. Direct trade with Europe was of importance, but gaining in significance among the delegates was the importance of opening and developing trade with the Amazon Valley in South America. Throughout all of the meetings over the years could be seen the struggle by southern businessmen to free the South from its heavy dependence on cotton and from its domination by northern commercial and financial interests.[20]

Following the Civil War, the commercial conventions did not resume immediately; however, meetings on matters of economic importance, some of them subjects inherited from the prewar conventions, did gradually start taking place. The matter of obstructions on the Tennessee River at Muscle Shoals and other places was the subject of a resolution at the River Convention held in St. Louis in 1866. This same concern was also the subject of resolutions passed at the Merchants' National Convention in Philadelphia in 1868, the National Board of Trade meeting in Cincinnati in 1868, the great International Direct Trade Convention held in Norfolk, Virginia, on October 14, 1868, and the Chattanooga convention of February 24, 1869. Prior to the New Orleans Convention of May 25, 1869, one had been held at Memphis on May 20. This convention numbered more than eleven hundred delegates, including groups from Illinois and Pennsylvania. This gathering heard another report on the improvement of the Tennessee River, as well as reports from committees on the Southern Pacific Railroad, direct trade, finance and banking, manufactures and mining, Mississippi River levees and improvements, river navigation, and agriculture and general business. From 1837 to 1869 these conventions served as a forum for business and civic leaders to identify and approach problems, establish priorities, publicize their concerns, and organize lobbying efforts for those matters requiring governmental action at the state and national levels. Consequently, one can hardly overestimate the value of Colonel Forshey's achievement at Memphis and New Orleans in elevating the issue of the improvement of Galveston's harbor to a matter of national attention.[21]

The Louisville Convention

The greatest of the commercial conventions of 1869 was held in Louisville on October 12. Although an extension of the New Orleans gathering, this meeting became in effect a national convention since the states and territories represented grew from twenty-one at New Orleans to thirty-one, including states from New England, the middle Atlantic, and midwestern regions. The number of delegates grew from 578 to more than 1,000. The selection of former president Millard Fillmore as president of the convention added to the national flavor of the meeting. Among those representing Texas were former governor Francis R. Lubbock and Colonel Forshey from Galveston; Colonel C. B. Shepard, Washington County; John F. Torrey, New Braunfels; Colonel J. M. Camp, third congressional district; F. G. Campbell, Jefferson; and D. W. Wells. Lubbock served as a vice president of the committee on permanent organization, and Forshey again was successful in having a committee on channels, bars, and harbors added to the thirteen other standing committees that presented reports to the convention.

These conventions, of course, were conducted with a great deal of pomp and ceremony. Speeches were held to a minimum, and order generally prevailed. The hosts were determined to show the best side of their cities, and at Louisville there was a four-hour parade put on by the merchants, manufacturers, businessmen, and citizens. The delegates elected a former president as their presiding officer, heard an expression of regret from sitting president Ulysses S. Grant that he could not attend, and passed a resolution expressing the sympathy of the convention to the family of former president Franklin Pierce, who had recently died. The committee reports were essentially those previously adopted at Memphis and New Orleans, and their presentation again did not provoke debate.[22]

Governor Lubbock and Colonel Forshey reported on their activities to the annual meeting of the chamber of commerce held at the

Harmony Hall on December 14, 1869. In addition to his work in support of the harbor improvement at Galveston, Forshey told of his activities to promote the Great Northern Railroad along the line of the 95th parallel (or meridian) to a connection with the Kansas roads. Forshey also spoke of the enthusiasm of the citizens of Kansas City and their interest in railroad connections to Texas. This contact would lead to a further expansion of Galveston's horizons. He spoke of his astonishment at the progress being made in Chicago, St. Louis, and other cities, and urged upon the chamber the necessity of keeping well posted in regard to the material progress going on to the north and west. A resolution was passed commending Lubbock and Forshey for their efforts on behalf of the city, but perhaps the best statement of the importance of their efforts in the commercial conventions was to be found in the annual report of the chamber's activities submitted by Secretary Samuel A. Edgerley. In regard to the conventions, he stated:

> We have also necessarily taken cognizance of those new but powerful agencies for good, the various Commercial Conventions held throughout the land, and have been ably represented at two of them—the one held in New Orleans in May last, and the other at Louisville in October. By this means the wants and necessities of our States, as well as its emporium, have been brought before a larger audience than possible in any other way, and by this means, also have we been able to exert an influence calculated to enable us to share in the many projected schemes for the advancement of our State on the road to prosperity.[23]

Inclusion in the Rivers and Harbors Bill

As its next step, the chamber of commerce sent a memorial, or petition, to Washington to the senators and members of Congress from the state of Texas, transmitting the report of Forshey's committee on harbors, channels, and bars of the Atlantic and gulf ports, which was adopted at the conventions. While not minimizing the claims of other ports, it stated that "we would respectfully ask your special and favorable consideration of that portion which relates to the coast of Texas, and above all to the facts, reasonings and urgent claims of Galveston Bay." It called attention to the current construction of a pile jetty started to prevent a closing of the Galveston Channel but said this was only a temporary measure taken by the citizens of Galveston until a permanent work by the government could be initiated.[24] In April the city's board of aldermen also submitted a petition to the Congress, providing more detail on the work undertaken by the board and describing its progress and cost. The memorial stated that the jetty was planned to extend three thousand feet into the bay but that less than fifteen hundred feet had been accomplished at a cost of $45,000. It was estimated that another $100,000 was needed to finish—an amount that the city could not afford. An accompanying article in the *Daily News* stated that about $50,000 remained of the funds appropriated by the city; however, the memorial requested that the federal government appropriate $100,000. Therefore, it appeared that the aldermen did not plan to issue the remaining bonds if the Congress voted funds. The *Daily News* also added that the presence of Galveston's congressional representative, General William T. Clark, on the House's commerce committee, which had the responsibility for the rivers and harbors bill, would help in bringing attention to the memorial.[25]

On July 11, 1870, Congress appropriated $25,000 to finance the dredging recommended by Major Miles D. McAlester following Lieutenant Stanton's 1868 study of the alternatives for improving Galveston Channel. By 1870 Major McAlester had died and his post as the Army Engineer at New Orleans had been filled by Captain Charles W. Howell on June 7, 1869.[26] As happened in 1867, another yellow fever epidemic interfered with the work of the Army Engineers. However, by December of 1870, the Chief of Engineers, General Humphreys, notified Representative Clark that the Army Engineers were ready "to commence the work of improvement at Galveston harbor at as early a day as practicable."[27] While there doubtlessly was frustration in Galveston over the amount of the appropriation and the delay in starting work, the inclusion of Galveston in the rivers and harbors bill for the first time was an act of major significance in the history of the city and the Texas gulf coast.

The History of Federal Involvement

Because of the critical significance that federal involvement would have in Galveston's history, it is important at this point to review the history of federal participation. The role of the federal government in the development and improvement of rivers and harbors evolved over the years. The first act was passed May 7, 1822. Prior to this time the federal government had been responsible only for safe navigation in bays and harbors, and the states had been responsible for all improvements to rivers and harbors. However, the necessity of the development of means of transportation had been recognized as early as *The Federalist Papers* by James Madison, John Jay, and Alexander Hamilton in 1791. The assumption by the First Congress in 1789 of the responsibility for lighthouses, beacons, and buoys was the first step in this evolution. President Thomas Jefferson expanded this concept in his annual message of 1806 when he made clear his conviction that the development of roads, rivers, and canals was essential to the economic harmony of the new nation.

The thrust toward wider federal responsibility for internal improvements was given further impetus by Secretary of Treasury Albert Gallatin's *Report on Roads and Canals* in 1808. The War of 1812 both interfered with congressional action and demonstrated the need for improved transportation throughout the country, and President Madison gave the matter priority again in his seventh annual message of December 5, 1815, when he called for a program of road and canal development.

The earliest steps were under way by 1822 when rivers and harbors were added to the previously supported turnpikes and canals as federal responsibilities. In the Senate three of the leading voices of the day—Daniel Webster of Massachusetts, John C. Calhoun of South Carolina, and Henry Clay of Kentucky—emerged as strong proponents of internal improvements. Clay saw the potential for federally funded projects as a means of combating the growing sectionalism taking place. In what he called his "American System," he proposed a tariff to protect the industrialists of the North, the proceeds of which would go to finance needed internal improvements in the agricultural South and West, enabling these sections better to transport their products to northern cities. The tariff carried, 107-102, in 1824. The annual rivers and harbors appropriations increased from $22,700 in 1822 to a pre–Civil War peak of $1,512,194 in 1838, in spite of opposition from President Andrew Jackson, who questioned the constitutionality, and from antitariff forces who attacked the improvements as well as the tariff. The South, of course, led the antitariff forces, threatening nullification and secession. In addition, that section stood to benefit least from Gallatin's proposal of East-West networks of canals, roads, and railroads. This opposition effectively ended the Era of National Projects.

The rivers and harbors suffered also, as appropriations between 1838 and 1861 usually were under $100,000 (except for $2,055,167 in 1853). Following the Civil War, however, there was a new interest in improvements, as $8,777,329 was approved in 1867. There is not a direct connection between the rivers and harbors bills and the commercial conventions where so many of the improvement projects were discussed and voted upon. There can be little doubt, however, that the conventions played a vital role in marshalling political support for the projects and making these recommendations known to members of Congress, as occurred in the matter of the improvement of Galveston Harbor.[28]

Multiple Approaches

Returning to Galveston, even while pursuing the pile jetty and seeking congressional support of the project, the businessmen kept their eyes and ears open to other schemes for improving the harbor. Colonel J. E. Gowan, who had earned a reputation by carrying heavy vessels over obstructions at Sebastopol, Russia, during the Crimean War and had lately been professionally engaged in Europe, visited Galveston on April 27, 1870, and addressed the chamber of commerce on his techniques. His plan used "an open dock of some two hundred feet in length by forty feet wide, in which the vessels to be raised would rest as in an ordinary dock." In his lecture Colonel Gowan described how he had raised sunken vessels at Gibraltar and Buffalo on Lake Erie as well as in the harbor of Sebastopol. For the movement of ships over sandbars, he said he would employ self-propelled pontoons so as to avoid the expense of tugs for towing the ships to and from the wharves. Although he estimated operating costs in the neighborhood of $40,000 per year, the initial capital investment would be approximately $300,000, and Colonel Gowan suggested requesting that amount from the state legislature. A committee of Colonel Alfred M. Hobby, Willard Richardson, John C. Wallis, J. W. Jockusch, and Zack Sabel was named to consider the proposal and to report back to the chamber membership. The committee submitted its report to a special meeting on April 29 and recommended that the chamber present the Gowan plan to the governor for action and that the chamber also pursue federal funds to reimburse the state. In support of their recommendation, the committee pointed out that the plan had been endorsed by Sir Charles Hartley, chief engineer for the commission to regulate the mouth of the Danube River, and had the endorsement of eminent practical men in London, New York, and New Orleans. The plan was so welcomed as a solution to the problem at the mouth of the Mississippi River that the Louisiana legislature approved $1 million to implement it. Although there was some disappointment expressed that the committee had not done any further investigation of the plan on its own, the recommendation was unanimously approved. Colonel Hobby was chosen to act as the agent of the chamber and to proceed to Austin to present the plan to Governor Edmund J. Davis and to seek suitable legislation.[29]

Colonels Gowan and Hobby met with the governor on May 9, 1870, and returned to Galveston to report that he was very interested in developments that could contribute to the commercial growth of the state. In June a bill was introduced in the Texas legislature incorporating a private company, the Texas Harbor Improvement and Dock Company, "to improve the navigation across the bars at Galveston and other Texas ports" and granting state aid for the same. The act proposed to incorporate the company for ninety years and set its capital stock not to exceed $2 million in shares of $100 each. The proposed company would be authorized to build the floating docks, apparently as promoted by Colonel Gowan, to purchase or lease shops, steamers, and real estate, and to establish wharves, depots, and landings. The initial construction would be financed by state bonds and repaid by company bonds issued to the state as docks were completed. As security, the company would mortgage all of its assets to the state. Fourteen incorporators were named, including six from Galveston: G. H. Sherwood, Barney Tiernan, John Sealy, George Flournoy, Thomas Chubb, and Colonel Gowan. The remaining Texas incorporators were W. S. Swymmer, N. B. Patten, J. J. Anderson, H. C. Rivers, J. S. Clark, R. B. Stapp, W. H. Nichols, and George Moore.[30]

Following the introduction of the bill in the legislature, Galveston had under way three initiatives aimed at harbor improvement: (1) the locally funded task of building the pile jetty east from Fort Point under the direction of Captain Fowler; (2) the effort through the rivers and harbors committee of the Congress, which obtained the appropriation of $25,000 on July 11, 1870; and (3) the effort in the Texas legislature. After its introduction, this latter bill was never mentioned again in the pages of the *Galveston Daily News*. One can only speculate in regard to the bill's demise in the legislature, but opposition to granting such rights to a private corporation or the difficulty of selling the bonds in the postwar financial market could have been contributors. With the city and the federal government already appropriating funds, the state legislators may have believed there was not a sound requirement for the state to act.

The action in Washington before Congress also received little attention in the *Daily News*. Little note was taken of the 1870 appropriation, and it was not until July 14, 1871, that attention was given to the fact that a second appropriation—this time $20,000—had been made on March 8, 1871. The *Daily News* expressed surprise that the sum of the two appropriations was sitting in the federal treasury unused, and questioned why the federal and the local funds could not be put to joint use. Apparently six months had passed since General Humphreys had announced that the Army Engineers were ready to go to work and Captain Charles Howell had asked for proposals without any signs of activity or progress from the Engineers. In his report to the Chief of Engineers, Howell would later explain that he had received no answers to his announcement because all of the dredges on the gulf coast were occupied. In April, 1871, he was authorized to purchase a dredge-boat, two dump-scows, and a tugboat. However, by the time he received them it was obvious that the scouring created across the Inner Bar by the pile jetty was working. The vessels were put to other use and the funds were applied to extending and strengthening the jetty.[31]

While seeking both federal and state aid for the harbor improvement, Galveston moved steadily ahead with its jetty. By July, 1870, a tour of the site with Captain Fowler revealed that it was approaching three thousand feet in length and that dry land had formed along the entire length of the gulf side of the breakwater, partly restoring the east end of the island to its earlier shape. On the north side, the Galveston Channel side, a current had been produced that scoured a twelve-foot channel through the Inner Bar, an increase of three feet since the beginning of the work. At this point it was believed that the pile jetty was strong enough to resist any action of the water because the accrual of sand was protecting it, and that the current in the channel was strong enough to maintain the channel without any artificial dredging. The main problem at this time seemed to be the prospects for the future issuance of city bonds because of the lowered rating brought about by the financial mismanagement practices of the board of aldermen. The terms under which the harbor improvement fund was created prevented any diversion by the board of the funds set aside for the payment of interest on those bonds already issued. However, it was becoming uncertain whether future appropriations could be made. Harbor improvement board president Henry Rosenberg reported that $53,740 of the $62,380 received by the board between July 1, 1869, and July 1, 1870, had been spent, leaving a balance of $8,630 for continued work. However, by January of 1871, the worst fears about the city's credit standing were coming true as it was announced that the latest harbor improvement bonds issued were discounted at 20 percent.[32]

The matter of Galveston Harbor was kept on the national agenda when the Southern Commercial Convention met at Cincinnati on October 4, 1871. Former governor James W. Throckmorton headed a Texas delegation that consisted of General George P. Buell of Waco and Colonel Forshey and David Richardson of Galveston. Twenty-five states were represented at this convention, including New York, Pennsylvania, Ohio, Michigan, Indiana, and Iowa, in addition to the usual southern states. Again Forshey had Galveston's case included in the report of the committee on seacoast harbors, emphasizing the port's importance to the area west of the Mississippi River. Forshey also, as chairman of the committee on translatitudinal railroads, proposed a federally supported railroad from St. Paul to Galveston, by way of Kansas City and Tyler, and specifically recommended for the Galveston and Great Northern Railroad as much aid as might be just and equitable.[33]

Events in 1871 presented a muddled picture. It is not clear that the harbor improvement board was able to extend farther the pile jetty, but it was certain that the depth over the Inner Bar was twelve feet, the same as the Outer Bar. In response to criticism that no bids had been received on the work to be funded by the $45,000 Congress had appropriated, the *Galveston Daily News* pointed out that no competent engineer believed that the work could be accomplished for that amount of money. Then, to make matters even more confusing, Captain Howell informed the president of a Baltimore steamship company that work would begin around September 15, 1871, to dredge the channel to a depth of twelve feet, a depth Captain Fowler had reported more than a year earlier. Captain Howell's statement also expressed the objective of attaining a width of eighty feet for the channel, which may have implied an improvement since width had not been mentioned in Fowler's report. But, again in contrast to Howell's statement, the *Daily News* in its annual review of events on September 1 clearly stated that ships drawing twelve feet were clearing the bar and coming to the wharves without the costly lightering expense. The New York Line was now handling the Galveston trade with five instead of six steamships, resulting in cost savings for all parties (except the lightering business, of course). According to this report, the Army Engineers were now putting together a new dredging machine to begin work on deepening the Outer Bar since work on the Inner Bar was complete.[34]

Attention Turns to the Outer Bar

On February 5, 1872, the board of aldermen approved a lengthy memorial, drafted by Aldermen James P. Cole, George Sealy, and James Moreau Brown, requesting the Congress to fund the necessary effort required to make the improvements in the Galveston Channel permanent. The document began with statistics on the increase of trade that had occurred at Galveston since 1867, a period in which imports had tripled and exports had doubled. It described the railroad network comprised of the Houston and Texas Central, the Houston and Great Northern, and the Galveston, Harrisburgh and San Antonio roads now facilitating commerce in and out of the port. The memorial emphasized that Galveston was the only port between New Orleans and Veracruz accommodating vessels drawing twelve feet as well as the coming importance of Galveston as the seaport for the entire midsection of the nation. The history and accomplishments of the local effort to improve the harbor were recited, including that since 1869 the city's board of harbor improvement had spent $120,000 increasing the depth over the Inner Bar from nine feet to twelve. It was recognized that this was only an experiment that had succeeded and that now the resources of the federal government were required to insure a permanent improvement that would benefit a large portion of the nation.

In addition to providing for the work in the Inner Channel, the memorial also requested "a careful and thorough survey of the entrance to the harbor, with a view to determining the practicability of increasing the depth of water on the bar [i.e., the Outer Bar blocking the Bolivar Channel]." This step, of course, was the first of a long-range plan to make Galveston a deep water port accessible to any size vessel. Although Galveston harbor had already received two small appropriations for harbor improvement, this memorial set the stage for a much broader federal involvement in Galveston's future; in effect, it was the proposal that would lead to a permanent marriage between Galveston and the Army Engineers, a marriage to be marked by many ups and downs, by many successes and failures, but nevertheless a permanent one, given the geography at Galveston and the Congress's charter to the Army Engineers to oversee the nation's rivers and harbors.[35]

Shortly after the memorial was approved, the city's effort to improve the harbor received another boost. The *Daily News* printed the text of Captain Howell's report of July 20, 1871, to the Chief of Engineers. The report reviewed the physical forces at work along the Texas coast—at least, as well as they were understood at the time—presented his ideas for two breakwaters at Galveston permanently to control the Inner Bar, and concluded with his recommendation that Galveston, the site with the greatest potential for development of a deep harbor, receive all of the funds appropriated for Texas in the rivers and harbors bill. Captain Howell did include some negative remarks about the success of Captain Fowler's pile jetty. However, the *Daily News* pointed out that Howell had changed his mind on a more recent visit to Galveston. In fact, in his report of July 20, 1872, he stated that the jetty had been a success and that the dredge, scows, and tug that he had purchased were not needed when they arrived to do the dredging that he had proposed earlier. Recognizing that the Galveston Channel was already twelve feet deep by eighty feet wide, he stated that the dredge had been loaned to J. S. Sellers and Company to improve the depth along the waterfront and the piers until September 1; then it would be used on Red Fish Bar in Galveston Bay and then at

Calcasieu Pass in Louisiana. His report said that the tugboat and $10,000 of the $30,000 requested for the fiscal year beginning July 1, 1872, would be used in making the survey of Bolivar Channel and the entrance to Galveston Harbor. The remaining $20,000 would be used to make improvements to the pile jetty to make it more permanent.[36]

Three Reports Are Issued

With this favorable report from Captain Howell, the concerned officials at Galveston took a series of other steps designed to support larger appropriations when the matter came before the Congress for action. First, Representative William T. Clark acknowledged receipt of the memorial in a letter to Mayor Albert Somerville and announced that he would present it to the House of Representatives. He added that it had already been presented to the Senate by Senator Morgan C. Hamilton. Representative Clark pledged his full support for seeking a larger appropriation in order for the pile jetty to be made more permanent. He also recognized that he would have former mayor James McKee and Patten to assist him. Since Congress could not act upon the memorial until it received the report from the secretary of war with the detailed plans and cost estimate of the Chief of Engineers, there was little McKee and Patten could do at the time. The support of two leading civil engineers, Albert Stein of Mobile and William J. McAlpine of New York, was sought.[37]

Stein began his report by commenting favorably on the plans contained in the 1871 Report of the Chief of Engineers, stating, "There is much occasion for encouragement in the recent report of the engineer officer. . . . It indicates a return to sounder principles than those which have, unfortunately, prevailed on our coast for many years in the execution of all the works of Harbor Improvement that have been attempted . . . But yet, there is abundant room for caution, and perhaps of amendment of the plan which seems to be proposed." Without explaining the specific reasons for the caution, Stein goes on to give his interpretation of the hydraulic principles at work on the Texas coast and his solutions:

> *The construction of piers in front of the entrance to the bay can not*
> *permanently lower the bar, or increase or improve the sailing over it*

unless they secure an increase of quantity of water admitted, or quantity of backwater.

The most effectual means of lowering the bar is by an additional amount of backwater, that is, water flowing outward from the bay to the Gulf in a single channel in the direction of the ebb. . . .

Nothing should be permitted that tends to lessen the quantity of water going into the bay of Galveston, or receptacle for the tidal water. The contraction of the entrance, or the erection of piers several miles long in front of the entrance to the bay, does necessarily imply a diminished quantity of water admitted into the tidal receptacle.[38]

He then went on to state very clearly that any obstruction to the flow of the flood tide into Galveston Bay, or any other bay, would proportionately reduce the amount of the ebb tide and its scouring action on the channel to the open sea. With no major river adding its volume and velocity to the flow ebbing from Galveston Bay, the scouring action would be dependent upon the water that previously entered the bay on the flood tide. Obstructions in the channel would only reduce the anticipated scouring action, especially if the piers contracted the entrance, admitting less water into the bay.

An increase in the scouring action should be achieved by increasing the amount of water admitted to the bay, thereby increasing the force of the ebb tide, Stein wrote. If piers in the gulf contributed to an increase of the flood tide rather than a decrease, that would be desirable. However, he pointed out, any benefit that might be achieved by piers constructed in front of the entrance could also be achieved "with much greater security, and for less cost, by employing the same methods, or methods similar to those which have proved effectual in other tidal rivers, for the improvement of the tidal receptacles." Stein did not explain what those other methods were.[39]

Stein's knowledge of the situation at Galveston was taken from Howell's report and was not based upon firsthand knowledge of the confluence of tides, currents, and winds affecting the Bolivar Channel and the Outer Bar. The behavior of the littoral current along the coast could have been especially foreign to him, and doubtlessly the physical circumstances at Mobile Bay were considerably different. Stein's seeming disagreement with Captain Howell at that point over piers was still only in a "potential state," since Howell had not yet finally located the piers and Stein was not opposed to piers per se but only to those piers so placed that they would obstruct the quantity of water entering the receptacle—Galveston Bay. Therefore, neither Stein nor McAlpine could be said to have been in disagreement with Howell in regard to piers at the time of the reports.

McAlpine's Report

McAlpine, who at the time was the president of the American Society of Civil Engineers and one of the world's most renowned engineers, spent ten days in Galveston in March, 1872, examining the sandbars and channels of the harbor. His report occupied five full columns on the front page of the *Daily News*. McAlpine generally supported Captain Howell and the logic of his plans without coming to any final conclusion. Since Howell was making additional surveys and had not yet made his own recommendations final McAlpine withheld a final judgment himself. But he did offer a lengthy discourse explaining the forces of nature at work in the area and agreeing with Captain Howell that Galveston was the best site on the Texas coast for further development. This conclusion was drawn from the fact that the area of the receptacle of the flood tide (Galveston Bay) was larger than Matagorda Bay, the next largest receptacle on the coast, and the distance the flood tide had to travel once inside Galveston Bay was also less. These two factors combined would create the strongest ebb tide to scour a channel through the Outer Bar.[40]

Without knowing the design of the permanent works (that is, piers, jetties) to be built by the Army Engineers, McAlpine did recommend the extension of the Fowler pile jetty seaward, "gradually deflecting its present line of northeast by a curve, to its intersection with Bolivar Channel, and terminating in a line nearly east." He continued, "This direction will tend to deflect the combined currents (littoral and from the bay) toward the Cylinder channel, where the bar is comparatively narrow, and can be more easily maintained."[41]

The issuance of the three reports within a year of each other was a very significant step in the history of the development of a deep water harbor at Galveston. Although it was not the last time that some of the nation's leading engineering minds would address the problem, it represented the major step of initiating a scientific study of all the forces of nature at work on the Texas coast—tides, winds, and currents and their interaction with the land and seabed—affecting the channels into the Gulf of Mexico and the sandbars limiting access through them.

If the Congress of the United States was to be expected to appropriate the taxpayers' money for the improvement of these channels, the testimony and supporting evidence of the best engineering minds available would be required to justify the expenditures. In addition to establishing that Galveston was the best site to develop, it would also have to be established that the technical problem of deepening the channel was well understood scientifically and that the proposed solution would offer the best prospects for accomplishing the objective. The reports by Captain Howell, McAlpine, and Stein did much to support Galveston's cause at that time. The attention of eminent engineers was, in itself, a very positive factor.

The Citizens Organize

In addition to the efforts made to find a technical solution to the problem of deep water, the businessmen and citizens of Galveston also began to organize the lobbying effort that would be required to push the legislation through the Congress. A citizens group met on July 9, 1872, under the chairmanship of Willard Richardson for the purpose of making the necessary arrangements to support the legislation in the next Congress. Colonels Alfred M. Hobby and William L. Moody were named at this meeting to a committee to carry out the objectives, and the city council and the chamber of commerce were requested to name their representatives. Mayor Albert Somerville and Alderman Henry Rosenberg were named to represent the city council and the chamber of commerce later named James Moreau Brown, Moritz Kopperl, and George P. Alford to the group. At the chamber of commerce's meeting of December 10, 1872, Secretary and Treasurer R. J. Hughes reported that the harbor survey discussed earlier by Captain Howell was under way with Lieutenant Henry M. Adams, assistant engineer to Howell in New Orleans, in charge of the survey party. Hughes also reported that a committee appointed to evaluate continued membership in the National Board of Trade had recommended postponement of action to withdraw. It was pointed out that Galveston might wish the support of that body when harbor improvement legislation came before Congress. George Ball, representative to that body, informed the chamber that the National Board of Trade's

Executive Council would hold its annual winter session in Washington, D.C., during the coming January and that Galveston would have the opportunity to present its interests at that time. Colonel Hobby was also elected president of the chamber of commerce for the following year.[42]

Although Galveston's plans to become the "Seaport of the Great West" date back to the end of the Civil War and a great deal of local initiative was demonstrated in the movement to improve the harbor, the threat of competition from a new port at the mouth of the Brazos River also served as a stimulus to move ahead. In March, 1872, the rumors began to circulate regarding the plans of the eastern financial combine of Dodge-Phelps-Taylor to invest millions in the new port. The impact of a new port at Velasco backed by huge amounts of eastern money on Galveston's future was clearly understood. "The effect upon this port," said the *Daily News,* "must be disastrous." In fact, Galveston stood to lose many millions in decreased property values whether the port was finished or not. Consequently, the matter of improving Galveston Harbor was no longer a pipe dream or something that could be left to idle chance. At the end of 1872 Galveston was faced with a very serious threat to its continued prosperity, a threat that was going to require a complete mobilization of the business and civic interests in Galveston to press the case for federal funds to deepen the channel through the Outer Bar.[43]

An Abundance of Plans

When the Missouri-Kansas-Texas (the MKT or Katy) Railroad crossed the Red River north of Denison and connected with the Houston and Texas Central (H&TC) on December 28, 1872, it was a historic day for Texas. It certainly was for Galveston. The combined lines, the H&TC and GH&H in Texas and the MKT across the Indian Territory, Kansas, and Missouri, provided a continuous link between Galveston and Hannibal. The isolation of Texas from the rest of the United States was over, and passengers and freight could now move easily in either direction between these points, and other connections were available at Hannibal for points north and east, such as St. Louis.[44]

Of course, this did not come as a surprise; the possible economic impact upon the towns of Texas and the ports of Houston and Galveston had been the subject of speculation in 1870. The *Daily News* put the question to its readers very directly: "But what is going to be the effect upon Galveston and Houston? Heretofore these towns have depended mainly on the advantages they have enjoyed as cotton, hide, and wool markets, and as places of wholesale and jobbing trade for the country. Will they be able to retain these advantages after our connection by railroad with much larger cities, such as New Orleans, Memphis and St. Louis, and the great cities of the West, and the Atlantic seaboard?"[45]

Galveston and Houston would have the advantage of being closer to the producers, but would the railroads nullify this advantage with rates that were not competitive with railroad transportation east of the Mississippi River? There already was some indication of this, and New Orleans had begun to lose some of its trade each year. As it turned out, the railroad penetration of Texas from the north and east was only the first step in a process that historian L. Tuffly Ellis labeled "The Revolutionizing of the Texas Cotton Trade, 1865–1885."[46] In his analysis of the effect of technological change upon Galveston's history, David G. McComb points out that it was this opening of North Texas to trade with Kansas City and St. Louis that was Galveston's main economic problem in the 1870s, "not rivalry with Houston or Charles Morgan, or the Wharf Company's monopoly."[47]

In spite of all of the planning and meetings, the proposals and options, the citizens of Galveston were unable to match the accomplishment of the H&TC with other lines to the east or west, which could offset any loss of trade that the city might suffer as a result of competition from Kansas City and St. Louis. No city could have thought much more about railroads during the six years following the Civil War than Galveston, yet they had not a mile of new track to show for their efforts.

On August 1, 1871, Captain S. H. Gilman, a well-known civil engineer interested in railroads, published a seventy-page pamphlet entitled *The Relation of Railroads to the Commerce of Galveston*. The pamphlet included a number of articles that had been published in the *Galveston Daily News* in the preceding months, plus Captain Gilman's own analysis of the importance of the sixteen railroads included for discussion. The pamphlet also included a map of the United States and Mexico on which he had superimposed the routes of the proposed sixteen railroads emanating from Galveston like the spokes of a wheel with Galveston at the hub. The map included all of the transcontinental railroads built or under discussion at that time. With its coast-to-coast connections, the sixteen lines running through Galveston, and the sea routes indicated, the map creates an impression of Galveston as the "Center of the Universe," a phrase once used in describing the Island City's potential. With the roads depicted only in various stages of becoming reality, it is difficult to call the map a master plan. Yet it would provide those coming in the future with a scheme for Galveston's rise to greatness.[48]

Railroad scams were everywhere in those days, and potential investors in Galveston were right to be cautious and not to leap at every opportunity that arose. Sparse population west of the Mississippi River, especially in Texas, made railroad profitability difficult. But the world was not standing still. It was critical that Galveston find a means to converge its energies on the option, or options, that seemed to offer the most benefits to the city and the port, along with the hope of a fair return to the investors.

Progress was being made through the commercial conventions and the local congressmen to have the need for harbor improvement recognized. But that would avail little without a network of railroads moving exports and imports in and out of the port. New ideas and new initiatives, and perhaps new leadership, would be required in the remainder of the decade if Galveston was to become the "Seaport of the Great West."

Chapter 3

Galveston's
"Kansas City Movement"

Events in 1873 and 1874 proved that the ambition of becoming the "Seaport for the Great West" was not an idle pipe dream peculiar to the businessmen and civic boosters of Galveston. Instead, it was a vision that other states were increasingly coming to share, and events were occurring that were beginning to move the dream toward reality. As the population of the states of the Midwest—Missouri, Kansas, Iowa, and Nebraska—began rapidly to increase after the Civil War, the agricultural production likewise rapidly grew, even beyond the needs of the region itself. Markets for the surplus were sought after on the East Coast and in Europe. Unless prices were high, however, the farmers often found that high transportation costs actually resulted in their losing money, with crops sometimes being burned in the fields.

Through the rest of the 1870s, the seeds planted in the years since the end of the Civil War began to sprout. Out of all the railroad planning that took place came a plan for Galveston's own road to the interior—the Gulf, Colorado and Santa Fe. Initially it was envisioned as a line that would span the wide-open spaces of western Texas to reach Santa Fe, New Mexico, where it would also connect with the Denver and Rio Grande and its line to Denver. Its incorporators envisioned the same commercial relationships with Santa Fe as those held by the backers of the Santa Fe Expedition thirty years earlier. Now the earlier dreams were expanded by the hopes of transporting the mineral wealth of the Rocky Mountains to Galveston for shipment to ports around the world.

In Kansas City, Missouri, other civic leaders seeking to make their city a commercial and transportation center for the surrounding grain fields in Kansas, Iowa, and Nebraska began looking to the Gulf of Mexico for cheaper means of moving the rapidly increasing crops to Atlantic and European ports. The rebellion by the farmers and merchants of this region against the high rates imposed by the railroads to the Atlantic Coast caused them to look to their new connection to the gulf over the connecting tracks of the Missouri, Kansas and Texas Railway, the Houston and Texas Central, and the Galveston, Houston and Henderson. In 1873 and in 1874 Galveston was visited first by political leaders and then by business leaders examining freight rates and facilities.

Thus, in addition to the links to the New West by connections to Santa Fe and Denver, there was now added to Galveston's potential the opportunity for new commercial relationships with the agricultural "heartland" of the New West. The city responded to what became known in Kansas City as the "Galveston movement" by taking steps to create commercial ties, soliciting favorable rates between Kansas City and Galveston by the three connecting railroads, continuing the plans to deepen the channels through the bars in the harbor, and seeking reduced wharfage rates at Galveston.

Kansas Looks to the Gulf

Before Kansas City grew to be the metropolis of the Plains, opening the way to the New West, the creation of the Santa Fe Trail in 1821, soon to be followed by the Oregon Trail, had established Independence and Westport, now suburbs of Kansas City, as the jumping-off points. Located at the juncture of the Missouri and Kansas Rivers, they represented the westernmost points easterners could travel by water. As Lorenzo Sherwood and Caleb G. Forshey had seen Galveston as the hub of a network of railroads extending spokelike in every direction, so had William Gilpin seen a future metropolis at the mouth of the Kansas River also becoming a transportation center. Initially he probably meant Independence, but by the 1850s Kansas City, built upon the bluffs actually overlooking the juncture of the rivers, had surpassed its neighbors and become Gilpin's focal point. His prophecy for this transportation center of the future was set forth in an article entitled "Mission of the North American People," in which he outlined the "natural advantages" of Kansas City's location and defined its geographically determined future. The developments that were leading to the transformation of the New West—the settlement of the Plains, the gold and other mineral discoveries in the Rocky Mountains, and the transcontinental railroad—all focused upon Kansas City. More important, Gilpin saw as an integral part of the rise of the Mississippi Valley to national dominance, a railroad connection between Kansas City and Galveston on the Gulf of Mexico as a means of enabling the West to escape the domination of the East.[1]

The ideas expressed by Gilpin received further amplification by another "city planner," Charles C. Spalding, in his book *Annals of the City of Kansas.* Spalding, acknowledging his debt to Gilpin by incorporating his ideas into his book, stressed that Kansas City's destiny depended upon railroads to fulfill the promise of its natural advantages. With railroads, he said, Kansas City stood to become the next American metropolis. Following Spalding, Johnston Lykins, a missionary to the Indians who gravitated toward the new profession of "town boosting," laid out a master plan of railroads radiating from Kansas City, including one to Galveston. Writing in the winter of 1855–56, Lykins proposed a road first up the Kansas River Valley to Fort Riley; then a Pacific road across the continent that would enable Kansas City to become "the San Francisco of the Eastern slope of the mountains"; the Galveston road; and finally one to the Great Lakes. Lykins, who had become the first president of the chamber of commerce, president of the Mechanics' Bank, commission merchant, and real estate developer, envisioned Kansas City becoming "the grand emporium of the West . . . greater than Babylon, Ninevah, or Thebes." Drawing upon the geographical determinism of Gilpin and Spalding, Lykins proclaimed that the laws of geography providing for major emporiums three to four hundred miles apart and the location of the rivers necessitated the rise to greatness of Kansas City. A Kansas City, Galveston, and Lake Superior Railroad was actually chartered in 1857 as part of Lykins's grand design, but the Panic of 1857 and then the war stopped all construction until the war ended.[2]

Lykins's plans were published in the *Enterprise,* a newspaper owned by Robert T. Van Horn, who would rise to become one of Kansas

City's greatest civic leaders and railroad advocates. By the 1870s, the roads that had been built had formed pooling arrangements, setting rates unfavorable to Kansas City merchants. In 1873 both Van Horn's newspaper, the *Journal of Commerce,* and the *Kansas City Times* were printing attacks on the railroads. As historian Charles N. Glaab points out: "Before 1870 Kansas City leaders had been almost exclusively concerned with attracting railroads to the city. Now they had to deal with them. During the decade, they reshaped old concepts relating to railroads and formulated plans for alternative methods of transportation. For the most part, their proposed solutions proved ineffectual, but this itself was significant, for it demonstrated the declining scope of local promotion in a period when business consolidation and monopoly were on the rise."[3] The most detailed presentation of the complaints against the railroads came from the Kansas City Board of Trade in 1873. Departing from the doctrine of "natural advantages," the board's report concluded that the margin between success and failure in business was bound up in freight rates and that cities could not leave such matters to the eastern corporations that controlled the railroads.

After determining that control of the rail routes to New York and Baltimore by the eastern corporations was enabling them to create the rate pools so detrimental to Kansas City merchants and the farmers of the region, the board of trade developed a three-part plan designed to provide competition to the railroads to the east. The first part called for the building of narrow-gauge railroads that would be cheaper to build and less expensive to maintain. Because of the lower costs, it was intended that the railroads be locally financed so that local interests could control the rates. The second part of the plan urged the establishment of barge lines on the Missouri River as a method of competition between Kansas City and St. Louis. The combination of narrow-gauge railroads radiating from Kansas City and the barges to St. Louis would enable Kansas City to service the grain farmers of a large region and to recapture the grain traffic that had been siphoned off by Chicago. To some extent, the two approaches— railroads and barges—reflected contradictory thinking, saying that, on one hand, railroads could create a transportation center, while at the same time relying upon the doctrine of "natural advantages" to maintain that waterways were required for the growth of great cities.[4]

The Delegation to Galveston

The third part of the board of trade's plan urged the search for outlets on the Gulf of Mexico as a means of shipping directly to Europe and avoiding the monopolistic railroad lines controlled by eastern interests. Drawing upon the ideas and writings of Gilpin, Spalding, and Lykins, the board reemphasized the importance of creating this competitive alternative to reliance upon the eastern railroads. Of course, the completion of the Katy to the Texas border in December, 1872, made this option a reality instead of a dream. A board delegation had already visited northern Texas, and another delegation from Kansas headed by Governor Thomas A. Osborn had made a tour of Texas, visiting Galveston on April 25 and 26, 1873. Lieutenant Governor E. B. Stover and twenty-seven other Kansas officials accompanied the governor to meet Galveston's business leaders and view the harbor facilities. Then on May 1, 1873, the Island City played host to Van Horn, J. L. Bittinger, editor of the *St. Joseph (Mo.) Herald,* and a small party of civic leaders from Kansas and Missouri. At the time of these visits the emphasis was upon opening new markets for Kansas City merchants, and the delegations gave favorable reports to the board of trade. After the Panic of 1873 hit in September, the emphasis shifted to supporting port and trade facilities in Galveston, and Van Horn's *Journal of Commerce* suggested that a commercial convention including representatives from Missouri, Iowa, Kansas, Nebraska, Arkansas, and Texas should be held for that purpose. Unfortunately, that convention was never held, and it would be another fifteen years before another deep water convention would be held to rally midwestern support for harbor improvements in Galveston.[5]

But the opportunity to reach a broader audience was not completely lost. As a result of the congressional convention at St. Louis and the excursion to Galveston held in May of 1873, Senator William Windom of Minnesota announced that his committee was coming to St. Louis to take testimony in its investigation of national transportation needs and facilities. Van Horn and William H. Powell were selected by the board of trade to present a memorial to Windom's committee on the requirements of Kansas City. Arguing that the farmers of the region now required new markets to absorb the surplus crops not required by the region itself, Van Horn and Powell concluded by stating that Kansas City required federal support of a railroad from Kansas City to Memphis in order to shorten that route by about two hundred miles, and needed federal support for the removal of obstructions at the mouth of the Mississippi River and improvement of the harbor at Galveston. Drawing upon the works of Gilpin, Spalding, and Lykins, the Van Horn–Powell memorial defined the plains region as the New West, listed its attributes, and reasoned that it must play a role in the shaping of national transportation policy. The benefits were obvious, stated the memorial: "If the port of Galveston was made accessible for ocean going vessels, the wheat and corn of the Missouri Valley would seek the ocean at 26 $\frac{1}{4}$ cents per bushel, and pay the same rate it does today to New York at 52 $\frac{1}{2}$ cents—adding a quarter of a dollar to the price of the 115,000,000 bushels of these crops produced in 1870—or more than $28,000,000 to the farmers of this New West every year."[6]

In the next two years a civic effort that became known as the "Galveston movement" sought to expand trade between the two cities, lower freight rates, and improve the harbor at Galveston. The first initiative taken in 1874 occurred when Colonel James E. Marsh of Kansas City appeared before the national board in support of an additional memorial urging the creation of a territorial government for the country known as the Indian Territory (the present state of Oklahoma) as a means of promoting commerce among the rapidly growing new areas of the nation. Marsh's memorial provided for the right of each Indian head of family to a homestead and for the dedication of revenues received from land sales to the provision of schools and social services to the Indians. However, the main purposes were clearly to open the Territory to settlement and right-of-ways for railroads.[7]

In May of 1874, a delegation of businessmen from Kansas City, headed by Van Horn, visited Galveston.[8] A reception was held aboard the Steamship *San Jacinto* of the Liverpool and Texas Steamship Line, which was taking on cargo in preparation for departure. Colonel Alfred M. Hobby, president of the chamber of commerce, and Van Horn exchanged greetings, observed the loading activities, and then proceeded to their accommodations at the Cosmopolitan Hotel. The visitors met with the chamber of commerce at the Cotton Exchange building, where they were greeted by William K. McAlpine, chairman of the Exchange. He pointed out that Galveston had been almost exclusively a cotton port until now, but that he had no doubt about the port's ability to handle the wheat crop as well. Galveston had increased its exports from a very small amount to 357,238 bales in the current season. The commission merchants and the capital to finance the buying and selling of the wheat crop were also available. Van Horn responded, pointing out that in 1870 the region produced 26 million bushels of wheat, 89 million of corn, 24 million bushels of oats, 6 million pounds of tobacco, 1.8 million tons of hay, 2.5 million hogs, 835,000 horses, and 116,000 mules. He stated the crops were worth $85 million and the livestock $26 million—a total of $111 million. Kansas City was seeking to increase the share of that production that it was shipping and needed Galveston's help. Van Horn said that, based upon the shorter distance to Galveston, Kansas City should be able to ship wheat to the gulf at 20 cents per bushel, compared with 36 cents per bushel to New York, 30 cents to Baltimore, and 24 cents to New Orleans. The basic problem, as Van Horn saw, would be getting the management of the railroads to share the view of the Kansas City businessmen and provide competitive rates.[9]

To stimulate further the interests of the businessmen of Galveston, Van Horn also referred to the other side of the coin—the importation through Galveston of products needed by Kansas City and the New West. He cited, for example, the 20,000 bags of coffee disposed of in Kansas City the previous year, $1,580,000 worth of hardware, $270,000 worth of queensware, $3,710,000 worth of groceries, and $1,910,000 worth of liquors. New York and Baltimore, he said, were already becoming shaky over the possibility of losing this two-way trade with the New West. Van Horn's speech was followed by replies from several of the Galveston businessmen present—Colonel Hobby, Gustave Rangel, J. M. Walthew, and J. B. Grinnan—and all agreed that Galveston could handle the grain trade and that obtaining favorable railroad rates was the only problem to be solved. The meeting ended with the appointment of a committee to work with the Kansas City delegation to prepare letters to the presidents of the Houston and Texas Central, the International and Great Northern, and the Galveston, Houston and Henderson Railroads urging the establishment of favorable rates. Named were chamber president Hobby, James Sorley, C. R. Hughes, Leander Cannon, Moritz Kopperl, M. Quin, Walthew, and Grinnan.[10]

Good news was quickly forthcoming. Upon leaving Galveston the

Kansas City delegation met with officials of the Houston and Texas Central in Houston and Vice President James A. Baker. The delegation chairman Edward Dunscomb informed Colonel Hobby that, in Baker's own words, the railroad will "give us such a rate of freight over their road as *will compel* the shipment of our produce this way. . . . That was all we could ask, all we expected." Added Dunscomb, "We go home with the satisfaction that our mission has not been and will not be without good results to your city—and ours."[11]

More results followed quickly when the *Kansas City Journal of Commerce* announced that the general freight agent of the Missouri, Kansas and Texas Railroad promised the Kansas City Board of Trade "to pro rate with the Houston and Texas Central on the most favorable rate that road might be induced to give, and that in the meantime the rate from this city to Houston and Galveston shall not be higher than the rate charged from St. Louis to the same points."[12]

In addition, the *Journal of Commerce* announced that both the MKT and the Atchison, Topeka and Santa Fe completed lines directly into Kansas City, bringing to thirteen the number of railroads providing freight and passenger service to the city. "We are today," proclaimed the *Journal,* "where the original system projected placed us—the center of the entire railway system of the trans-Mississippi country—without rivalry and without competition."[13] Thus Kansas City moved another step closer to becoming that transportation center envisioned by Gilpin, Spalding, and Lykins. With one of those spokes radiating from Kansas City reaching to Galveston, the future prospects for both cities were looking very bright and their business communities were very aware of their burgeoning potentials. But it was not only in Kansas City and Galveston that the potential of the new relationship was being recognized. In late May and June the *Galveston Daily News* carried reprints of articles in the *Atchison Champion,* the *Tyler Index,* the *Topeka Commonwealth,* the *Buffalo (N.Y.) Courier,* the *Spring Hill (Mo.) Progress,* the *Denver Tribune,* the *Carrollton Record,* the *Omaha Republican,* and the *Lawrence Journal,* which recited the recent events and commented upon the coming changes in trading patterns.[14]

A Delegation to Kansas City

On June 15, 1874, a delegation led by Mayor Charles W. Hurley left Galveston for Houston, where it met a delegation from that city and departed on the H&TC for Kansas City. Joining Mayor Hurley for the trip were city alderman Patrick H. Hennesy, D. C. Stone, Leander Cannon, John D. Rogers, James Sorley, Julius Frederich, Noah N. John, Garland B. Miller, Alfred P. Luckett, John J. Hand, George Flournoy, Charles Evans, and B. R. Davis. The Houston delegation was composed of T. W. House, John Shearn, George L. Porter, John T. Brady, Henry S. Fox, C. S. Longcope, and George W. Kidd. A dispatch from Kansas City stated that plans for the combined delegations included dinner at the Coates House, entertainment at the Opera House, a general meeting with the board of trade followed by a banquet, and finally an excursion on the Kansas Pacific Railroad. The representatives of Galveston and Houston assured the hosts of their ability to handle the grain trade of the region, and Van Horn informed the visitors that he had been authorized by Robinson of the MKT and J. Waldo of the H&TC that their railroads would carry the products of Kansas and Missouri to the gulf for at least 3 cents per bushel less than it could be done to Atlantic ports, although they were not ready to set a specific rate.[15]

An invitation by the city of Denver, which many of the delegates accepted, added a new dimension to the trade talks previously held. Now the territories of the Rocky Mountain region had been added to the states of the Missouri Valley. The delegates were now encompassing the "Great West" as defined by Willard Richardson in those seminal editorials published in 1866, which had reoriented Galveston from its antebellum past as a southern cotton port—Charleston West—toward a new future as the port for that half of the United States west of the Mississippi River. The visit, of course, gave businessmen of both the gulf coast and the Rockies a chance to meet, and gave those from the flat coastal prairies a chance to enjoy the grandeur and climate of the Denver area. But it also provided all the opportunity to sense the real significance of the newly chartered (May, 1873) Gulf, Colorado and Santa Fe Railroad in its role as the connecting link between Denver and Galveston. The visit also provided those from the gulf coast their chance to have their first meeting with John Evans, the former governor of the Territory of Colorado, a great civic leader and businessman who would later play an extremely important role in Galveston's effort to achieve a deep water harbor.[16]

Although sumptuous banquets, lengthy speeches, and bottles of champagne were standard fare for such excursions at that time, there is ample evidence that both hosts and visitors found time to do business. Mayor Hurley, who also was the agent for the Black Star Line of Liverpool, announced that Dr. Dunscomb, the head of the Kansas City delegation, would serve as his representative in that city, offering through bills of lading at the lowest going rates. The following day an advertisement for the Hammerslough Company explained the benefits to be derived from "The Galveston Movement," including an increase in population and property values, increased profits for farmers, better markets, cheap transportation, and "no more hard times."[17]

A dispatch from Houston announced that the delegations, while en route home, had formed a new organization, the New West and Gulf Coast Association, and named George Flournoy as chairman and George W. Kidd as secretary. In Kansas City it was announced that J. D. Bancroft, cashier of the First National Bank, had joined the company of Gillespie and Bancroft to own and operate a new grain elevator nearing completion. The sudden increase in shipments to the gulf over the MKT lines had caught the attention of St. Louis, and lower rates were being offered. Another dispatch from Houston carried more information about the new association being organized, and indicated that the merchants of Kansas City, Sedalia, Fort Scott, Lawrence, Topeka, Junction City, Denver, Atchison, St. Joe, Omaha, Council Bluffs, and Lincoln would be invited to join with those of Houston, Galveston, Austin, Dallas, San Antonio, and other Texas cities in the formation of the association. Quickly, numerous advertisements by Houston and Galveston businesses, including the National Bank of Texas and merchants John Collins, L. T. Botto and Brothers, and Evans and Company of Galveston appeared in the *Kansas City Times*. This initiative on the part of the gulf coast businessmen testifies to the seriousness of their purpose of greatly expanding two-way trade with Kansas City and the New West.[18]

Omaha Included

The visits to Kansas City and Denver were not the end of Galveston's promotional efforts. In December, 1874, Charles W. Hayes, the business reporter for the *Galveston Daily News,* visited Omaha, Nebraska, as an unofficial representative of the Galveston business community, providing information about Galveston to the newspapers of the region, stimulating interest in an excursion to Galveston, and also involving himself directly in the effort to obtain railroad rates that would make the outlet to the gulf competitive with the eastern railroads to the Atlantic Coast. Hayes admitted that his purpose in remaining behind after the visit to Kansas City was to visit St. Joseph, Missouri, and Atchison and Leavenworth, Kansas, to report on business conditions to the *Daily News*. However, at St. Joseph he found the businessmen unenthusiastic about trade with Galveston and lacking the enterprising spirit found in Kansas City. He also found them to be taking a "show me" attitude toward freight rates that would be cheaper than East Coast rates. Therefore, he took it upon himself to contact Colonel J. F. Barnard, general superintendent, and George Olds, the general freight agent, of the Kansas City, St. Joe, and Council Bluffs Railroad, to see what reductions they would make in order to compete successfully with the eastern railroads. The officials replied with rates to Kansas City of 10 cents per hundred pounds from St. Joe; 20 cents from Council Bluffs; and 25 cents from Omaha. This was a big reduction, which translated into rates to Galveston of 70 cents per hundred pounds ($140 per car) from St. Joe, 80 cents per hundred pounds ($160 per car) from Council Bluffs, and 85 cents per hundred pounds ($170 per car) from Omaha. Hayes tested these rates by asking three of Galveston's largest coffee importers to send samples to Kansas City along with the prices of delivering them. Before the samples could arrive, New Orleans stepped in with a rate of 55 cents per hundred pounds ($110 per car) from that city to St. Joe on freight, and quoted coffee prices $1/4$ to $1/2$ cent lower than the Galveston market. Stymied at this point, Hayes was now forced to turn to the MKT and the H&TC to fulfill their earlier promises of such low rates that they would compel producers to seek the outlet to the gulf. His initial step was frustrated when the MKT official in Kansas City told him he did not have the power to act and he did not receive any answer from general manager J. Waldo of the H&TC.[19]

While these events were taking place, Hayes related, momentum developed for an excursion to Galveston by the merchants of Omaha and the surrounding region. In fact, before the visit by the Galveston businessmen to Kansas City, Barnard had already introduced the idea and was organizing a delegation of representatives from cities along the line of the Kansas City, St. Joe and Council Bluffs Railroad, stretching from Kansas City to Minneapolis, St. Paul and Duluth. By December, the Merchants Club of Omaha, whom Hayes described in his dispatch as far more enterprising than those of St. Joe, decided that the time had come for the excursion. Barnard offered free transportation to Galveston and back, said that he or Olds would accompany the group, and placed Hayes in charge of making all of the arrangements.

An Omaha delegation was quickly selected, comprised of men whom Hayes described as "prominent businessmen of commanding influence and wealth." They included delegation chairman John I. Redick; T. L. Kimball, Union Pacific Railroad; Colonel R. H. Wilbur; O. P. Henford, miller; S. R. Johnson, wholesale grocer; W. P. Wilcox, merchant; John C. Clark; Dr. George L. Miller, editor and proprietor of the *Herald*; A. D. Balcombe, manager of the *Republican*; M. Dunham, general dealer; and A. J. Simpson, carriage manufacturer. In addition, the Merchants Club sent a letter to Waldo suggesting that the establishment of competitive rates by the H&TC and the connecting roads, that is, the MKT and the GH&H, would "attract a current of trade in your direction that would be vastly renumerative." Specifically, the letter stated that the current rates on carloads of grain and flour were $75 between Omaha and St. Louis and Omaha and Chicago and $140 to New York. It suggested that a rate of $80 between Kansas City and Galveston would have a very favorable impact on the volume of trade. To insure that the readers at home fully understood the import of the happenings in Omaha, Hayes gave them the following admonishment:

> *This movement, so auspiciously inaugurated, if properly directed and encouraged by the city of Galveston, will result in making her the grandest commercial city in the South. Every citizen of Galveston should take a deep interest in founding a trade that will be beneficial alike to poor as well as the rich, and it should command the earnest attention of every live man in the city, whether in or out of business. Our railroads and shipping interest should put forth herculean efforts to encourage and foster this trade. Nothing should be overlooked or left undone that will tend to make this grand scheme a permanent and lasting success. Now is the time for our city to strike hard and steady blows, and create such an impression upon the minds of our distinguished visitors, who will soon be your guests, as will at once result in the establishment of a large and permanent trade.[20]*

Before the delegation could arrive in Galveston, Hayes received a satisfactory reply from Waldo on rate reductions. Combined with the rates north from Kansas City offered by Olds, Hayes reported that the rates on coffee, sugar, and molasses from Galveston would be $120 per car to St. Joseph, $130 per car to Council Bluffs, and $140 per car to Omaha.[21]

The delegation arrived in Galveston on January 6, 1875, with elaborate arrangements made for greetings, transportation, entertainment, and accommodations at the Grand Southern Hotel.[22] Representatives from Omaha, Plattsmouth, and Nebraska City, Nebraska; St. Joseph, Missouri; Atchison, Kansas; Council Bluffs, Iowa, and elsewhere met formally with their Galveston hosts at the Cotton Exchange on the afternoon of January 8, 1875. Colonel Hobby and Hayes gave welcoming remarks, and R. F. Montgomery of Council Bluffs, who had been elected chairman of the twenty-seven-man group, responded. The speeches that followed stated the many benefits to be gained by the farmers and merchants of the New West by having a shorter distance and cheaper rates to get their produce to market. Statistics were presented on the volume of all the crops produced in the various states represented. Of course, freight rates on the connecting railroads was the most important topic, but others mentioned were the need for the deep water channel, narrowing the wide gauge on the GH&H, lowering wharfage rates, and opening the Indian Territory that separated Texas from the states of the New West. At the end of the day a transportation committee was named, consisting of the following: O. P. Hurford, W. W. Marsh, S. R. Johnson, and Ezra Millard of Omaha; Charles Headrie, T. J. Evans, and E. S. Shuegart of Council Bluffs; M. Kerr of St. Joseph; Mayor Thomas Murphy of Atchison; Dr. John Black of Plattsmouth; and James Sorley, Moritz Kopperl, and J. M. Walthew of Galveston. This committee met to discuss rates and named a subcommittee that met with freight agents Robinson of the MKT and Waldo of the H&TC to negotiate. The negotiation did not produce the rates that all of the delegates would have liked to hear; rather, the subcommittee report stated that the freight agents assured the subcommittee members that rates would be lowered once the trade materialized.[23]

Progress did not occur as rapidly as everyone had hoped. Soon after the Panic of 1873 began in September, a severe slowdown in business occurred all across the country. The railroads that had promised the competitive rates failed to deliver. But the effort made to establish commercial relations with the western states was by no means a failure. When better economic times returned, the community of interests identified at this time and the personal contacts made would serve as a foundation for significant leaps forward. The important accomplishment of the exchange of excursions was in that both Galveston and the western states saw the Island City as the port of the future. In time the pieces would all fall into place.

Chapter 4

The Army Engineers Try—and Fail

The efforts to achieve deep water continued in parallel with the attempts to establish commercial relations with Kansas City and Omaha. The year 1873 would be filled with action for the citizens of Galveston on the local, state, and national levels as an all-out effort was launched to bring deep water to the city. Attempting to leave no stone unturned, the new lobbying program expanded beyond local-level memorials to Congress to include memorials from the state. The new approach also expanded beyond the sending of memorials to include excursions to Galveston and the presence in Washington of representatives to push the cause.

The tone for the year was set early in a January editorial in the *Daily News* that pointed out that the wealth of Galveston already accounted for 10 percent of the state's tax revenue and that this could be significantly increased by improving the harbor and enabling the city to capture a larger share of commerce from outside the state. The example of New Orleans was cited, and it was pointed out that the railroads already built, those under construction, and those in the planning stage—all converging on Galveston—would do for the city what the Mississippi River had done for New Orleans. Both the state and national governments would benefit from the increased taxes and customs levies that the increased commerce through Galveston would provide. With all of the engineering surveys agreeing that Galveston was the best natural harbor west of the Mississippi for improvement, the *Daily News* emphasized that it was now time for both state and federal government to fund a twenty-foot channel through the Outer Bar, a task that was beyond Galveston's ability.[1]

On March 12, 1873, the chamber of commerce passed a strong resolution to support the Army Engineers and the cause of harbor improvement. The resolution named President Alfred M. Hobby and members James Moreau Brown, Moritz Kopperl, and George P. Alford to a standing committee to cooperate with the Engineers, the city's board of harbor improvement, and any other group working toward a deeper channel.[2] Shortly after that event, board of harbor improvement president Henry Rosenberg submitted his report to outgoing mayor Albert Somerville, stating that the board had temporarily suspended its operations and that the Army Engineers had taken over the responsibility for the pile jetty. This action, unless the incoming mayor implemented a new initiative, would leave the chamber of commerce in the driver's seat to lead the effort to press for the deeper channel.[3]

The initial action taken occurred at the state level when both houses of the Texas legislature passed a resolution urging the consideration by the Congress of the United States for the deepening of Galveston Harbor. The resolution not only pointed out Galveston's increasing importance as a port for the imports and exports of the western United States, it also emphasized the growing commerce between the West Indies, Central America, and Brazil on the one hand and Galveston on the other. The savings to be realized in this trade by eliminating the lightering charges then incurred made deepening the channel through the bar a matter of national importance, claimed the resolution. It was soon introduced in the U.S. House of Representatives by Congressman Charles Sabin of Houston, where it was referred to the committee on commerce and manufactures. The Texas legislature also passed an act authorizing the Galveston City Council to issue $500,000 in bonds to be known as "Galveston Bar and Harbor Improvement Bonds," and to carry on such works as might be advantageous to the commerce of the city. The control and expenditure of the funds was placed in the hands of the board of harbor improvement, and were to be used for projects undertaken solely by the board, or by the board in cooperation with the authorities of the United States.[4]

In addition to action on the legislative front, the city engaged in very important "public relations" activities. As mentioned earlier, on the weekend of April 25 and 26, 1873, the city played host of a large group of excursionists from the rapidly growing state of Kansas. Taking advantage of the newly established link to Texas provided by the connection of the Missouri-Kansas-Texas and the Houston and Texas Central railroads, Governor Thomas A. Osborn, Lieutenant Governor E. S. Stiver, and more than two dozen state officials and members of the legislature and their wives visited the "Queen City of the Gulf" to view its assets and enjoy its hospitality. Mayor Charles W. Hurley and Colonel Hobby welcomed the visitors, accompanied by many of the city's leading citizens.[5]

During their visit the guests were given a cruise aboard the steamer *Josephine* through the harbor and into the gulf, and tours of the Texas Cotton Press, the *Galveston Daily News,* the Opera House, the beach, and the residence of Mayor Hurley. Independently, the guests had opportunities to visit many of the city's large wholesale houses and acquaint themselves with large stocks available at Galveston and the prices. On Saturday evening, the Kansans met in the parlor of the Exchange Hotel and passed several resolutions, expressing their gratitude to Mayor Hurley and the other hosts and to the officials of the steamship lines and railroads who extended courtesies to them. More important, they also expressed their hope for the day in the future when the products of Kansas and its neighboring states would have access to the sea at Galveston with the advantage of eight hundred fewer miles of rail transportation than to the port of New York.[6]

Congressional Visitors

The visit of the Kansans gave the citizens of Galveston a good chance to develop their hospitality skills, and another opportunity to use them came quickly. A delegation of congressmen passing through Texas on their way to New Orleans visited the city on May 20 and 21, 1873, to see and hear of its splendors. The businessmen and civic leaders spared no effort to impress their guests, who came from all over the country. "No such an occasion has transpired since Galveston has been a city as that of the reception and entertainment of the Congressional and other visitors yesterday," said the *Galveston Daily News* in opening its description of the proceedings. Although ample time was devoted to sightseeing, speech making, and dining, appropriate time was also set aside for the business at hand, the matter of Galveston harbor. After being toured around the Strand and other city sights, the visitors were taken to the Opera House where they were the guests of the chamber of commerce. There the visitors had the opportunity to examine charts and drawings of the gulf and the bay and to hear explanations of the current conditions and the projected improvements that the Congress would be asked to finance. Colonel Hobby, president of the chamber, and John S. Thrasher, John S. Sellers, James Sorley, and others were on hand to satisfy the visitors' requests for additional information.[7]

The visit began even before the guests reached Galveston. A delegation from the Galveston Chamber of Commerce met the visitors at Corsicana, and their servants began serving lunch and wine—all the way to Galveston. The visitors were also greeted, first, with envelopes including the itinerary of their visit and names of all the members of the reception committee and subcommittees, and second, with a packet of four cards—one for a hotel room, a welcome to the rooms of the Gulf City Club, another welcome to the rooms of the Harmony Club, and the fourth a Morgan line ticket for the steamship excursion to New Orleans. Upon arrival at Galveston the guests were met by carriages to escort them to their hotels. The carriages remained at their disposal for the duration of their visit. That evening, Tuesday, May 20, the festivities were held at the Opera House. Welcoming speeches were made by General Thomas N. Waul of Galveston and Senator James W. Flanagan of Henderson, one of Texas's Reconstruction senators. Responses were offered by Congressmen G. S. Orth of Indiana, S. S. Marshall of Illinois, and Judge James R. Wilson of Indiana. In light of the hostilities that had only recently ended, apparently there was some apprehension on the part of the hosts regarding the views that northern congressmen might hold. But, according to the *Daily News,* this apprehension was unwarranted:

> *Without the slightest intention of personal criticism we would express*
> *our thorough gratification at hearing the able and manly response of the*
> *Hon. G. S. Orth to the welcome extended by General Waul on behalf of*
> *the citizens of Galveston. Judge Orth is a Republican; he is a prominent*

representative of his party in Congress, and might have been regarded, antecedently, as either inimical or coldly affected to us. None who listened to the impassioned and spontaneous utterances of this wonderfully eloquent man, will deny that such ideas were foreign to the feeling of the speaker. No clearer or cordial expression of amity could possibly haven been made, and, coming from such a man on such an occasion, we think it memorable in itself, and weighted with good tidings for the future.[8]

The Army Engineers Act

Once the "politicking" was over, it was time to go to work. The report on Galveston Harbor, containing the results of the surveys and examinations made by Lieutenant Henry M. Adams (who had graduated first in his class at West Point in 1866) and his civilian assistant, H. E. Ripley, were submitted to Captain Charles W. Howell (who had graduated first in the class of 1863) in New Orleans in June, in time to support the submission of Howell's report and recommendations to the Army Chief of Engineers, General Andrew A. Humphreys, who was a founding member of the National Academy of Sciences. Supporting data for all of the engineer projects to be submitted to Congress were required in Washington in order to be included in the Annual Report of the Chief of Engineers (ARCE). Colonel Hobby, president of the chamber of commerce, was very busy preparing the economic and statistical information needed to justify the expenditure to the Congress. This information, of course, would include the steps taken by Galveston first to help itself by improving the channel over the Inner Bar.[9]

The wheels of the government bureaucracy did not turn quite as fast as hoped for, however. When visited by Colonel John S. Thrasher in early October on behalf of the chamber of commerce, General Humphreys had not yet received the report from Captain Howell. Consequently, Thrasher stopped at New Orleans on his return trip to see Howell, who assured him that the report on Galveston harbor would be completed in time to be included in addenda to the ARCE. When the middle of December arrived and Howell's report still had not been received in Washington, the *Daily News* took a more strident tone and recommended that Mayor Charles Hurley; Henry Rosenberg, as president of the harbor improvement board; and Colonel Hobby, as president of the chamber of commerce, be designated by the city council as a delegation to go to New Orleans to see whether or not the report on Galveston could be submitted to the Chief of Engineers by January 1, 1874, in order to be included in the addenda. Describing the situation as "inexplicable," the *Daily News* proclaimed that extraordinary action was necessary to get the Galveston appropriation before the Congress.

While Galveston's anxiety was justified, Captain Howell's problem was not so mysterious. At that time the matter of deepening the mouth of the Mississippi River was one of major concern, and Howell and the Army Engineers were under considerable pressure to find a workable solution. Almost forty years of dredging on the Mississippi had produced a depth of only fifteen and one-half feet at considerable cost, and the impact on trade through New Orleans was enormous. Receiving considerable attention in New Orleans as a solution was the idea of a new outlet to the sea for the Mississippi—the Fort St. Phillip Canal. But the Merchants' Exchange of New Orleans was now promoting another approach—the construction of jetties proposed by civil engineer James B. Eads on the Southwest Pass of the Mississippi. These jetties, maintained Eads, who had achieved worldwide recognition as the designer of the bridge over the Mississippi at St. Louis, would produce a channel twenty-six feet deep with guaranteed results. Doubtlessly the presence of these competing plans was generating a major problem for Captain Howell. In addition the Army Engineers were conducting analyses of the mouths of the Rhone, Rhine, and Danube Rivers in Europe to see what could be learned from the experiences at those locations. All of this information was creating a major workload problem for Howell and his staff as they attempted to arrive at recommendations on the Mississippi—before they could arrive at plans for Galveston.[10]

Captain Howell's Plan

In spite of the logical obstacles, Captain Howell did complete his report and recommendations on the Galveston Harbor and submitted them to the Chief of Engineers on December 30, 1873. The plan envisioned two parallel jetties on opposite sides of the Bolivar Channel extending into the Gulf of Mexico. The basic cost of the design would be $531,866 for submerged jetties. However, the cost would increase to $1,144,951 to raise the tops of the jetties above mean low tide if that proved necessary. With a contingency factor added, the total cost rose to $1,259,446. The report requested $500,000 to cover the work that would be accomplished during the government fiscal year beginning July 1, 1874, and ending June 30, 1875. The basic building block of the jetties was to be the gabion, a basket or cage filled with earth or rocks employed in the construction of military fortifications and adapted to a new use. The gabions were to be constructed from the brush plentiful in the Texas countryside. Pieces of the brush were to be woven into baskets six feet tall and six feet in diameter to be filled with sand and covered with cement. These blocks would be laid side by side to form the jetty (or gabionade), and, if necessary, a second row would be placed atop the first.

The basic objective of employing the gabion instead of stone was to reduce the cost of the jetties to an amount that Congress would approve. The jetties planned to be constructed in this manner were to be approximately three and four miles long, 16,200 feet for the jetty on the Bolivar Peninsula side of the channel and 20,800 feet on the Galveston Island side. In addition to these jetties extending into the Gulf of Mexico, the plan also included two dams 2,600 and 20,100 feet long, also made of gabions, to connect Pelican Island and Pelican Spit and extend to West Bay parallel to Galveston Island and the Galveston Harbor Channel. The dams would serve to throw all of the water to fill West Bay through Galveston Harbor for the purpose of widening the harbor on the flood tide and having the ebb tide flowing out through the harbor deepening the channel through the Inner Bar at the entrance to Galveston Harbor. The plan also included one more jetty, 5,000 feet long, "to cut off all the flood-tide that would find its way over the shoal the jetty covers, and to carry the full volume of the tide into the harbor to widen and extend it opposite the city front." Since the chart accompanying Captain Howell's report was not included in the published record, it is difficult to locate precisely the position of this jetty and its relationship to the dams intended to steer the flood tide into the Harbor Channel.[11]

Captain Howell estimated that a gabion could be constructed for $30. However, 12,333 gabions were required for the two jetties into the gulf, thus a cost of $369,990. Adding $38,744 for the cost of the sand filling, the total cost of the jetties was put at $408,734 for a single-layer, submerged design. The dams, involving 4,250 gabions at $15.80 and 950 at $30, added another $102,470. The third jetty, with only 1,250 gabions, came to $20,662. The total for all of these components came to $531,866. However, the estimate submitted included the cost of adding a second row of gabions on top of the first, $613,084, even though there was no certainty at the time that this step would become necessary. Adding to the basic cost for the one row and applying a 10 percent contingency factor, the total estimate for the entire project came to $1,259,446. The plan for jetties and dams was based upon the results of the survey and examination made by Lieutenant Adams and Ripley in 1872–73, and the report defined the very difficult circumstances presented by the entrance to Galveston Harbor and Bay. In describing the soil conditions, the report said the following:

> The upper stratum of Galveston Island, Bolivar Peninsula, Pelican Spit and Island, and of the bars, is of the fine rounded sand peculiar to the islands forming the condon littoral of the Gulf coast. It has all of the characteristics of quicksand, is easily moved, when dry, by the wind; the littoral current moves it back and forth along the coast; waves and tidal currents, where it is exposed to their action on the bars, shift it with every change in direction of wind and velocity of current, making frequent changes in the shape of the bars and the channels across them. . . . It affords the least desireable of all foundations on which an engineer may be obliged to build.[12]

The report also compared data from the survey charts of 1841, 1851, 1867, and 1872 to illustrate the changes that had taken place in both the shorelines and the various channels in Bolivar Pass. For example, the northeast point of Galveston Island (Fort Point) had moved 1,200 yards to the west of its position in 1841. Pelican Spit had also moved to the west along with Fort Point, and the Inner Bar, which did not exist in 1841, had been created between Fort Point and Pelican Spit. In 1841 the Galveston Harbor Channel (along the north side of the island) and Bolivar Channel were connected by a thirty-foot channel, which the formation of the Inner Bar had reduced to a nine-foot channel. Also changed since 1841 was Bolivar Channel, which actually consisted of four channels: a central (cylinder) channel; swash channels on both the Galveston and Bolivar sides; and a fourth channel following the shore of Galveston Island used by the deepest draught vessels and properly considered the main channel. It was concluded that most of the changes to the shorelines and channels had been caused by the effect of the winds upon the currents and tides and the changes in directions and velocities of the currents and tides. Although the prevailing winds were from the southeast and east, a high degree of variability was experienced through the year, each direction having a different impact on the currents and tides. The combination of unfavorable foundation and highly variable winds, producing an ever-changing topography, presented the Army Engineers with a formidable challenge.[13]

The experimental nature of the approach proposed by Captain Howell was underlined by the fact that the project was referred to a board of distinguished Army Engineers for evaluation before submission to Congress by General Humphreys.[14] The board was comprised of three lieutenant-colonels, each of whom already had notable accomplishments and had outstanding careers yet ahead of them: Zebulon B. Tower, Horatio G. Wright, and John Newton. Howell was also named to the board to insure a full treatment of his concepts. Although the board members essentially agreed with Captain Howell in the analysis of the conditions at Galveston and his recommended concept, they concluded that the highly experimental nature of the project be recognized from the beginning and that a trial be conducted first by constructing the inner end of the jetty on the Fort Point side. If successful, this first step could then be followed by an additional test—building the inner end of the jetty on the Bolivar Peninsula side as well as two hundred to five hundred feet of jetty near the bar in the most exposed position. For this experimental construction, the board recommended an appropriation of $60,000 for the fiscal year beginning July 1, 1874.[15]

In addition to recommending an experimental, or prototype, program, the board also made some modifications to Captain Howell's design. First, they recommended increasing the thickness of the gabions from four to six feet, raising the cost from $30.00 to $40.00. They also added covers and bottoms to the gabions to prevent any loss of the sand-filling by the action of the sea, and the covering of the heads of the gabions with asphalt for additional protection. The dams and jetty inside the bay proposed to improve the Inner Bar were deleted from the project since no work would commence there until the feasibility of deepening the water over the Outer Bar had been proven.

The additions and deletions resulted in a net increase of $500,000 to Captain Howell's estimate of $1.2 million. Captain Howell dissented from the findings of the majority of the board, stating that he had more confidence in the design proposed and the original cost estimate. However, since the idea of testing the concept before proceeding had been accepted by General Humphreys and recommended to Congress, the debate over the final design and eventual cost became moot. More important at this point than exact costs was the promise that the gabion technique held out for the reduction of jetty costs over previous methods. The technique, if successful, would have wide application on the coasts of the United States and would enable the undertaking of improvement projects that would have been out of the question because of prohibitive costs.[16]

Hutchings Prods the Engineers

While the plans for the jetties and the necessary appropriation were going through the required processes in Washington, the concerned parties in Galveston were not leaving their city's future to chance. At the request of Mayor Hurley, John H. Hutchings, one of the city's leading businessmen and a partner in Ball, Hutchings and Company, went to visit Washington on his return from a trip north to determine the status of Captain Howell's plans. In a report back to the city, Hutchings stated that Congressman Asa H. Willie had informed him that Captain Howell's plans had been well received in the Army Engineers headquarters and that a favorable outcome was anticipated. Hutchings also reported that he was gratified by the interest shown in Galveston by Texas Senators Morgan C. Hamilton and James W. Flanagan and Representatives DeWitt C. Giddings, Roger Q. Mills, John Hancock, and William S. Herndon. The effects of the Panic of 1873 were being felt in the Congress, Hutchings observed, and he offered this hopeful opinion: "Retrenchment and economy are now in the mouth of everyone, and it is an unpropitious time to bring forward claims to new appropriations. But, notwithstanding this virtuous spasm, I shall be grievously disappointed if Judge Willie and our delegation do not secure such an appropriation to our bar as will be an earnest commencement to its improvement, and the work once adopted and undertaken, the government will carry it through."

Hutchings also found favor for Galveston among Republican congressmen he visited and, perhaps even more important, considerable respect for the ability of the Texas delegation among the Republicans.[17] The information received and reported back by Hutchings was essentially correct. The modification of the plan by the Board of Engineers occurred after his January visit, but this approach, seeking only $60,000 for the first year instead of $500,000, no doubt contributed to the bill's attractiveness. On the evening of June 19, 1874, the Senate passed the Rivers and Harbors Appropriation containing the appropriation for Galveston, after Judge Willie successfully steered the proposal through the usually turbulent legislative waters. The public announcement of the recommendations of the board was made on February 17, 1874, but the House commerce committee had already announced its determination not to undertake any new projects in the coming fiscal year. In the meantime it was reported that Judge Willie was spending much time at the war department examining the maps and plans for the works in order to prepare himself to advocate the project before both the commerce committee and the full House of Representatives. When he finally introduced the matter "incidentally" to the committee, he found no opposition. "On the other hand," reported the *Daily News*, "several members of the committee spoke in very appreciative terms of the growing importance of Galveston, and indicated their willingness to treat the matter generously."[18]

Congressman Willie's Support

Judge Willie's speech to the House in support of the appropriation was delivered in late April and presented the economic justification for the expenditure on Galveston. Imports for the past fiscal year amounted to $30 million and exports to $37 million. These amounts represented a tenfold increase in imports and a doubling of exports in the last five years. As a consequence, customs duties collected at Galveston had risen from $184,177 for the year ending June 30, 1869, to $682,934 for the year ending June 30, 1872. Cotton, of course, was the prime export commodity. During the commercial year ending September 1, 1873, Galveston had shipped 388,802 bales, an increase of 60,000 bales over the previous year. Since that date,

816,267 bales had been received for shipment by April 11, 1874, and an estimated 400,000 additional bales were expected by September 1, 1874. This growth in commerce, said Judge Willie, had been accompanied by a population increase from 14,000 in 1870 to 34,350 in the census just completed.[19]

Both of these increases could be attributed to extension and multiplication of railroads in the early 1870s terminating in Galveston, especially the connection with the MKT, which brought the city into contact with the grain fields of the Midwest. Production of wheat, rye, corn, oats, barley, hay, and tobacco in the Kansas-Missouri-Iowa region was well established by 1870 and new statistics would show marked increases through 1873 when available. When the grain, cotton, and cattle of Texas and Arkansas are added to the output of the midwestern states, said Willie, the port of Galveston lies within easy reach of great wealth. This commerce had already made Galveston the eighth United States port in exports, ranking behind New York, New Orleans, Savannah, San Francisco, Boston, Philadelphia, and Baltimore.[20]

Willie then came to his "punch line." The producers of the West were annually paying a $28 million tax on their grain, the amount that could be saved in transportation costs by using the port of Galveston and cutting rail costs to the Atlantic Coast in half. To this must be added the savings to be realized on all of the other products now moved by rail, plus a corresponding increase to the value of their lands. "Could the largest sized vessels be brought to our wharves," Willie pointed out, "elevators would be erected, and cars for the transportation of grain in bulk constructed, and the farmers of Western Iowa, Nebraska, Western Missouri, and Kansas, and all other sections located convenient to our port could put their grains in market with expedition and economy, and find renumerative returns for that which now rots upon their hands or is consumed for fuel." Clearly, the answer was to improve the harbor at Galveston, the most accessible and economical port for the western farmers. By the end of May, Judge Willie had assurances from both houses of Congress that the appropriation for Galveston had no enemies, and the path was cleared for the final vote in June.[21]

Lieutenant James B. Quinn was assigned to Galveston by Captain Howell in New Orleans to manage the experimental project. Quinn, who graduated from West Point in 1866 and, as did many of the engineer officers, ranked high in his class, announced after his arrival that by the latter part of November, fifteen hundred feet of these gabions would have been constructed, commencing at the end of the existing pile jetty and extending northeast out to where the water reached a depth of fourteen or fifteen feet. This effort would use approximately $35,000 of the congressional appropriation. The remaining $25,000 would be used in a further extension two to three hundred feet southeast in the direction of the Outer Bar, provided that the initial phase was successful. This construction, when completed, would provide an ample test of feasibility of the gabion design, according to Lieutenant Quinn, who also added that the test would be completed in time for congressional action on the appropriation required to continue the work after July 1, 1875.[22]

Lieutenant Quinn's Problems

But Lieutenant Quinn's plans for rapid progress immediately following his August arrival were frustrated by the problem of obtaining materials, especially the brush from which the frames of the gabions were to be constructed. Owners whose lands contained the desired brush were located by mid-September, but when these landowners became aware they had a valuable commodity their prices began to rise appreciably. Lieutenant Quinn attributed this behavior to the experience of the landowners during the Civil War, when the government was willing to pay liberally for badly needed supplies. It is also possible, however, that the effects of the Panic of 1873 were affecting the prices the farmers were receiving for other products and the demand for the brush was a convenient way to offset these losses. Nevertheless, it was the middle of October before Lieutenant Quinn was able to negotiate acceptable prices and the brush began arriving at the work site at Fort Point.[23] In the meantime Lieutenant Quinn and his staff kept their people busy building accommodations for the workmen, storage facilities for the materials, and devices, such as platforms, to be used in the building and placing of the gabions. Once materials began to arrive in necessary quantities, the construction progress moved swiftly. Enough of the gabions had been placed by December 9 that when the gabions withstood three days of "fierce storms" on December 4, 5, and 6, Lieutenant Quinn felt justified in formally reporting to Captain Howell in New Orleans that the gabion design concept had been adequately proven to be feasible and in requesting an additional $100,000 for the fiscal year ending June 30, 1875, and $300,000 for the fiscal year commencing July 1, 1875. In his report, Lieutenant Quinn gave the following description of the status of the gabions following the storms:

> We entertained no hopes whatever of finding any of the gabions in place or even in the vicinity of the place where they had been sunk.
>
> An examination made as soon on the following Monday as the subsidence of the sea would permit, disclosed the important facts—
>
> That the gabions were substantially in the same position they had been put;
>
> That they had not been undermined or settled any; That the sand had banked up against them on either side; and
>
> That they were quite effectual in arresting the current produced by the tide, quiet water existing in rear of the jettee [sic] they formed.[24]

In addition to claiming that the gabions had passed their test, Lieutenant Quinn went even further by recommending that the design of the jetty use only one row of gabions instead of the two that Captain Howell had indicated might be necessary. The Howell plan placed the two rows in a "quincunx form," with two alternating rows supporting each other, as follows:

O O O O O
O O O O O

The only negative aspect to Lieutenant Quinn's report, if it could be called that, was his raising the cost estimate per gabion from Captain Howell's $30 to $50, based upon the actual experience gained in building them. However, the recommendation to change the plan from two rows to one, reducing the number of gabions by 7,000, resulted in a net decrease in the total cost of the two jetties. Knowing that his recommendations might be looked upon in Washington as the effort of an exuberant young officer trying to improve his efficiency rating and chances for promotion, Lieutenant Quinn solicited the support of another West Pointer, General Braxton Bragg, who at this time was the chief engineer of the Gulf, Colorado and Santa Fe Railroad in Galveston. General Bragg issued a public statement, which Lieutenant Quinn included in his report, that confirmed the observations, conclusions, and recommendations of the report.[25]

Another Board Review

Events moved rapidly once Captain Howell received Lieutenant Quinn's report. He transmitted the document with his endorsement to General Humphreys on December 14, 1874, and shortly afterwards Congressman Willie introduced legislation in the House of Representatives to appropriate immediately the $400,000 recommended by Lieutenant Quinn for the combined fiscal years. General Humphreys did not, however, move quite as rapidly as Judge Willie did. He referred the report to the same Board of Engineers that had reviewed the project the year before—Colonels Zebulon Tower, Horatio G. Wright, and John Newton. The board recommended that the project continue on an experimental basis but expressed the view that the results thus far were not decisive. The fact that the gabions became so rapidly embedded by accumulations of sand may have been owing, observed the board members, to a favorable position of the jetty, and they were not certain the same accumulation would occur for every position of the jetty proposed and under all the varied phases of wind, wave, and current. Furthermore, they said, any sand-embankments thus formed would have to be tested by exposure to gales from all quarters before their permanence could be assured. General Humphreys submitted his recommendation to Secretary of War William W. Belknap on January 13, 1875, asking that the experiment continue and $400,000 be appropriated for the current and ensuing fiscal years (as Congressman Willie requested) in order that the work would not have to be interrupted when the currently available funds were expended. The following day Secretary Belknap endorsed the recommendation of the Chief of Engineers and forwarded it to the House of Representatives.[26]

When the rivers and harbors appropriation bill was reported out of the House commerce committee at the end of February, the amount requested by the Chief of Engineers had been reduced to $150,000, as was the practice of the committee every year when acting upon the requested amounts. Congressman Willie, however, did not look upon this reduction as a cause for disappointment. In a letter to his constituents, he pointed out that the amount would provide approximately $10,000 per month for the period between the adjournment of Congress in 1875 to the end of the government fiscal year in June, 1876, and the work could progress. He also reported that a supportive resolution from the Kansas legislature and similar actions anticipated by other state and municipal bodies would strengthen Galveston's position during the process in Washington.[27]

Senator Maxey Investigates

Galveston's fortunes received another boost in May when Senator Samuel Bell Maxey of Paris, recently elected by the Texas legislature to replace James W. Flanagan, visited to acquaint himself with the city and its need for a deep water channel to the gulf. Maxey was a member of West Point's class of 1846, which included Generals Ulysses S. Grant and George Pickett among others. As were many of his classmates, Maxey was decorated for his service in the Mexican War and later served as a Confederate general in command of forces in the Indian Territory. Because of his engineering education, Maxey was also uniquely qualified to understand the nature of the work undertaken by the Army Engineers to construct the jetties.[28]

Senator Maxey arrived on May 13, 1875, on the 9:30 P.M. train and was met at the station by representatives of the chamber of commerce and the Cotton Exchange—Colonel Hobby, William K. McAlpine, and Lieutenant Quinn. The visitors were escorted to the Southern Hotel where they were permitted a full night's rest before the carriages arrived after lunch the next day to carry them to Fort Point. Maxey engaged in lengthy discussion with Lieutenant Quinn over the design of the gabions under construction in the shops. Later Colonel Hobby put the visitors aboard boats and took them out to the point where the gabions were being placed in the water, where they were able to witness the entire operation of sinking, securing, and adjusting the huge "crates," as they were called by the visitors. Those not quite as interested in the technicalities of gabion construction as Senator Maxey and Lieutenant Quinn, were fascinated by the diving operation taking place. It was a matter of great concern to all whether or not the divers would come up again after their periods beneath the waves. In his letter of thanks to Colonel Hobby, Senator Maxey described the future that he foresaw for Galveston as the commercial center for Texas and the New West. The commerce of Texas would be based upon the state providing beef, flour, wool, cotton, and leather

to the world and Galveston becoming a large importer of manufactured goods from Europe and coffee from South America.[29]

The 1875 Hurricane

Events in the spring of 1875 marked the high point of the experiment
of the gabionade jetty. Everything went well until a hurricane hit the
Texas coast September 15–17. The damage to Galveston was severe,
but Indianola on Matagorda Bay, then a rival seaport to Galveston,
was completely destroyed. The Army Engineers works, a compound
of buildings located at Fort Point where the gabions were constructed
and the workers housed, was completely destroyed. The eastern tip of
the island was cut off by a new channel across the island and the
workers had to be rescued from their stranded position.[30]

The work resumed and attracted attention in a national engineering journal in May, 1876. At this time another bright young Army
Engineer, Lieutenant Charles E. L. B. Davis, later a brigadier-general,
was assigned to supervise the works under Captain Howell in New
Orleans.[31] But inadequate appropriations caused work to stop in both
1876 and 1877. While the Fort Point jetty was completed, work on
the Bolivar side continued to be plagued by stoppages and storms. At
the end of 1879, a Board of Engineers reviewing the project some six
and a half years and $477,000 later, with little accomplished, con-
cluded: "There is no very cheap way of building jetties into the ocean."
The construction of the gabionades was halted and the Corps of Engineers began to look for a new technique. In summing up the experiment, historian Lynn Alperin concluded that the problem with the
inadequate appropriations and subsequent work stoppages, which
resulted in deterioration of the work completed, were the result of
"the tentative nature of the government's commitment to civil improvements" at that time.[32]

Fourteen Years and Few Results

The years 1873–79 were a difficult period for Galveston and its plans
to expand its commercial relations beyond the confines of Texas. To
say that time had been lost would not be completely true. Because of
the severity of the depression that followed the Panic of 1873, progress
had been stopped throughout the nation, and business began to return to normal only in the last years of the decade.

There were signs that lessons had been learned the hard way. The future had already arrived in the case of the Gulf, Colorado and Santa Fe Railway Company (GC&SF), where George Sealy had assumed the leading role and was on the verge of making the railroad a major player in Texas during the dynamic decade that lay ahead. It is difficult to fault the GC&SF presidents of the seventies, given all of the obstacles they faced. But they were full-time bankers and merchants and part-time railroad executives, and the competition to be brought on by outside railroad interests would no longer tolerate that style of management.

The jetties project was also facing changes. The Army Corps of Engineers was looking for a new technique to replace the gabion concept, and there were signs that the corps was considering changing its management style so that the project would receive more attention from senior managers. In addition, the lack of adequate annual appropriations from Congress for the Engineers made it obvious to the citizens of Galveston that that funding pattern could no longer continue and that a lobbying effort by the city to support the Chief of Engineers before Congress was becoming necessary. Again, there would be an opportunity for new leadership to rise to the occasion to meet the challenges of the times.

Galveston's progress thus far was largely owing to the presence of the Engineers trained at the U.S. Military Academy at West Point. The bankers, merchants, and attorneys were fortunate to have had the likes of Caleb G. Forshey and Albert M. Lea, both of whom had moved on, to help Galveston broaden its horizons. Both of these men had been thinking about railroads for twenty years, and their contribution was of immense importance. The presence of General Braxton Bragg, the first chief engineer of the GC&SF, and General X. B. DeBray as city engineer was important. The Corps of Engineers had sent some of its brightest young officers to direct the jetty work, and their experience would serve as a foundation for the corps to build upon in the next decade. The role of these West Point–trained engineers was not mere accident; the need for a supply of men with such education had been recognized and planned for early in the century. President Thomas Jefferson proposed a scientific and engineering college, which he called the United States Military Academy, to Congress in 1802. Congress passed the act on March 16, 1802, creating a military academy for ten cadets. Jefferson and his colleagues saw the need that the country would have in the future for internal improvements—roads, canals, bridges, harbors, and so forth—to bring the sprawling country together and to make it function efficiently.[33]

Historian William Goetzmann, who has written three studies of the roles of scientists and engineers in exploration, sees the role played by the Army Corps of Engineers in the nineteenth century in broader terms than that of builders. He described this role as follows: "The Corps acted as a focus for national enthusiasms. . . . It was the expression of a general spirit of Romanticism that both governed its purpose and prescribed its methods. . . . it was an instrument of self-conscious nationalism. Each of its projects was related to the development of the nation, and its work in the West was part of a grandiose urge toward continental fulfillment."[34]

Perhaps no location in the country would benefit more from President Jefferson's foresight than Galveston had by 1879 and would continue to benefit in the coming years. Little did the city know as 1879 closed that it was on the verge of a new period that would see the nation's best—financiers, railroad executives, engineers, even a former president and eventually a sitting president—come to the island to witness its progress, to enjoy its hospitality, or to do business.

Chapter 5

⪻ *Gould and Huntington* ⪼
Seek a Gulf Port

The explosion of railroad building in the 1880s worked to Galveston's advantage by making a deep water port on the Gulf of Mexico all the more important. Agricultural interests in the states west of the Mississippi wanted ports closer than those on the Atlantic Coast; Jay Gould was interested in steamship lines to supplement his railroad connections to Mexico; and Collis P. Huntington was seeking a land-sea route for moving California's huge wheat crop to the Atlantic states and Europe as quickly and cheaply as possible. Linking all of this new interest in Galveston was the absolute necessity of deep water—a channel through the Outer Bar allowing the passage of ships requiring twenty-five feet of water over the bar. What had been a matter of largely local concern was now becoming a matter of concern to powerful financial circles.

Jay Gould's two visits to Galveston—on March 7, 1881, and May 5, 1883—served multiple purposes, but the greatest single result was the added thrust given to the deep water movement. At the time of the first visit, Gould was deeply involved in the consolidation of his Southwestern System, under the title of the Missouri Pacific, and its extension into Mexico. Gould and General Grenville Dodge, who was in charge of building the Texas and Pacific for Gould, had already been negotiating for the purchase of the GC&SF before coming to Galveston. In spite of the fact that the negotiations had not gone anywhere, all was well when Gould and his party arrived for the first visit. Traveling by a special train composed of the president's coaches of the Iron Mountain and Missouri Pacific roads plus a baggage car, the Gould party arrived shortly after lunch on the seventh. Since all of the public conveyances had been commandeered for electioneering purposes, the party first walked to the Western Union offices. From there they proceeded to the Cotton Exchange, where they were met by a large gathering of the exchange board and other business leaders. Gould was accompanied by General Thomas T. Eckert, vice president and general manager of Western Union Telegraph Company; Samuel Sloan, president of Delaware, Lackawanna and Michigan Railroad; Henry G. Marquand, president of St. Louis, Iron Mountain and Southern Railroad; A. A. Talmadge, general manager of Missouri Pacific Railroad; and R. S. Hayes, president of International and Great Northern Railroad. Commenting upon Gould himself, his small stature, and his quiet voice, the *Daily News* reporter observed that "had it not been known that he actually was Jay Gould, he could have been the least conspicuous and least noticed of the visitors."[1]

Gould himself was reticent, referring the reporter to General Eckert as "someone you ought to see." Gould did confirm that the information in a recent interview in the *New York Herald* was correct, and the *Daily News* reprinted it as part of its coverage. It was determined that Gould was contemplating a steamship line to Mexico and South America with Galveston as its terminal. In contrast to earlier reports that Gould would make the mouth of the Brazos his gulf port, it now appeared that Galveston was the favored spot and that railroad connections and terminal facilities were possibilities as well as the steamship line.[2] General Eckert, in his interview, was effusive in his praise for the future of Texas and the Southwest. The moneyed circles in New York, he said, had been focused on the Northwest for some years, and now the Southwest was becoming a particularly inviting field for investment.[3]

Gould's own interest in the Southwest and Mexico was brought out in the *Herald* interview. Denying that railroads were overbuilding, he pointed out that his line would connect with Mexican lines at El Paso and Laredo and that he foresaw an immense foreign market developing in Mexico for American manufactured goods and machinery. He thought that the Mexican mining industry would be given new impulse because they did not have the new and improved mining machinery available in the United States. He also believed that the Mexican fears of American encroachment would subside as trade grew and its benefits became obvious.[4]

In addition to the subjects relative to Galveston and its role, Gould also took the opportunity to expound on the nature of corporations and on the proper role of the states in regulating corporations. It has been suggested that one of Gould's purposes, perhaps his major one, in visiting Texas at this time was to attack pending railroad and telegraph regulation measures coming before the Texas legislature.[5]

Gould Stirs Rumors

The months following the Gould visit were rife with rumor and speculation. Some of the continuing speculation pertained to the plan for the steamship line. The remainder focused on the persistent rumors surrounding the GC&SF. Shortly after Gould left, it was revealed "that he had made the proposition to the people of the city that if they would subscribe $100,000 he would duplicate the sum for the establishment of a daily line of steamers," the interest being offered for the sole purpose of securing activity on the part of the people of Galveston in behalf of the successful operation of the line.[6] Colonel J. M. Eddy, general superintendent of construction for Gould's Missouri Pacific, visited Galveston on March 28, 1881, to negotiate for the sale of fourteen blocks of ground on the bay front. In an interview, Colonel Eddy stated, "I don't think that the people of Galveston should let us pay too much for the grounds that we need." Again, the possibility of building at the mouth of the Brazos was raised and Eddy also discussed his plans to inspect that area.[7]

Circumstances were much the same when Gould and a similar traveling party returned to Galveston May 5, 1883, for another visit. Nothing had transpired in the way of a steamship line and terminal facilities. However, friction had developed between the Missouri Pacific lines and the GC&SF over the acceptance of passengers. While Gould and the party toured the city, H. M. Hoxie met with John Sealy, the general manager of the GC&SF at the time. Presumably relations between the lines were discussed, but no public statements were made. However, Gould was still enthusiastic about Galveston's possibilities if deep water was acquired, and he advised the citizens to take hold of the matter and to see to it that a channel was secured.[8]

Since Gould was a man known for employing devious strategies and tactics to achieve what he wanted, it is difficult to know exactly what he had in mind for Galveston and if any great opportunities were lost by the city. The most certain thing was that he hoped to buy the GC&SF, or to obtain a controlling interest, to avoid having to build a line from the Texas and Pacific at Fort Worth to the Gulf. Whether he was serious about the steamship line or whether that was a ploy to induce the GC&SF management to bring him in will never be known. What is known is that he tried for the next two years to drive the GC&SF out of business, until poor economic conditions and crop failures forced all of the Texas railroads to form the Texas Traffic Association, or the Texas Pool, to eliminate competition between them.

Huntington Eyes Galveston

Huntington and his partners, Leland Stanford, Mark Hopkins, and Charles Crocker, had become famous with the building of the first transcontinental railroad. They had built the Central Pacific from Sacramento over and through the Sierra Nevada Mountains to meet the Union Pacific at Promontory Point, Utah, on May 10, 1869. The Big Four, as the partners became known, merged the Central Pacific with the Southern Pacific and began building lines to the San Joaquin Valley and Los Angeles. The San Francisco–to–Los Angeles line was completed on September 5, 1876, beginning a long and often controversial period of domination of rail transportation in California.

But Huntington's plans extended far beyond the borders of California, or even the Pacific Coast. California's agricultural importance had grown to significant proportions by 1880, and the Southern Pacific had its eye on both eastern and European markets for the products. California's wheat production had passed twenty-nine million bushels by 1880 and would increase to forty million bushels by 1890, making the state second in wheat production behind Minnesota's fifty-two million. Huntington's goal was to seek a port on the Gulf of Mexico to serve as a terminal for a land-sea network to the East Coast and Europe. With this goal in mind, he began to push the Southern Pacific eastward. Galveston was well aware of the plans and recognized that New Orleans, with its deeper harbor, held an advantage over the Texas port in spite of its being three hundred miles closer than New Orleans. By 1877 the Southern Pacific had reached Yuma, Arizona, where Hopkins would die the following year. In 1878 the tracks reached Tucson, Arizona, and were extended to El Paso, Texas, on May 19, 1881. At this point Huntington was poised to begin to play a major role in the burgeoning Texas railroad scene.[9]

Huntington did this by acquiring Colonel Tom Peirce's Galveston, Harrisburg and San Antonio on June 3, 1881, and announcing that the GH&SA would start building west to meet the Southern Pacific coming east. This announcement was followed shortly by the news that he added the Texas and New Orleans (Houston to Orange) and the Louisiana Western (Orange to Vermillion, Louisiana). The remaining 143 miles to New Orleans, covered by the Morgan Company line, would be the final link. Although the Morgan estate initially refused to sell the line to Huntington, it was soon reported that they had entered into an agreement known as the California-Pacific combination. Although Galveston held out hopes that some of the Pacific Coast traffic would find its way to its wharves, it was obvious at this point that the lack of a deep water harbor was giving Huntington no other choice but to opt for terminal facilities at New Orleans.[10]

In an unusual move for the ordinarily tight-lipped business leaders of the day, Huntington published a statement of the intentions of the Southern Pacific. He cited the following as the reasons for the eastward expansion of the road: a short rail line between the Pacific Ocean and the Gulf of Mexico; service to the mining industries in the Mexican states of Sonora and Chihuahua; the desirability of a "Southern alternative" route between the Atlantic Coast and the Pacific; and a more direct union between the growing network of roads in Louisiana, Texas, and Mexico with those of the Pacific Coast.

The statement included an analysis of international trading patterns, pointing out that ships make triangular voyages via Australia to San Francisco because of insufficient return cargoes. The analysis also stated that in 1880 there was a surplus of 400,000 tons of wheat and equivalent flour left unshipped because the available grain ships and inland transportation were inadequate. It concluded that the route with the shortest land carriage and a single inexpensive transfer at a gulf port would have a very decided advantage for certain higher classes of freights passing in either direction and westbound passengers.[11]

The statement next compared the relative advantages of the Texas and Pacific, building across Northern Texas to El Paso, with the proposed southern route through San Antonio and Houston. The southern route clearly passed through more settled country and possessed the advantage of lower and more equable grades. In addition, San Antonio was destined to become a great agricultural center and Houston was a railroad center of importance already. With the additional advantage of the anticipated connecting roads coming from Mexico, the southern route was shown to be superior. If deep water harbors were to be achieved at the Texas ports, three hundred miles closer to California than New Orleans, the advantage would be even greater.[12]

Huntington's First Visit

March 21, 1882, became one of the significant milestones in Galveston's economic development when Huntington visited the island for the first time. In spite of the recent developments regarding access to and facilities in New Orleans, Huntington left no doubt as to his future hopes for Galveston as a great port once twenty-five feet of water had been obtained over the bar. He had fixed on twenty-five feet after discussions with leading shipping interests led him to believe that eight-thousand-ton ships requiring twenty-five feet had been decided upon as the most fitting for sea business. Accompanied by Thomas W. Peirce, president of the GH&SA, he visited the Cotton Exchange, Major Samuel M. Mansfield's office, the Strand, the site of the harbor works, and the beach during their three-hour visit. Among those who visited with him were Moritz Kopperl, Leon Blum, Julius Kaufman, Julius Runge, and Gustave Mayhoff. Having made his arrangement with the GH&H for access to the island, Huntington made it abundantly clear that the next move was up to Galveston. "You must have twenty-five feet of water on your bar—do not stop at twenty feet," he warned. He added, perhaps with more understanding than he was aware of, that perhaps the channel between the jetties should be narrowed.

Not much time during the visit was devoted to railroad affairs, but part of the interview dealt with railroad politics. As had Gould before him, he stopped in Austin, spending an hour with the governor, Oran M. Roberts. He was pleased with the head of Texas affairs. He favored laws preventing discrimination but thought attempts to regulate freights by legislative action would lead to disaster. He expressed his hope of completing the San Francisco to Galveston and New Orleans line by September, and revealed his three proposals to improve the quality of the GH&SA roadbed and trackage in order that it could carry the heavy tonnage that he expected after the line opened.[13]

Huntington left Galveston without any announcements or indications of any specific moves on his part. However, by July the rumors had begun to fly. First, it was reported that Gould and Huntington were negotiating with Charles Whitney, the president of the Morgan interests, to purchase the H&TC. This was quickly followed by additional rumors that the H&TC had already surveyed the land and bay around Virginia Point, and that three dredge boats were now being ordered up to cut a channel to Virginia Point. The plan here was that, having been shut out of facilities on the Island itself, Gould and Huntington would build wharf facilities at Virginia Point to reach the channel, and an extension would be built from the GH&H to the wharves. It was recognized that while such a move might not be to the benefit of all interests in Galveston, it would be in the greater interests of both Galveston and the state to have such an enlargement and cheapening of port facilities. In addition, the solution to the problem of the twenty-five-foot channel to the gulf would then become of vital interest to the Gould-Huntington faction. The rumors may have been nothing more than another negotiating ploy by the Gould and Huntington people to strengthen their hand, since nothing materialized.[14]

In 1883 Huntington completed the final efforts in his transcontinental connection. On January 12, the Southern Pacific, building eastward, and the Galveston, Harrisburg, and San Antonio, building westward, met at the Pecos River where the Golden Spike was driven. On February 6, the first train from New Orleans reached San Antonio, and on February 7, the first train from Los Angeles reached there. Next Huntington announced his purchase of Morgan's Louisiana and Texas Railroad and Steamship Company (the sea-rail network built and operated so successfully by Charles Morgan until his death) for $7.5 million, or $150 per share. This purchase gave Huntington the Vermillion–New Orleans connection for his railroad, the Morgan fleet of ships, and a controlling interest of 400,000 shares of stock in the H&TC railroad with its Texas Central branch running northwest from Waco and its connection to Paris under construction. The acquisition was soon followed by reports that all ships would be taken off the New Orleans to Galveston run. Instead, freight would be hauled from New Orleans by rail to Clinton and then by ship to the ports of the Western Gulf.

This news was quickly followed by rumors that the GC&SF was negotiating with the Southern Pacific to use Galveston as the port instead of Clinton, with the GC&SF serving the Southern Pacific's interests and providing terminal facilities at its property at the east end of the harbor.[15]

These negotiations did not produce results, and the matter of Virginia Point arose again with the report that the Huntington interests had made a conditional purchase of a tract of land there. Again reference was made to the opposition by local interests without being specific. Since the partners of the Ball, Hutchings Company who dominated the GC&SF directory also dominated the Wharf Company, it would appear unlikely that the Wharf Company was creating obstacles for the entry of the Southern Pacific. Eventually it would be George Sealy who would play the largest role in bringing Southern Pacific facilities to the island. Again, the "conditional" purchase may have been only another tactic employed by Huntington to force better terms. By October it was revealed that Huntington had taken a lease on the Galveston Flats, the area west of the Wharf Company waterfront property. No terms were revealed and nothing was said about the demise of the opposition. The move was looked upon as proof that Huntington was earnest in his attempt to make Galveston the grand terminal of his Southern Pacific system, even to the extent that his company would dredge a deep water channel to the gulf when it finally appeared that all other means had failed.[16]

Huntington Returns

The next spring Huntington was back again, staying overnight at the Beach Hotel and receiving courtesy calls from prominent citizens and leading businessmen. Although he was not available for an interview, it was reported that he advised the Galvestonians to go for the Eads bill if that was what they wanted and not to accept anything less. No business discussions were reported, as usual, but again it is likely that limited talks took place.[17] Huntington's involvement with Galveston was carried a step further in September when the Southern Pacific leased additional wharfage and warehouse facilities in order to use the port for transferring freights brought by Huntington ships from New York bound for the interior. The freight would be carried to Houston over the GH&H to connections with the H&TC and the

GH&SA of the Southern Pacific system. This development left Galveston with a double line of steamers from Galveston to New York, such as it had before Morgan pulled out of Galveston and began to use Clinton as his port.[18]

In the meantime Huntington had incorporated the Southern Pacific in the state of Kentucky on March 17, 1884, and completed the transcontinental network of roads under his ownership, becoming the first to do so. While purchasing and building the Southern Pacific from San Francisco to New Orleans, Huntington was also extending the Chesapeake and Ohio to Memphis. This provided a connection of 1,120 miles between Memphis and Newport News. The 455-mile gap between Memphis and New Orleans was achieved by consolidating four roads—the Tennessee Southern, the New Orleans and Baton Rouge, the Vicksburg and Memphis, and the New Orleans and Mississippi Valley—into a single new line, the Louisville, New Orleans and Texas. With this transaction completed, the Huntington line stretched 4,070 miles from San Francisco to Newport News and brought him further national acclaim.[19]

In spite of these accomplishments, the slowdown in business across the nation was affecting Huntington and his roads as well as everyone else. With the end of 1884 the emphasis would shift from expansion to holding on. By 1885 the fates of the Gould and Huntington systems and the GC&SF would be bound together by the lengthy negotiations for shares of a dwindling market. As he repeatedly warned his Galveston contacts, he would not begin grain movements from California to Galveston until a twenty-five-foot depth had been reached over the Outer Bar by the Army Engineers.

Chapter 6

The Deep Water Committee Attacks

Major events in 1880 brought about a new phase in the pursuit of deep water, and the decade of the 1880s opened on a positive note. In January Moritz Kopperl disclosed that he had been informed by Representative John H. Reagan that the U.S. Army Corps of Engineers planned to raise the rank of the officer in charge of the harbor improvement works at Galveston. In addition, he said, General Horatio Wright, the Chief of Engineers, would send a three-man commission headed by General Quincy Gillmore to examine the harbor question at Galveston and prepare a report. This news was quickly followed by the announcement that Major Samuel M. Mansfield, currently involved in jetty construction on the Great Lakes at Chicago and Michigan City, had been reassigned to Galveston to replace Lieutenant Davis and would be in charge of all Texas projects except Sabine Pass and Blue Buck River.[1]

The other major event was the one-hour stopover by James B. Eads, who was on his way to his project at the Isthmus of Tehuantepec. Eads met with an interested group at the Cotton Exchange and expressed his belief that what had been accomplished at New Orleans, where his jetties had given thirty feet of water across the bars at the mouth of the Mississippi River, could also be accomplished at Galveston if men, minds, and money were properly employed. While asserting that he had no warfare to wage with the Corps of Engineers, he stated that a private contract was the proper method of accomplishing such a project. Implicit in Eads's remarks was the understanding that a private contractor would be provided the funds to complete the job and that he would not be subjected to the annual and inadequate appropriations that Congress provided the Corps of Engineers out of the "pork barrel," the rivers and harbors appropriation.[2]

The years 1880–86 were extremely busy as the Engineers continued work on the jetties, employing a new method, and the citizens of Galveston, along with Captain Eads and the Texas delegation in Congress, carried on an extensive lobbying campaign in Washington, D.C. The construction activities of the Corps of Engineers have been previously described in Lynn Alperin's excellent book, *Custodians of the Coast*. The life of Eads, who won worldwide fame in 1874 with the completion of the bridge over the Mississippi River at St. Louis, is described in his biography, *The Road to the Sea*, by Florence Dorsey. Therefore, this book will focus on the lobbying activities of the deep water committee.[3]

According to Alperin, these years for the Engineers were similar to the previous experience with the gabion jetties. First, inadequate appropriations from Congress hobbled the continuity of the work. The brush mattress design of the jetties presented the same difficulties working out in the open Gulf of Mexico in deep water as had the gabions. There was considerable displeasure in Galveston with the lack of progress made during the early eighties, and Major Mansfield was the subject of a scathing attack by former mayor Lorenzo C. Fisher. The dissatisfaction brought forth more criticism plus numerous suggestions on how to do the job.[4]

The whole situation was worsened by the organization of the congressional committees, according to a dispatch from Washington. Prior to the Forty-fourth Congress, Texas and the South received virtually nothing in the rivers and harbors appropriation from the commerce committee. This began to change in the Forty-fourth and Forty-fifth Congresses when three-fifths were allocated below the Ohio River. The current Congress would be equally difficult. The committee was appointed by a speaker who opposed all appropriations for rivers and harbors. Chairman Reagan and the member from Louisiana were the only southerners. They could expect support from the members from Kentucky, West Virginia, Virginia, and Missouri. The remaining nine members of the fifteen-man committee would not be very supportive. In the Senate, Richard Coke of Texas was newly appointed to the commerce committee and now in a position to work as hard as Reagan had for a fair share of the appropriations.[5]

Major Mansfield's First Report

Major Mansfield's first report, prepared by assistant engineer Henry C. Ripley on July 3, 1880, contained the new plans and estimates for brush mattress jetties modeled on those built for the improvement of the River Maas at Rotterdam. Both the south (Galveston) and the north (Bolivar) jetties began at points offshore and extended some distance underwater, gradually sloping upward until they reached the water surface. The top continued for another distance at the surface before again sloping underwater down to the foundation mattresses at the outer end. The south jetty would have a length of 15,330 feet, consisting of a section five feet below the water 4,080 feet long; a sloping section 6,140 feet long; a section at the surface of the water 4,740 feet long; and another sloping section 370 feet long. The north jetty would have a first section starting near the end of the gabionade and sloping upwards for 2,260 feet to the water surface; a section of 5,530 feet at the water level; and a third section of 300 feet sloping down to the foundation mattress. Ripley explained that the jetties began some distance from the shore in order to confine the ebb current to a single channel across the bar while providing as little obstruction as possible to the admission of water into the bay during flood tide.[6]

Judging by the columns of the *Daily News,* December of 1880 was an exciting month in Galveston. Major Mansfield granted an interview upon his return from Washington, pleased with the acceptance of his recommendations at headquarters and confident that the system of piers and dykes used successfully in the west of The Netherlands would work. He had $175,000 unused from the previous appropriation to start with, and he was sure that by the end of 1881 he would have demonstrated to all the Doubting Thomases that twenty-five feet over the bar was inevitable. Only an unsympathetic and stingy Congress could stop him. One *Daily News* article quoted from the *New York Maritime Register,* a journal devoted to the maritime commerce of the country as a whole, which saw the harbor improvement at Galveston as "one that deserves the help of the National Government."

A reprint from the *London Anglo-American Times* saw the matter of deep water at Galveston as of possibly equal importance to the Panama Canal project.[7]

The thrust of Jay Gould into Texas and the stories in December regarding his railroad consolidation plans and their impact on Texas gave the *Daily News* material for a series of editorials on the relevance of these events to deep water at Galveston. The presence of General Grenville Dodge, president of the Texas and Pacific Construction Company and one of Gould's top executives, in Galveston late in December provided a direct link between the twin issues of railroad development and harbor improvement. In addition to negotiating with the Gulf, Colorado and Santa Fe Railroad, General Dodge was also communicating Gould's interest in terminal facilities. Galveston definitely was at a crossroads in its economic development, and a new future was just around the corner for the taking as 1880 came to an end.[8]

Coke and Reagan Visit

When Representative Reagan came November 15, the *Daily News* used the occasion, perhaps at his suggestion, to again call for the naming of a permanent deep water committee and organization to support the legislation. At this time Huntington and Gould were about to complete the negotiation of their very important agreement, and it was becoming evident that soon there would be two California-to-New Orleans roads—the Huntington line through San Antonio and Houston and the Gould line through Fort Worth and Dallas. Without a deep water harbor, Galveston stood to be totally bypassed, with New Orleans receiving all of the benefits.

Reagan was followed two weeks later by Senator Coke, who spent much of the day with Major Mansfield investigating the progress of the work and acquainting himself with the plans of the engineers and the results that had been attained. He spoke highly of the work and Galveston in his remarks at the end of the day, in which he pointed out to those assembled that each Texas port project would stand on its own and that Galveston's appropriation would not be increased at the expense of another. There were remarks also by several local citizens, including newly elected Mayor L. C. Fisher and Colonel William L. Moody, who spoke out publicly for the first time on the deep water issue. He said that he never felt there was actually any hostility to the deep water effort but that he felt there was a coldness and indifference on the subject that would hamper vigorous prosecution of the project. The next interview with Colonel Mansfield in late December, while not revising any of his previous projections, found the engineer stating that his currently available funding would expire in March and he probably would have to stop work until the next appropriation became available in September. In other words, deep water might be delayed. He noted that having $100,000 to work with through the summer would avoid a big delay.[9]

Perhaps the most important event that took place in 1881 was the publication by the *Daily News* of two letters by attorney Robert G. Street, who attacked not Major Mansfield and his performance during 1881 but the entire federal appropriation process, the pork barrel nature of the rivers and harbors bill, and the waste involved in annual appropriations inadequate for the most efficient and timely accomplishment of a project. As an alternative he proposed a contract with a private contractor, such as Eads had at South Pass, on a "no water, no pay" basis, whereby the contractor would raise his own funding and be reimbursed as he met specified goals. Under this approach, the government would not interfere with the contractors, as it did with the Corps of Engineers, and the contractor would have no excuses for nonperformance. At the time of publication in December of 1881, a year after Eads's short one-hour stopover in Galveston, these letters were only the expression of an idea. However, as events were to unfold over the next several years, the idea would take a firmer and firmer hold on the thinking of Galveston.[10]

Huntington's First Visit

Huntington's first visit to Galveston on March 20 came one month after the delegation to Washington returned. Kopperl, Blum, Runge, and others played host to him and no doubt informed him of events in Washington and how promising things looked. Huntington, for his part, stressed the importance of achieving a depth of twenty-five feet in order that the port could receive eight-thousand-ton ships then being discussed in shipping circles as the desired size. His forecast of the tremendous future Galveston would have with deep water produced considerable optimism throughout the remainder of 1882 following the final passage of the rivers and harbors bill. With the railroad plans under way providing connections to Denver, the Pacific Coast, and Mexico, there seemed no limit to Galveston's increasing use as a port of international commerce if the city obtained deep water. With deep water, the Gulf, Colorado and Santa Fe could also become the backbone of a great southwestern railroad system with its principal financial and commercial domicile and terminus at Galveston. It was reported that eighteen feet would lure Chicago interests to invest in a first-class grain elevator and put themselves in line to accommodate the grain trade that would seek Galveston as an outlet.[11]

Two sour notes marked the beginning of 1883. The Washington correspondent of the *Daily News* wrote that not much in the way of appropriations should be expected during the present session of Congress. He expressed the view that enough would be voted to keep the Corps of Engineers employed at a moderate rate, which would be frustrating to officers like Major Mansfield and to cities like Galveston. This "dribble" of public funds would amount only to a wasteful extravagance.[12] The other bad news came in a letter from James Eads to Street, who had written on his own to find out where Eads stood in regards to taking on the job at Galveston. Eads had been in Europe from April to November after his doctors warned him that his health was endangered. Although improved, he was advised by the doctors to do as little as possible for the next year. But, he added, he would not involve himself in another project dependent upon government funding, such as the South Pass jetties. Unless Galveston were to find an alternate method of using local and state financing, it would have to be content with the current system and just hope for the best some day. In a closing sentence, he stated that the technique used on the River Maas had proved to be a failure.[13]

Local optimism was augmented by news from New York City that an effort would be made in "influential quarters" there to help Galveston obtain a sufficient appropriation in a bill separate from the rivers and harbors bill to be paid to a contractor when actual results were obtained. Presumably these quarters would be the Huntington organization. The article also stated that Captain Eads had regained his health and would accept the task at Galveston if called upon. The *Daily News* vouched for the substance of the dispatch from New York and called for the city council and the Cotton Exchange to contact Eads. A week later the mayor announced a committee composed of aldermen Ed

Ketchum, C. C. Allen, Wright Cuney, F. D. Mitchell, and Louis Falkenthal and citizens C. G. Wells, Julius Runge, W. L. Moody, Morris Lasker, and Street. Moritz Kopperl, who might have been appointed because of his earlier involvement, had died earlier in the year. A letter was prepared and approved immediately and was sent to Eads in London along with endorsements from the city council, merchants, shipping firms, the Cotton Exchange, and each of the banks. Eads was asked to submit a cost estimate, a completion date for a certain depth of water, and an estimate of annual cost for maintenance of the depth specified.[14]

Mayor Fulton received Eads's reply on December 27, 1883. He estimated a depth of at least twenty feet in two years with an additional two or three feet per year until a thirty-foot depth had been achieved. He estimated the total cost at $7.5 million with additional $100,000 per year to maintain the depth as desirable. He also estimated that the tidal action after completion of the jetties would eventually reach thirty-five or perhaps forty feet. He explained that the cost would be much more than South Pass because of the distance required to reach thirty-feet in the Gulf of Mexico, and because of the increased exposure of the works to sudden storms. Of course, he would only undertake the task if assured of having complete freedom to plan and execute as he saw fit.[15]

Ketchum's Committee Reports

With Eads's willingness to accept a contract if offered, the deep water movement took a new turn. The difficulty of getting separate legislation, outside of the rivers and harbors appropriation, through Congress would only serve to aggravate the differences back home. Both the Texas congressional delegation and the Galveston deep water delegation would find their tasks much more difficult than they had imagined during the excitement immediately following Eads's reply.

The Ketchum committee completed its report to the city council on January 2, 1884, with four actions: first, it endorsed Eads's proposal; second, it requested that the state legislature be memorialized to ask the Texas congressional delegation to urge the passage of a bill based on the proposal; third, it asked that two thousand copies of the memorial be distributed to governmental, trade, labor, and commercial organizations; and four, it asked that a delegation be named to promote the passage of the bill through Congress. The report was approved by the city council at its meeting of January 8, a meeting that was interrupted by one of Galveston's periodic fires but not until after this important business was transacted. The committee met again on the twelfth to continue its work and named Moody, Wells, Runge, Street, and Alfred H. Belo to a delegation to present the bill before Congress. The committee also requested the assistance of four prominent Texans already in Washington—the Honorable John Peter Smith of Fort Worth; the Honorable J. M. Lindsay of Gainesville; the Honorable C. C. Binkley of Sherman; and Walter Gresham, who was already there supporting the bill for the Santa Fe Railroad right-of-way through the Indian Territory.[16]

The committee's plan was approved by the city council on January 23, and immediately the delegation to Washington began planning for support it would receive from parties outside of Galveston. Colonel Belo was informed by Charles Fowler, the Morgan agent in Galveston, that Morgan president A. C. Hutchinson had made arrangements for the delegation to meet with the Huntington and Gould interests in New York before going to Washington. Huntington replied: "Referring to President Hutchinson's inquiry, I would suggest that your selected friends should come here with the papers at once and a meeting with interested parties will be arranged at once. Galveston must show her earnestness with us."[17] The following day Fowler informed Colonel Belo of another telegram from Huntington stating that Captain Eads's counsel, Alex C. Cochrane, had returned to St. Louis and would meet with the delegation en route to Washington.[18] Colonel Belo also heard from John C. Brown, the general solicitor of the Missouri Pacific Railway, that he would arrange the Gould-Huntington meeting.[19]

In Washington the Texas congressional delegation was already making preparations. Representative James B. Belford of Colorado was being discussed as someone of prominence from the West who could introduce the bill not as a local measure of relief but as a work of national character in which the entire western half of the country was interested. Belford had established his credentials as a western spokesman by his remarks on the report of the Mississippi River commission when he attacked the eastern financial interests for their domination of southern and western areas. A draft of the text of the bill was prepared by Representatives Thomas P. Ochiltree of Galveston and Charles Sabin of Houston, in conjunction with Colonel Cochrane, who handled all of Eads's government business.[20]

Preparations in Washington

The delegation arrived in Washington on February 17, 1884, and began visiting the Texas congressmen immediately. On the twentieth, Representative Ochiltree arranged for the committee to meet with his old friend President Chester Arthur and his cabinet. As the *Daily News* dispatch described it, "Before Major Ochiltree's presence all guards and barriers disappeared as if by magic." The major explained the national importance of the harbor improvement at Galveston, and the president, who had vetoed the rivers and harbors bill of 1882, assured the group that the improvement of Galveston did not come within any objection he had to river and harbor appropriations and that he recognized it as a great national work.[21]

The Texas congressional delegation finally decided to have Representative John H. Reagan introduce the bill in the House and, on Senator Coke's motion, to have Senator Maxey introduce it in the Senate. They also had a session with Cochrane to work out the final details of the act. On Wednesday, February 27, Senator Maxey made the introduction and Representative Reagan repeated the action in the House on the following Monday. In the rivers and harbors committee, action on Major Mansfield's request for Galveston was temporarily passed over, pending the outcome of the Eads bill.[22]

Major Mansfield grudgingly consented to an interview on March 19, 1884, when pressed by the *Daily News* reporter. He did not wish to talk, but gradually opened up and stated that he could complete the job for less than 10 percent of Eads's estimated $7.5 million. He said the South Jetty is completed and the North Jetty could probably be done in one season for the 10 percent. He bluntly stated that he would produce twenty-five feet over the bar by that time, with another five or ten feet in a matter of time. As the interview progressed, he became more agitated, eventually blurting:

> *The fact of the matter is, the people are beginning to be unreasonable. The News, for instance, which forces public opinion, is continually impugning my motives and covertly insinuating against my plans and methods. Now do you suppose that these gentlemen who went to Wash-*

ington to strive to make the government enter into a contract with Captain Eads know any more about this matter than I do, who have made it a life study? Mr. Moody is a merchant, Mr. Wells is a cotton factor, Colonel Belo is a newspaper publisher and Colonel Street is a lawyer. It is very easy for these gentlemen to sit in their offices and indulge in plausible abstractions.[23]

The *Daily News* responded editorially the next day, setting forth its objective of being completely fair to Mansfield, but pointing out that if he needed only $700,000 to complete a guaranteed job, he need go no further than the Strand for the money. However, the *Daily News* also pointed out that the previous year he had promised eighteen feet upon completion of the South Jetty, and now he was asking for more money because he claimed the North Jetty was also needed. Coincidentally, the final report of the Chief of Engineers for June 30, 1883, was published that same day containing Mansfield's statement about no measurable progress in the last two years, which was contradicted in his interview the day before when he stated that an additional depth of two feet had been obtained. The major was clearly vulnerable.[24]

On March 31 Reagan and Maxey received letters from Eads in London repeating the statement made in his reply to the Galveston committee in December: he would not appear before Congress. He would take the proposed contract and complete the job, but Texas and Galveston interests would have to secure the passage of the bill on their own. The delegation met, along with Moody and Gresham, on April 2 to discuss the new predicament and passed two resolutions—one that it was impracticable to pursue the Eads bill and the other that the only practicable thing left to do was to pursue the largest attainable appropriation through the Corps of Engineers. With Colonel Mansfield's evaluation of the "Eads Plan" due to be released, it was felt that Captain Eads had to be there to support his own position.[25]

Eads Will Appear

Major Mansfield's report followed on April 4, essentially repeating what he had said in the interview—that he could finish the North Jetty for $700,000 and provide deep water. Eads proposed two feet in two years and eight months with partial payments of $2 million out of the total of $7.5 million. He failed to see any advantage to it, and the new chief engineer, General John Newton, supported his position. But, just as Major Mansfield reacted strongly at the time of his interview when he felt that his professional integrity had been attacked, so did Captain Eads when he returned from England and read the Mansfield and Newton reports and their criticism of his plans. Eads immediately wrote to the *Daily News* a letter in which he pointed out that in 1874 Major Howell, as the district engineer, and General Newton, as a member of the engineer review board, had fought against his plans for the jetties at South Pass, which eventually provided a depth of thirty-three feet, whereas their plan for the Fort St. Phillip Canal would have been a total failure, devastating commerce on the Mississippi River. Never completely willing to give up, the Eads supporters in Galveston quickly met with Cochrane and James Andrews, another Eads attorney, in Galveston in hopes that the fight could be continued and made plans to meet Eads in New Orleans. It must have brought great joy to certain quarters when the New Orleans delegation—Richard S. Willis, J. D. Skinner, Street, and Moody—wired back that Eads had agreed to place his proposition before the Texas delegation and Congress himself.[26]

Colonel Moody Elected

Captain Eads's decision to go to Washington and fight before Congress brought yet another new phase to the effort to obtain the passage of the Eads bill. His decision seemed to prompt a new vigor in the citizens of Galveston, who promptly prepared a petition naming a permanent deep water committee to manage the affair. The deep water committee held a meeting May 9, 1884, naming a twenty-three-man general committee and selecting officers and committees. Colonel Moody was chosen chairman; Clinton G. Wells, vice-chairman; Robert G. Street, secretary; and James D. Skinner, treasurer. Other members of the general committee were Richard S. Willis, John H. Hutchings, John D. Rogers, Sampson Heidenheimer, Julius Runge, Isaac Blum, John C. Wallis, Henry Rosenberg, D. Theodore Ayers, Harris Kempner, Walter Gresham, Colonel A. H. Belo, Mayor Roger L. Fulton, John L. Darragh, Morris Lasker, James Moreau Brown, Charles L. Cleveland, Lorenzo C. Fisher, and James Sorley. Named to the finance committee were Moody, Willis, Runge, Wells, Skinner, and Heidenheimer. Selected for the delegation to meet Eads in St. Louis and proceed on to Washington were Moody, Willis, Runge, Cleveland, and Sorley. Belo and Gresham were requested to cooperate with the delegation, as was Colonel Elbert S. Jemison of New York. Blum and Heidenheimer were requested to cooperate with the delegation while in the North. The delegation left May 10, 1884, for its meeting with Eads on the twelfth. Moody immediately wrote Cochrane and Senator Maxey to notify them of arrival times in St. Louis and Washington and also to inform them that Galveston was now solidly behind the Eads bill.[27]

The delegation, along with Eads and Cochrane, arrived on the fourteenth and met immediately with the Texas delegation. Everyone was inspired by Eads's energy and faith in his plans. In a meeting on the fifteenth it was decided to remove the appropriation for Galveston from the pending rivers and harbors bill in order to clear the way for the Eads bill. Representative Ochiltree took the responsibility to strike Galveston from the bill. Ochiltree started receiving telegrams, thought to be from his friends, warning him not to, but he maintained his belief that Galveston overwhelmingly wanted the Eads bill.[28]

It was decided, however, that the removal of Galveston's appropriation from the bill would not occur until after Eads's testimony. If the Galveston appropriation were out of the rivers and harbors bill, General Newton would have no cause to confront Eads. With it in the bill, it was thought that he would have to defend the Engineers' position.[29] Nevertheless, General Newton, in a letter to committee chairman Albert S. Willis declined the invitation. Reminding the chairman that the Engineers had submitted their report on the Eads bill to the Senate on March 27, the general stated, "I do not think an oral discussion in which are engaged a number of persons of opposing views is the best means of solving a question involving engineering matters both theoretical and practical as well as important economic considerations." Instead, he felt that his office should remain in readiness to provide information on such points as may be referred to it.[30] Perhaps Newton felt a certain futility in a face-to-face encounter. In an earlier interview he was described as not being positive as to the results on the Galveston bars, believing that there was something that might be called wild in any positive statement or calculation by any person on the subject.[31]

Eads's Appearance

Captain Eads appeared before the House rivers and harbors committee for four hours on May 22 and attacked technical aspects of the Engineers' work. He pointed out that the Engineers had entirely overlooked the effect of friction and wave action in the location of their jetties and that they did not consider the effect of wave action in determining the height of their jetties. He explained: "The wave action would be sufficiently energetic to level down and obliterate any channel which the current might be able to excavate, but it will be shown that the height to which they determined the jetties would be built must expose any channel excavated between them to serious interruption, if not obliteration, by the sands which would be transported from the outer side of the jetties into the jetty channel." In addition to the height of the jetties, he also criticized the gaps between the jetties and the shore, which would act as enormous outlets for the lateral escape of the water.[32]

About half of Eads's time before the committee was devoted to a scholarly treatise on hydraulics, and the other half was devoted to questioning by the members of the committee. In his presentation, Eads methodically went about defining the laws of hydraulics applicable to the deepening of the channels at the mouth of the Mississippi River and Galveston Bay, and citing those specific laws that the Engineers had overlooked when opposing his plans for jetties at South Pass and were still overlooking in their construction of the jetties at Galveston. He pointed out how the Engineers' efforts at Galveston were doomed to fail because the jetties, according to the laws of hydraulics, were too far apart, were not built high enough above mean high tide, and were not built continuously from shore, thus leaving a gap. Where applicable, he used examples of the successful work at South Pass to prove the validity of the laws and to illustrate that the Engineers had not learned from the lesson. He hit strongly upon the point that General Newton, now the Chief of Engineers, was a member of the commission that fought against his plans at South Pass and was apparently still committed to methods that would not work.[33] Eads returned to New York immediately after the hearings, as he had plans to return to London. But upon arrival he wired Colonel Moody that he had deferred sailing and would be back in Washington the following week to support the effort.[34]

Through the secretary of the treasury, the chief of the bureau of statistics Joseph Nimmo was asked to prepare a report on the trade and commerce of the western states and what impact a deep water port on the Gulf of Mexico could have on that trade. The committee members, each with his assigned tasks, rolled up their sleeves to prepare for their appearance before the rivers and harbors committee scheduled the following week. In the meantime, Senator Coke and Representative Ochiltree both had to turn their attention to the right-of-way bill for the Gulf, Colorado and Santa Fe Railway that Walter Gresham was nursing through Congress. Coke was scheduled to introduce it on June 2.[35]

Demonstrating his political sensitivity as well as his technical astuteness, Eads provided Moody his analysis of the potential votes on the rivers and harbors committee. Chairman Albert S. Willis and Representatives Clifton R. Breckinridge, James T. Jones, Jeremiah Murphy, Newton Blanchard, Eben F. Stone of Massachusetts, and David Henderson of Iowa were certain supporters, he thought, and Charles A. Sumner of California, Julius Houseman of Michigan, and Henry G. Runleigh of New York very probable. Representatives Thomas M. Bayne of Pennsylvania and Joseph Rankin of Wisconsin were certain to be against the bill, leaving Eustace Gibson of West Virginia and James S. Robinson as doubtful. "I think you should get your Texas friends to make an effort to capture Gibson and Robinson at once," Eads advised.[36] The "capturing," however, would have to be accomplished by Colonel Moody and Judge Cleveland, because Richard S. Willis and James D. Skinner returned to Galveston June 4, and Sorley went on to New York City. Willis and Skinner were both very optimistic upon their return to Galveston. An early adjournment because of the coming political conventions would mean that a favorable report would be the most that could be hoped for during the convention, but a favorable report would place the bill on the calendar for action at the winter session. It was also thought that the delays would actually strengthen the chances of the bill.[37]

Colonel Moody's Testimony

Colonel Moody's appearance before the rivers and harbors committee on June 7 with the results of the Galveston delegation's "homework" was the next event. His presentation was a direct attack upon the record of the Engineers, based upon their own official reports. In thirteen points, he directed the attention of the committee to inconsistencies, questionable statements, milestones missed, and revisions of previous plans, that is, the need for the North Jetty. In conclusion, he stated the people of Galveston were justified in believing that this ten-year record of failure would never produce results. At this point, not much was said of the problem of "inadequate appropriations," a legitimate cause of some of the difficulties encountered by the Engineers, perhaps because this problem was attributable to the committee.[38]

The Texans made their points. On June 10, 1884, the House sitting as a committee of the whole voted to strike the $250,000 appropriation from the rivers and harbors bill. There was opposition from Representative William D. Kelley of Pennsylvania, Representative John D. White of Kentucky, and Chairman Albert S. Willis of the rivers and harbors committee, but the amendment carried. The bridges were burned! It was the Eads bill or nothing.[39]

Just as it was needed, a boost to Galveston's hopes came from Nimmo's report, transmitted to the secretary of war on June 18 and presented to the Senate by Senator Coke the next day. The conclusion of the report read as follows:

> The foregoing facts and conclusions appear clearly to prove that the proposed improvement at Galveston Harbor is a work of great national importance. At no time since the annexation of Texas has the condition of national affairs been as favorable as the present time for the adoption of measures for the support to the Southern States, and more especially those bordering on the Gulf of Mexico, the greatly needed harbor facilities, and at the same time of adopting a measure the effect of which will be to exercise an important and extensive regulating influence over the internal commerce of the country.[40]

Supported by twenty statistical appendices, the report established the case for the contention of Galveston that a deep water harbor on the Gulf of Mexico was not a local interest matter but rather one of national importance. Citing Galveston's strategic geographical location, it established the case for a harbor there to serve the interests of trade from the Midwest, the Pacific Slope, and Mexico. Nimmo's report added one more weapon to the arsenal employed by the Galveston delegation.

Eads Before the Senate Committee

Finally, Captain Eads got his second chance to present his story to the Congress. A hearing by the Senate commerce committee on June 30, 1884, provided the occasion. According to the Washington dispatch to the *Daily News,* "In the discussion preceding the vote Captain Eads again handled General Newton and the engineer corps without gloves." Senator Coke said Eads routed Newton on every point and forced him frequently to disclaim responsibility for the statements and views expressed concerning the Galveston works in the reports of the officers in charge. Eads performance resulted in a 9–2 vote in the committee to report the bill favorably, and Senator Coke was instructed to report the bill and have it placed on the calendar. A written report on the bill was to be presented at the beginning of the winter session. Senators Coke and Maxey, the rest of the Texas congressional delegation, and the committee from Galveston all drew praise for the very successful effort. With this accomplished, Eads announced he was returning to London but planned to be in Galveston in October. The passage of the Santa Fe bill gave Galveston another triumph to celebrate, and Judge Cleveland and Walter Gresham left for home.[41]

Once Congress adjourned and everyone was awaiting the December session, there was an opportunity to rest up and prepare for the difficult task ahead. In this interim the biggest event to take place was Captain Eads's visit to Galveston on November 17, 1884. The party, which traveled in a special car attached to the regular Missouri Pacific train, included Senator Coke; Representative Reagan; Representative Clifton R. Breckinridge of Arkansas; Alex C. Cochrane, counsel to Eads; James Anderson, Eads's chief engineer; and the Honorable D. H. Armstrong, former senator from Missouri. The party was met by a reception committee of members of the deep water committee and the Washington delegation—Moody, Hutchings, Brown, Gresham, Street, Fulton, Wells, and Representative Ochiltree, as well as a large crowd of interested and appreciative citizens. After lunch at the Tremont House, Eads was taken aboard a tug for a tour of the channel with Captain Fowler, the most informed man on the harbor and channel, acting as Eads's tour guide. The trip to the outer bar took an hour with soundings being made along the way. With the tide running high, a depth of fourteen and a half feet was found on the bar. Ochiltree had wanted to cross over the submerged jetty, where the tide was six to nine feet. Since the tug drew eight and a half, Reagan asked to be put out in a lifeboat before crossing, which caused Ochiltree to change his mind, forgoing what he thought would have been an excellent point to make in the coming congressional debate.[42]

Moody and Gresham, who had already spent much of the year in Washington, left for the capital again on December 3, 1884, along with a newcomer to the effort, Dr. T. C. Thompson. The "Texas team" went to work right away. Senator Coke attempted to have the bill brought up on Monday, December 15, but commerce committee chairman Benton McMillan, who had voted against reporting it favorably, managed to delay it until January 8, 1885, because of the holidays. Nevertheless, the team kept up its efforts. Copies of the December 1 deep water issue of the *Galveston Daily News* were placed on all of the congressmen's desks. Senator Coke had two thousand copies of the map in Nimmo's report printed and had it incorporated in the report of the commerce committee on the Eads bill. A memorial from the Denver Chamber of Commerce supporting the Eads bill was presented in the Senate. But a major change in strategy was taken by the Texas congressional delegation on December 15 when they voted to unite in an effort to have the provisions of the Eads bill reincorporated into the rivers and harbors bill in order to increase the chances of its being passed in this session. Another meeting was held on the eighteenth in the rooms of the Galveston delegation at the Metropolitan Hotel, at which time the Texas delegation hosted other congressmen favorably disposed toward the bill, including Representatives William S. Rosecrans, Pleasant B. Tully, and Barclay Henly of California; Lewis Handback of Kansas; and Clifton R. Breckinridge of Arkansas. Eads addressed the group, but, surprisingly, there was no discussion at this time of going back to the rivers and harbors appropriation after Ochiltree deliberately had it stricken out.[43]

Colonel Moody, who had remained in Washington, was corresponding with members of the deep water committee urging return of Gresham and Dr. Thompson as well as the presence of Congressman-elect William H. Crain, chosen when Ochiltree decided not to run. He was also saying that no other delegation would be necessary at this time and the resources of the committee should be saved for the important occasions. The House rivers and harbors committee continued to work during the Christmas holidays and agreed upon the amounts to be appropriated for all projects except Galveston and two or three gulf ports. January 6, 1885, was established as the date to meet again to complete the bill. The *Daily News* reported from a reliable source that the committee was not satisfied with the government work at Galveston and other points and, although no other provisions had been discussed yet, appeared to be disposed to try a different plan. So as 1884 ended, there was optimism in regard to the Senate; and even in the House, where the situation would be difficult, there was a ray of hope.[44]

Opponents Become Active

January, 1885, was to be a difficult month, but the opposing forces were to make it much more difficult than it had to be. Letters to the editors that criticized the Eads plan and ridiculed the Galveston committee were showing up in such papers as the *Fort Worth Gazette,* the *Galveston Record,* and the *Houston Journal,* a staunch deep water supporter. A Greenback organ, the *National View,* published an article attacking the Wharf Company as being the chief beneficiary of deep water because of its monopoly and outrageous rates. The Eads bill was attacked at a meeting held in Dallas to support the bill, and a resolution was passed to the effect that the city of Galveston should totally buy the Wharf Company and provide free wharfage thereafter. A report from Washington said the Galveston committee had too many things to do other than answer the false charges in the Texas newspapers. The letters were described as coming from "the literary bureau of the professional blackmailers who constitute an element of the Washington lobby and resort to this and worse methods to extort from all who sought important legislation by Congress."[45]

The *Philadelphia Times* joined in the attack on the Wharf Company "which owns the entire wharfage system at Galveston, owns the banks and railroads, and runs the city government."[46] In the Washington press, false stories from Texas were published, such as a report that the Texas legislature had failed to pass a resolution favoring the harbor at Galveston.[47] Colonel Moody indicated all of this harassment perhaps was having some effect upon him, which prompted deep water committee member Hutchings to write him a very supportive letter.[48]

All of this external activity by the opposition had to be coped with in addition to the obstacles within the system. In a meeting on January 7 the rivers and harbors committee itself failed to reach a decision as to whether or not they would hear arguments from the Texas delegation in favor of incorporating the Eads bill into the rivers and harbors bill. On the following day, it was decided not to hear the Texas delegation, as this would open the door to all delegations wishing to be heard. But in addition to that action, the committee decided unanimously to incorporate a provision for a commission of experts to investigate the government system of submerged jetties along the gulf coast. Chairman Willis said he did not know what impact this would have on the Eads matter but that he did contemplate Eads being a member of the commission. While this may have been a favorable step on one hand, on the other it was looked upon as placing the Eads provision in an awkward position. Senator Maxey attacked the idea of commission as unnecessary and dilatory since there already was ample evidence of the failure of the Engineers.[49]

New Obstacles Arise

As time passed, it became more evident that it would be extremely difficult to get the Eads bill on the calendar in the winter session and that the only real hope was incorporation in the rivers and harbors bill. Besides, Eads was now growing impatient and saying that his agreement would expire with the current session. On the seventeenth the committee voted to report the bill without any provision for Galveston, leaving that issue to be taken up the next day. However, two more obstacles arose the next day. Representative Thomas M. Bayne of Pennsylvania introduced a bill previously shown to Colonel Moody by one of the lobbyists, Robert Alexander, who threatened him with having the bill introduced. It provided for a commission of three Army Engineers and three civilian engineers to conduct a survey of Galveston harbor and to advertise for plans and specifications for the improvement of the harbor and the maintenance of the specified depth. A contract would be let to the lowest responsible bidder and the commission would recommend whether or not the Chief of Engineers would supervise the work. The bill also provided that no appropriation or contract would be made until the commission had reported to Congress.[50]

The second obstacle that arose on the nineteenth was a report from General Newton, requested earlier, reiterating his previous position that the Eads proposal was excessively expensive and essentially defending the statements made in the previous year by Major Mansfield. This time he also questioned giving away such power over a navigable waterway by the government without any supervision over the contractor's plans, such as Eads had demanded in the bill. Three more days of delay were purchased by the opposition with these tactics, causing Eads to write to Colonel Moody in response to his letter, "When in the deepest distress I notice that your love of humor never forsakes you."[51] On January 22 the committee took up the matter again with Bayne leading the opposition, supported by Representatives Gibson of West Virginia and Stone of Massachusetts. Representative Blanchard led the defense and twice defeated the opposition on other resolutions.[52]

The next day, however, the Eads proposition began a roller-coaster ride through the legislative process that could serve as a textbook lesson in what can happen when politics—"the art of the possible"— runs its course. What comes out of the pipeline hardly resembles what went in. First, either the evening of Friday the twenty-third, or early Saturday before the committee met, a subcommittee composed of Representatives Willis, Breckinridge, John R. Thomas, and Blanchard met with the Texas delegation and informed them that the Eads bill as it was could not pass the committee, either separately or as a part of the river and harbors bill. Out of this session came a revised proposal, to be part of the rivers and harbors bill, providing for a $1 million appropriation, total control by Eads, and a salary for Eads of $5,000 per year and $3,000 for every foot of water over the bar. The Texas delegation and the Galveston committee accepted the compromise, and it was passed the evening of Saturday the twenty-fourth by the rivers and harbors committee. Senators Maxey and Coke and Representatives Mills, Ochiltree, Reagan, and Wellborn all thought the measure exceedingly favorable to Galveston, even though there was no certainty of follow-on appropriations to complete the job.

Colonel Moody left Washington to carry the news of the revised bill to Eads in Pittsburgh and planned to return on Monday. Instead, Eads came back with Moody on Monday and immediately met with Willis, Blanchard, and Breckinridge, where Eads declined the terms approved on Saturday. He countered with a proposition to take charge of the work for a commission of 3 percent of the expenditures. He also proposed an appropriation of $1 million, that he furnish the engineering force, and that he should receive $1.5 million in case the government abandoned the project. The rivers and harbors committee met late Monday and rejected most of Eads's proposal. They agreed that Eads would have control of the job but indicated that the Chief of Engineers would provide the engineering force, that the appropriation would total $500,000, and that the salary would be $10,000 per year and $5,000 per foot. Eads accepted these terms and also stipulated that the $5,000 per foot should not be paid until a depth of twenty-five feet over the bar had been reached.[53]

Eastern Opposition

The Galveston City Council, which was being kept informed by Representative Ochiltree, voted to give Eads $10,000 per foot, whereupon the rivers and harbors committee changed the salary on January 27 back to $5,000 per year with $3,000 per foot. At the same time it increased the appropriation to $750,000 and voted to report the bill. Again it was necessary for Colonel Moody to relay the news to Eads and hope that it would be acceptable. While waiting for word from Eads, the bill was reported on Wednesday the twenty-eighth with no further changes.[54]

With the bill finally before the full House of Representatives, the barrage of opposition from northern and eastern interests could really begin. The *New York Times* led the attack on Galveston Harbor while Representative William T. Price of Wisconsin, in the opening debate on the rivers and harbors bill, criticized the amount going to southern states, and to Texas in particular. The *Chicago Tribune* added its voice to the opposition, citing the benefits to be accrued by the Wharf Company and lack of commercial importance to Galveston. It was not to be expected that the trunk railroad lines to the east and the eastern seaports who stood to lose by having the trade of the West deflected toward the Gulf of Mexico were going to tolerate competition that they could prevent. The flak from the professional lobbyists was bad enough, but it really became difficult when the commercial forces of the East brought their strength to bear on the congressional process.[55]

This force was felt in the first hearings in the full House, and by February 5, the rivers and harbors committee was meeting again to deal with the opposition. Three amendments were approved to be presented to the House, one to eliminate any reference to Eads in the bill, another to direct the United States Harbor Board to make an examination of Galveston Harbor and report plans to the secretary of war, and the third to reduce the appropriation for Galveston back to $500,000. Again the Texas congressional delegation agreed to accept the terms of the proposed amendments as the best that could be achieved. At this point, however, having lost the total appropriation, the private contract, and Eads, Colonel Moody, and his delegation may have been ready to return home. The situation continued to decline on February 9 when the House voted to take up the post office appropriation, leaving the rivers and harbors bill with Galveston not yet considered. As if he didn't have enough trouble with his enemies, Colonel Moody now also began to have trouble with his friends. Jens Moller, part of "another delegation" sent to Washington by Mayor Fulton at the request of Representative Ochiltree, wired Fulton that "he was now working in harmony with General Newton and Rep. Rosecrans of California to get as much as possible on the government's plan."[56]

The Washington dispatch of the *Daily News* of February 11 began, "The friends of the river and harbor bill are despondent in regard to its prospects." With only seventeen working days remaining in the session, the post office appropriation was still under consideration, and several other appropriation bills, including the legislative, the sundry civil, and deficiency, remained to be acted upon. Hardly any time would be left to complete the rivers and harbors bill. In addition, Speaker of the House Samuel J. Randall of Pennsylvania was understood to be bent upon its defeat. The bill finally got back to the floor of the House on February 18 to be battered again. The makeup of the harbor board became a point of contention, but the board survived an amendment to strike it completely. Another amendment was offered requiring the Wharf Company, the City Company, and the Gulf, Colorado and Santa Fe Railway to build a breakwater around the east end of the island to connect with the government works. This was introduced by Representative William S. Holman of Indiana, who said he did it at the insistence of a very intelligent gentleman—Robert Alexander, the lobbyist who earlier threatened to fight Galveston if Colonel Moody did not hire him! With the House sitting as a committee of the whole, the amendments were rejected and the $500,000 remained in the committee report.

But in the session on February 24, matters became even worse for Galveston. Filibustering tactics by Republicans were hampering the activity, and friends of the rivers and harbors bill were yielding on any and all amendments, trying to keep something alive. One of the amendments struck out the harbor board, which virtually eliminated the Galveston provision since it was dependent upon a report by the board to continue. But there was still life! Chairman Willis drafted a revised rivers and harbors bill, totaling only $5 million, with each project to receive a prorated share based upon its previous year's amount. Galveston Harbor, which had been stricken, was to be included in the previous year at the original amount of $250,000, meaning its prorated share would be about $100,000 in the current year.[57]

The Bill Dies in the Senate

In early March attention shifted to the battleground in the Senate, where the rivers and harbors bill again had to vie with appropriation bills for time on the calendar. In addition to the scheduling problem, the Senate was known to look unfavorably upon the House bill and would need time to change it. On March 5, 1885, the bill was tabled, and with that Galveston lost its only chance for any appropriation in that session. With that action the last remaining members of the Galveston delegation, Colonel Moody and Dr. Thompson, left Washington for New York. Later Moody would provide the citizens of Galveston with a complete and lengthy explanation of what had happened, in his view, in a letter to the *Daily News*. Moody's letter explained the reasons behind the decisions made at each step of the way. First, the separate measure was abandoned because it would have been impossible to pass in a short session. Once part of the rivers and harbors bill, it invited opposition because it threatened the entire bill by swelling the total amount. The next plan was to have a separate bill voted on by the rivers and harbors committee, excluded from the rivers and harbors appropriation. Senator Coke was confident this would pass the Senate and, if favorably reported in the House, could be renewed in the next session with a high degree of confidence. However, Eads blunted this move when he said he would not renew his proposal in another session. From this point on the changes to the bill that have already been related occurred as congressmen with pet projects in their districts moved to protect their interests and voted to eliminate anything that would jeopardize the rivers and harbors bill as a whole. Since the projects originated with the Chief of Engineers and had to be recommended by him, these congressmen were subject to a great deal of pressure from the Engineers and their contractors—the nation's first "military-industrial complex"—not to disturb the status quo. Eads himself was a point of bitter contention because his name was involved not only with the harbor at Galveston but also with the Mississippi River commission. The intense opposition to Eads by the Army Engineers, going back to the fight over the mouth of the Mississippi, virtually assured the defeat of any measure involving him.[58]

Speaking of the professional lobbyists who misrepresented the Galveston committee and of the Texas newspapers who printed their slander, Moody wrote, "But for one to absent himself from his business for months, make a sacrifice of his personal money and his personal comfort, working with an honest purpose to benefit not only himself, but every man, woman and child in his state, and then have it said of him that he is conspiring to rob the government and enrich himself by a steal well, it is a little bit rough and of such slanderers I can but say: Father, do not forgive them for thou knowest they lie."[59] Having vented his feelings on this part of the experience, Colonel Moody went on the real issue: Was it a mistake to abandon Major Mansfield and the government plan? He admitted that the city would probably have wound up with $500,000 from the two sessions of Congress to continue the work on the jetties if the Eads plan had never been submitted, and this certainly would have helped the laboring men, the contractors, and supplying merchants at a time when Galveston needed the business. However, he said he was still confident that this appropriation would have been a waste of money and would have only caused further delay in the achievement of real deep water. In summing up what had been accomplished, he wrote: "It has led to a discussion and agitation of the matter, which have convinced the people of every section of our country of the national importance of an outlet on the Texas coast. It has educated the people of our own State and city to its necessity. The public criticism and overwhelming evidence of the failure of the government plan is a guarantee against further expenditures except on plans which will lead to success."[60] He praised Senators Coke and Maxey and Representatives Reagan, Mills, and Ochiltree for their staunch support and concluded by saying that the effort had not been in vain, that interest had been so aroused that by some plan or some agency Galveston would have a deep water harbor before too many years.[61]

Eads Vindicated

The remainder of 1885 after the defeat in March and all of 1886 were given over to postmortem critiques of what went wrong before Congress and how to proceed in the future. The Texas congressional delegation was of the opinion that there was no way to get through the House successfully other than to be a part of the rivers and harbors bill.

The most important thing that happened during this period was the report of the Board of Engineers established by General Newton on July 25, 1885, to review the entire experience at Galveston and to make recommendations for the next move. The board, comprised of Lieutenant Colonels J. C. Duane, Henry L. Abbott, and Cyrus B. Comstock, all brevet brigadier generals, reported their findings on February 25, 1886.[62] In Washington the *National Republican* in its analysis of the report was critical because "this board does not give Captain Eads the least credit for the unanswerable logic with which he pointed out the errors in hydraulic engineering which their brother officers have made." It cited the following conclusions as complete vindication of Eads:

1. *The board admits that 61 per cent in the height of the substantial and completed jetty of Maj. Mansfield is wholly destroyed already and that the works must be built of stone and concrete.*
2. *That the jetties should be five feet above low tide.*
3. *That they should extend out to 30 feet of water, about 10 ¼ miles, and have no openings to let the tide flow into the bay.*
4. *That they reduce the width of the opening from 12,000 feet to 7,000 feet.*
5. *The report estimated the cost at $7,000,000 without any guarantee of success (compared to Eads' cost of $7,750,000, guaranteed).*[63]

It is possible that both General Newton and the board had been influenced by the war of words that had taken place in 1885 between Lieutenant Colonel William E. Merrill and Eads. That started on January 31, 1885, when General Newton added to his presentation to Congress a paper written by Merrill critical of remarks that Elmer Corthell, at that time Eads's assistant, made before the American Society of Civil Engineers.[64] Eads responded with a letter to the *New York Times* on March 8, 1885.[65] This provoked a response by Merrill on April 11, 1885. The exchange ended with Eads's own appearance before the Society of Engineers on May 6, 1885. The fray had also been joined by Representative Clifton R. Breckinridge of Arkansas, who launched a blistering attack on Merrill and the Army Engineers.[66] These articles were all very lengthy and technical, and could be the subject of a book in themselves.

The Backers Regroup

Some organizational activity was accomplished during 1885–86 that may have laid the groundwork for things to come. First, Senator Maxey and Congressmen Crain, Stewart, and James F. Miller came to Galveston for a two-day conference with those who had been active in the deep water movement: Colonel Moody, Walter Gresham, George Sealy, Seth Shepherd, Charles L. Cleveland, Harris Kempner, Leon Blum, Judge William P. Ballinger, A. J. Walker, John C. Wallis, John D. Rogers, John H. Hutchings, Dr. T. C. Thompson, and T. William English. Considerable discussion took place on all aspects of the problem at hand. Of particular note were the comments offered by Senator Maxey about the attention Galveston received during the congressional debates. "There never was a great measure carried through on earth without educating the people up to it," he remarked. He went on, "You have got to convince the whole American people of the great measure, because it involves the interests of thousands and hundreds of thousands of people." He referred specifically to what had been accomplished already through the New York papers. While no particular plans were made at this meeting for an educational campaign, Senator Maxey's remarks must have made an impression on the group, especially Walter Gresham.[67]

On February 18, 1886, a meeting was held at Gresham's office bringing together the city council deep water committee, chaired by

Charles Fowler, the 1886 committee chaired by Richard S. Willis, and the 1883 committee that Moody chaired. The group received a preview of the coming engineer board report on the twenty-fifth from Congressman Crain, who also asked about Galveston's preference. After considerable discussion, the group approved a reply drafted by Colonel Moody stating that the separate bill was preferred but leaving the door open to accept the best that the Texas delegation could negotiate in the next Congress.[68]

Stuck with the Driblet System

Within a week of each other in 1886, Galveston reached two major milestones in the development of its land-sea transportation network. On February 26 the Board of Engineers submitted the report calling for a new approach to the construction of the jetties to provide deep water for Galveston Harbor. On March 3, President George Sealy completed the stock swap that merged the Gulf, Colorado and Santa Fe Railway with the Atchison, Topeka and Santa Fe. For the stockholders of the GC&SF, it may be said that the transaction was an end in itself. They had converted their investment in a bankrupt railroad between Galveston and Richmond into a valuable investment in one of the nation's major systems. For the people of Galveston, it meant a new connection with the wheat fields of the Great Plains. The Engineers' report meant the end of bankrupt designs of jetty construction and a new beginning, borrowing heavily from the ideas of James B. Eads, that promised to bring a twenty-five to thirty-foot deep water channel through the Outer Bar and to open the port to the world's largest ships in order that they might transport the cotton of Texas and the wheat of the Midwest around the globe.

With the GC&SF now part of the vast Santa Fe system and the GH&H part of Gould's Southwestern System, consolidated under the Missouri Pacific banner, almost all of the state's major railroads fed into Galveston. The MKT was building toward Houston, and the International and Great Northern (I&GN)—both Gould lines—connected to the GH&H at Houston. Only the Southern Pacific (SP)—which by now had taken over the Galveston, Harrisburg and San Antonio (GH&SA), the Texas and New Orleans (T&NO), and the H&TC—did not enter Galveston directly, but the SP did have an agreement to use the GH&H tracks. All that was left to complete Galveston's ties to a network of railroads blanketing the western United States was for the Corps of Engineers to deepen the channel to twenty-five feet, and Huntington would be ready to enter Galveston and build the terminal facilities for the Southern Pacific that he had been proposing since 1878.

A number of other railroad connections for Galveston were discussed during the 1880s that could have expanded the city's commercial possibilities, especially General William J. Palmer's Texas-Mexican line that would have connected at Laredo with his line to Mexico City. None of these materialized, possibly because they were never really needed. The directors of the GC&SF had had the foresight to build their road to Fort Worth through the region that would become the most populated and most agriculturally productive area of Texas. The extension to San Angelo also was a good choice, enabling GC&SF president Sealy to make his offer of delivering large cargoes of Texas cattle when he was negotiating with the Burlington and Alton in the early eighties.

On the other hand, the business community of Galveston had received extensive training in what was to be expected when one went before the Congress of the United States seeking large amounts of money for a local project. They were now aware that only a massive effort presenting the jetties project as a national requirement would muster the necessary votes to overcome the formidable opposition that was sure to attack any future proposal.

Chapter 7

⁓ *Denver Needs a Port* ⁓

When the Gulf and the Atchison roads met at Purcell in 1887 to give Galveston its own direct line through Fort Worth across the Indian Territory into Kansas City and the Midwest, an era of new economic possibilities opened. When the first through train from Fort Worth arrived in Denver on March 27, 1888, those possibilities were greatly expanded. Galveston now had the railroad connections required to become the seaport for all of those states between the Mississippi River and the Rocky Mountains. In August, 1888, all of those states would meet in the greatest convention of its kind ever held in the United States in support of deep water for the harbor at Galveston.

As Galveston moved toward the new era, the *Daily News* set the theme immediately with an editorial entitled "Denver and Galveston." The occasion that brought it about was the announcement in Denver by former governor John Evans that the Denver, Texas and Gulf Railway (DT&G), the successor to the Denver and New Orleans (D&NO), would soon have rail connections to Galveston. Twenty years, almost to the day, after Willard Richardson's epic editorial, "Galveston and the Great West," a major step in the realization was on the verge of accomplishment, and another—deep water at Galveston—was moving into a new phase of attack.[1]

With the DT&G connecting to the GC&SF at Fort Worth and the completion of the GC&SF and Atchison, Topeka and Santa Fe (AT&SF)

connection at Purcell in the Indian Territory, two huge steps had been taken toward giving Galveston the network of railroad lines that it would need to serve the vast region west of the Mississippi, as Richardson had envisioned. As the railroad network took shape, Galveston's approach to the problem of obtaining an appropriation from Congress large enough to complete the jetty system began to expand until it would become truly an effort by the western states. To these states, at the time completely dependent upon the pool that monopolized transportation to the Atlantic Coast, a connection to Galveston meant having a seaport one thousand miles closer than New York for their exports and a competitive market for their imports.[2]

These two railroad developments would prove to be very strong factors in the coming years in the deep water committee's renewed struggle for the congressional appropriation. Now these railroads—their executives, civic leaders in their states, and their congressmen—would become valuable allies in Galveston's efforts. The concept advanced by the deep water committee—that Galveston Harbor was a matter of national importance—would now become a working principle rather than a lofty idea as Colorado and Kansas joined Texas to obtain congressional support for an internal improvement important to all of the western states.

Governor Evans was to become one of the most important outsiders in Galveston's history. He was a man of enormous prestige in the West in the years following the Civil War, his impact felt in many ways. None would be more important than his role in marshaling the support of the western states for deep water at Galveston. Evans, whose governorship of the Colorado Territory ended in 1865, had become involved with railroads, along with many other business and civic enterprises, in 1869 when he built the Denver and Pacific line to connect Denver with Cheyenne after the Union Pacific had bypassed Denver. This act by the Union Pacific frustrated a dream Evans developed, while governor, of Denver becoming the hub of a railroad network covering the entire West, with the transcontinental Union Pacific the heart of the system. When that plan collapsed, he fell back to a scheme of Denver still being the hub of a system of north-south roads that would connect the region with the harbors on the Gulf of Mexico.[3] The Panic of 1873, of course, stymied railroad building in Colorado as well as it did everywhere else, and it was not until 1881 that Evans was able to implement his plan for connecting Denver to the Gulf of Mexico. On October 13, 1881, he addressed a large gathering of Denver's leading capitalists and merchants, most of whom were already stockholders in the Denver and New Orleans Railroad that he was announcing. In his speech, he spelled out all of the economic benefits to be received by Denver from having connections to the Gulf of Mexico. All of the products of the Rocky Mountains and Western Plains regions would be able to reach the sea over a shorter distance and at cheaper rates than connections to the Atlantic Coast provided. In addition, the West would have access to imports from Europe and South America without having to go through the eastern merchants as well as eastern railroads. In announcing the plans for the D&NO, Evans and his associates were challenging the transcontinentals—the Union Pacific and the Santa Fe—and offering direct competition to General William Palmer's Denver and Rio Grande, since both lines would serve Denver, Pueblo and Trinidad on their respective ways to El Paso and Fort Worth. Why would anyone believe that he could successfully challenge such formidable opposition? According to one historian, "The reason, incredible as it was, lay in the man himself."[4]

John Evans was a dynamic business and civic leader in Ohio, Indiana, and Illinois before he moved west. He went to medical school in Ohio, practiced in Indiana, where he also helped found the first hospital for the mentally ill, and later joined the faculty at Chicago's Rush Medical College. After he moved to Chicago, he played a leading role in the founding of Northwestern University at the suburb of Evanston, named for him, fourteen miles north of Chicago. Then he started the Chicago and Evanston railway to enable people to go back and forth from Chicago. After becoming the second governor of the Colorado Territory in 1862, in addition to his railroad building activities, he also found time to start the Colorado Seminary, which became the University of Denver. Richard C. Overton described him this way: "What excited Evans were broad objectives and long-run goals. . . . his real talent, and consequently his zeal, lay in formulating large schemes, selling them to the community, and watching them, if they succeeded, quicken the pulse of trade and contribute to the general development of society."[5]

Railroad Competition in Colorado

As soon as the D&NO was ready to start moving passengers and freight, its troubles with its competitors began. The Union Pacific, the Santa Fe, and the Denver and Rio Grande refused to do business with the newcomer. By 1883, things were so bad that Evans took his complaints to the Denver Board of Trade. His opponents controlled all of the lines out of Colorado, and lines within the state inevitably had to cross their tracks. Evans asked those in attendance, "Has any combination of corporations, or their agents, a right to conspire to break the [competitive] enterprise down in order to prevent the people [of Colorado] from enjoying the benefits of its operation?"[6]

Evans continued with the following charges: "I care not how they be clothed with power . . . by conspiring together and intimidation and threatening other outrages upon individual merchants, or by bribery and discriminations in favor of others, to drive away from our road its legitimate share of patronage, it is a crime against us and an outrageous crime against the people."[7] Following the speech the membership voted to give at least one-third of their shipments between Denver, Colorado Springs and Pueblo to the D&NO. Determined to pursue his dream of the connection with the gulf in spite of the strong opposition, Evans next submitted a memorial to Congress on November 30, 1883, maintaining that Congress had authority over the roads by virtue of its power to appoint part of the board of directors of one line and having made large land grants to two others involved. He then repeated in detail the charges made earlier, pointed out that no existing legislation prevented the actions causing his protest, and appealed to Congress to remedy the situation.[8]

Not content to wait upon federal action, Evans went back to the Denver Board of Trade, meeting with the chamber of commerce to seek a resolution asking the legislature to pass regulations prohibiting the discriminations and other actions taken by his opponents. A resolution was passed in March, 1884, but it was not until April, 1885, that the legislature passed an emergency act to regulate railroads and named William B. Felkner as commissioner. Felkner promptly heard Evans's case but ruled against him, demonstrating, according to Overton, that "the combined influence of the Rio Grande, the Union Pacific, the Burlington, and the Santa Fe was still stronger that the state's disposition to take remedial action."[9]

Undaunted, Evans reorganized the D&NO on May 28, 1885, as the Denver, Texas and Gulf, which began operating the D&NO properties on January 1, 1886. News of the reorganization received attention in Galveston on April 17, 1886, when the *Daily News* reported on the events completed and Evans's plans for the future. No specific dates were given; it was only stated that a road would be completed by the end of the year to the Canadian River in the Panhandle of Texas, where it would meet the Fort Worth and Denver City (FW&DC) building north from Fort Worth.

The Texas line had had its struggles also, beginning with the Panic of 1873. There was also the problem of the Indian Wars in the Panhandle, which ended in 1875 when Colonels Ranald Mackenzie and Nelson Miles routed the Indians at Palo Duro Canyon and took them to the reservations in the Indian Territory. But now both railroads were building toward each other again, and the connection with the Gulf, Colorado and Santa Fe (now part of the Atchison) would provide Denver's link to the Gulf of Mexico. The article, a dispatch from the Denver *Tribune-Republican* of April 13, 1886, said this about Evans: "Governor Evans has worked long and hard on this project, and has overcome countless difficulties which would have discouraged most men. He has been confident from the first that he would succeed in the end, though he has seen one plan after another destroyed by un-looked for opposition."[10] An example of Evans's confidence is provided by the fact that members of the Colorado congressional delegation—Senators Nathaniel P. Hill and Thomas Bowen and Representative James B. Belford—were corresponding with Evans as early as March of 1884 regarding support of the bill for a deep water harbor at Galveston. Belford was under consideration by members of the Texas delegation to introduce the Galveston bill in January, 1884.[11]

Evans made his third address to the board of trade and chamber of commerce on August 12, 1886, providing the members with a complete picture of the new company, the detailed plans for all of its branches in Colorado, and its determination to complete the line to Fort Worth and the Gulf of Mexico. Half of the speech was devoted to the anticipated business that would result from the line to the gulf, including cattle moving to northern pastures, coke, coal, minerals, imports from Europe and South America, southern products such as lumber, and tourists planning to enjoy vacations in the Rocky Mountains. The opportunities were boundless, and Evans had lost none of his enthusiasm in spite of the struggle with the other railroads.[12]

After several transactions and maneuvers, Evans signed an agreement on February 15, 1887, that provided a means of closing the 481-mile gap between Pueblo (the end of the Denver, Texas and Gulf) and Quanah, Texas (the end of the Fort Worth and Denver City), by creating a new company, the Denver, Texas and Fort Worth to build from Pueblo to the point where it crossed the Texas–New Mexico border at Texline. The FW&DC would continue to build from Quanah to Texline. This accomplishment, again spelled out in detail by Overton in *Gulf to the Rockies,* finally resulted in Evans being able to escape the noose set for him by the Union Pacific, the Santa Fe, and the Rio Grande and to put the Gulf road on a firm footing. The occasion was celebrated with a large chamber of commerce banquet honoring Evans. The president of the chamber recalled all of the achievements of Evans in his lifetime, stating that

> *the greatest and most important project of your life to this city was the organization of the Denver & New Orleans, now the Denver, Texas and Gulf Railroad, which will place us as near tide-water as Chicago and much nearer than Omaha or Kansas City. You had comparatively easy sailing with this enterprise until you reached Pueblo, when opposition of the strongest character made its appearance. This together with the depression of the money markets in the East made it tedious and difficult for you, but after meeting with disappointment after disappointment, and overcoming obstacle after obstacle with your well known stick-to-it-iveness, you have succeeded, and we rejoice with you tonight that the battle is over and the victory is won.[13]*

On the evening of March 27, 1888, the first through train from Fort Worth across the Texas Panhandle arrived in Denver. The occasion was marked by the publication of a special edition by the *Rocky Mountain Daily News* giving the history of the line and profiles on each of the companies. Also marking the event was Evans's fourth address to the chamber of commerce, at which he could announce that Denver's railroad crisis had passed. In his speech Evans made the statement that Denver, along with New York for the Atlantic states, Chicago for the western states, and San Francisco for the Pacific states and territories, had now become one of the four centers of business in the United States. As the hub of the Rocky Mountain states and territories, with rail connections extending in every direction, Denver would now be the metropolis and distribution center for a large part of the nation. He added, "Denver is the only port of entry or delivery within 600 miles to the east and over 800 miles in every other direction. We not only have the facilities for distributing, but also for importing from all countries and by all the important sea ports in the United States— more especially being nearest by way of New Orleans and Galveston on the gulf, and Laredo and El Paso on the Mexican border."[14]

The completion of the line also completely upset the balance of power in Evans's war with the other railroads. This was evidenced by the meeting of the Colorado Traffic Association held in Galveston on April 9, 1888, at which the association invited Evans's Denver, Texas and Fort Worth (the parent company of the Denver, Texas and Gulf and the Fort Worth and Denver City) to join the association and comply with its rates. Representing Evans, General Grenville M. Dodge, the original builder of the Union Pacific who had joined Evans to complete the Colorado line, declined and opened the way for a new and very different chapter of the war. Dodge and his executives announced a new set of rates between New York and Colorado via the Morgan Line to Galveston and the Houston and Texas Central railroad from there to Fort Worth. Immediately the Missouri Pacific and the Atchison had to lower their competing rates from New York to Galveston via the Mallory Line and the GC&SF to Colorado connections in Fort Worth or in Kansas. Negotiations among all of the Colorado parties would continue throughout the summer of 1888 until workable compromises were reached.[15]

The stage was now set for Denver and Galveston, in a remarkable convergence of interests, to make a push for the final step in their decades-old dream. For Galveston it would be another milestone in the long effort that began with the excursions to Kansas City and Denver back in 1873. Evans and Walter Gresham would now stage the great Interstate Deep Water Convention in Denver to gather all of the political, civic, and business leaders of the western states and unite them in pursuit of what had become the highest priority internal improvement project for these states.

184

Galveston Harbor in 1874. At that time the wharves consisted of piers that extended from the island across the mud flats to the Galveston Channel where the ships could tie up.

Captain Charles Fowler, harbor pilot, shipping agent, and manager of the 1870 pile jetty project.

Fabrication of the gabions, 1875, clearly showing how the wicker baskets were made. From Howell and Quinn scrapbook, Rosenberg Library

Colonel William L. Moody, chairman of the first deep water committee.

Walter Gresham, organizer and driving force behind the Interstate Deep Water Committee and director of its lobbying efforts in Washington in support of the deep water appropriation.

Grain Elevator A was built during the 1880s to accommodate the increased grain trade the port began to handle during that decade.

The South Jetty from eastern Galveston Island during construction, showing the railroad cars that carried rocks and more track for the continuation of the jetty.

President Benjamin Harrison (right, center) *and Texas Governor James Stephen Hogg are shown with a group of Galveston residents aboard a ship in the harbor during the president's visit. Those greeting the distinguished visitors included F. M. Gilbough, Colonel William H. Sinclair, Leo N. Levi, Henry M. Trueheart, Robert B. Hawley (later a congressman), Peirce Levine, C. Nicolini (the Italian consul), and Julius Runge. The whiskered gentleman to the right of the president is Secretary of Agriculture Rush, the former governor of Illinois.*

Willard Richardson, the dynamic and visionary publisher of the Galveston Daily News *until his death in 1875.*

Most of the cotton and shipping community were present for this luncheon at the Cotton Exchange building on February 28, 1895, celebrating the receipt of the 1,500,000th bale of cotton during the current season. Present were Exchange members, consuls of foreign governments, public officials, railroad officials, shipping agents, and other interested parties.

Members of the Galveston Cotton Exchange gather during the late 1890s. Colonel Moody, past president, is seated at right center holding his hat. The young man standing four places to his left with his hat tilted back on his head is I. H. Kempner.

GALVESTON HARBOR, FROM PIER U, Looking WEST

Galveston Harbor, ca. 1900. By the turn of the century, the wharves had a much different appearance. Bulkheads had been built along the channel, and the space behind the bulkheads was filled in, burying the old mud flats. Warehouses were built near the bulkheads to service the much larger ships coming to the port.

Chapter 8

The Western States
Are Aroused

In spite of the significant victory achieved in the Army Engineers' report, the deep water committee went into hibernation and very little was heard from it during the remainder of 1886. It was as if everything had to be left to the Engineers while one hoped for the best. A rivers and harbors bill was signed August 5, 1886, in the closing days of the session, after earlier indications in June and July that reform-minded President Grover Cleveland would veto the bill. It provided $300,000 for Galveston after the entire bill was reduced by 25 percent before the final vote.[1] During the bill's year there, several proposals were put forth in the Texas legislature by Alexander W. Terrell, John Hancock, and DeWitt C. Giddings for various means of state aid to Galveston, with public lands as the basis of a plan of state action. Nothing came of the proposals, however.[2]

A flurry of activity arose in February of 1887 when Andrew Onderdonk, a contractor from New York City, submitted a proposal to dredge a channel 20 feet deep and 250 feet wide across the bar for $500,000, the job to be completed in six months with no payments due until the work was completed. Judge Street drafted an amendment to the state constitution that would permit local financing of such a project, but Colonel A. M. Shannon, as might be expected, proposed throwing the job open to bids and giving local contractors a chance to keep the profits at home.[3]

Proposals and Propositions

The Onderdonk proposal was presented to the city council at a regular meeting by Mayor Roger L. Fulton and referred to the committee on harbors and wharves. Also referred to the committee on that day was another proposal that had an interesting history. It came from William M. Douglas and was presented to the city council by a large group of businessmen that included Moody, Kempner, Skinner, Samuel M. Penland, and Captain William Scrimgeour, who had been involved with the deep water movement, and many others who had not.[4]

Douglas was a former employee of the Army Engineers, or was about to become a former employee at the time of the city council meeting. He had first became involved with Moody and the deep water committee in March, 1885, when he wrote to Colonel Moody that he was holding certain papers bearing upon the matter of improving the harbor and asked Moody if he would like to see them. This letter was quickly followed by another in which he said he would deliver the "papers" and also proposed an approach for handling the matter. He suggested that Moody and associates request that he present the Army Engineers' plans to the deep water committee with the objective that the committee and the Engineers might be able to harmonize their differences. Douglas would receive additional salary for his work in preparing drawings, estimates, and so forth.[5]

A month later Douglas wrote again, informing Moody that Major Mansfield was going to reduce his salary on June 30 and requesting Moody to offer him something. In a postscript, he said, "I could make out a case for your side worth to you more than imaginable."[6] In another letter the next day Douglas told Moody that Major Mansfield had authorized his stepson to pass on the bad news for fear Douglas might quit immediately. After June, Douglas wrote, the workload will be down and Mansfield could do as he wished with him.[7]

In his next letter Douglas informed Moody that Major Mansfield held back the "papers" and told him that he did wrong in showing them to Moody, which only proved to Douglas that they were valuable. In this letter, Douglas also relayed the interesting information that the Chief of Engineers had offered Major Mansfield a transfer, which was refused because he wanted to stick it out at Galveston. Douglas again offered to give the "papers" to Moody, who apparently refused to take them unless Mansfield approved.[8]

In another letter on the same day that may have caused Moody to question Douglas's motives, Douglas asked Moody to loan him thirty-five dollars to help cover the cost of the birth of his daughter. He explained this was necessary because he lost most of his savings in the failure of the Island City Bank.[9]

Douglas had also told Moody that he was preparing to send a copy of the "papers" to Colonel Merrill, who at that time was preparing his article for the American Society of Civil Engineers, and suggested that Moody might then want to have them submitted to the committee on rivers and harbors. This probably occurred because later Elmer Corthell, Eads's assistant, returned the package to Moody, stating that Eads had received them from Representative Clifton R. Breckinridge but had never had time to examine them. He added that Douglas should be given great credit for the judgment, skill, and neatness shown in "this valuable compilation of facts."[10] Since the papers would have reached Eads after his May, 1885, speech to the American Society of Civil Engineers (ASCE), his last work on the jetties at Galveston, it is doubtful they served any real purpose.

Douglas, meanwhile, continued to work in the office of the Engineers in spite of his difficulties. In October of 1886, he requested Moody's assistance in his presentation of a proposal to the newly appointed committee on a seawall and beach erosion, headed by Judge Robert M. Franklin. It may have been this proposal that was presented to city council, since Douglas saw the three issues—deep water, a seawall, and the prevention of beach erosion—as interrelated.[11] There is no doubt that the cheap price of a deep channel had aroused interest in Galveston, and when Colonel Moody, as president of the Cotton Exchange, called a noon meeting on February 10 to discuss the proposal from Onderdonk, more than one hundred of the city's leading citizens came to participate.[12]

Many issues—old and new—were brought up during the meeting, and several resolutions and amendments to the resolutions were offered. Judge Street, more convinced than ever that only state aid would produce deep water, led off with his resolution for the constitutional amendment. Franklin suggested the naming of a commission to handle all harbor improvement business, something he had once before proposed to no avail. Sealy proposed that the funds raised be turned over to the Army Engineers, who would carry out the work. Colonel Moody still opposed putting the Engineers in charge rather than a private contractor, but he and Sealy compromised on the wording: "work to be done in harmony with the Bureau of [Army] Engineers." The last part of the three-part resolution passed at the meeting called for a five-man committee to present the resolution to the city council and to take the follow-up action to promote the purposes sought. Immediately after the meeting, Moody, who had been elected chairman of the meeting, named Street, Judge Ballinger, John C. Wallis, Dr. T. C. Thompson, and Harris Kempner to the committee.[13]

In an interview March 31, 1887, Street explained that Walter Gresham, now Galveston's representative in the legislature, had submitted both the proposed amendment to the constitution, which would have required approval by the people in the general election in November of 1888, and the proposed amendment to the existing law authorizing cities to improve their harbors, but it appeared that neither could be passed during the current session because of the business already before the legislature and the pressure for an immediate adjournment. Street further explained that amending the existing law did not take the place of the constitutional amendment since it would provide for the expenditure of $500,000 for a twenty-foot channel as a temporary measure while the means of obtaining a thirty-foot channel was being developed.[14]

Major Ernst's New Plans

While the citizens of Galveston were pursuing their plans for a local effort, the government engineers were pushing ahead with their own. Major Oswald H. Ernst, who had replaced Major Mansfield on November 22, 1886, announced his plans on March 2, 1887, for resuming work utilizing the $300,000 appropriated in 1886 and anticipating another $200,000 in the 1887 bill. At the time of the announcement, the bill had passed Congress and was awaiting the president's signature, but it was uncertain what action would be taken at the White House. Major Ernst planned to publish specifications as soon as the fate of the bill was known, and he expected to receive bids by April 15 and to commence work in June. He planned to issue a contract for the total work instead of subdividing the work among several contractors, and to advertise nationally in order to secure the best possible bids. Technically, the plan was to use the existing South Jetty, then four to six feet underwater, as a foundation for the continuation of the work and to raise the level of the new South Jetty to five feet above the surface of the water. The new design called for the use of an inside casing of clay, held in place initially by a line of pilings on each side, as a substitute for the brush mattress, to avoid destruction by the teredo. Small stones, or riprap, would be placed around the clay casing to secure it.[15]

The use of clay would be the basis of a claim to be submitted by Douglas, who had recently been fired by Major Ernst, to the secretary of war, maintaining that it was his idea to use clay instead of the more expensive stone and that he should receive a royalty from its use. This information was provided in a letter to Moody requesting financial assistance until he could find other employment and also start receiving benefits from the claim.[16]

It came as no real surprise when President Cleveland pocket-vetoed the rivers and harbors bill as the congressional session expired on March 4, 1887. The president, hostile to the spoils system and to "politics as usual," had just signed the Interstate Commerce Act, offending another special interest group, on February 7, 1887. Colonel Moody saw the veto of the "corrupt and futile system of river and harbor work throughout the country" as a benefit and said that it enhanced his good opinion of "that gentleman's honesty and integrity in showing a determination to revolutionize the system." Moody stuck to his previous view that the government driblet system was only prolonging the day Galveston would have deep water and regarded the defeat as moving one step closer to the accomplishment of a practical result. George Sealy generally agreed with Moody's view, adding that the defeat of the bill "would more thoroughly crystallize the idea and that it behooves us in the present emergency to help ourselves." Major Ernst said that his plans would remain the same and the work would go as far as $300,000 could carry it.[17]

Senator Maxey Is Defeated, Eads Dies

In January the deep water cause had received another setback when Senator Maxey, a staunch supporter, was defeated by Representative Reagan for reelection by the Texas legislature. In a tense and hard-fought struggle that lasted six days, Reagan won over Maxey after one representative falsely announced that Reagan needed only one vote to win and he was switching his. Actually Reagan needed five, but the stampede was on and he wound up with 102 votes, far more than the 69 needed to win. Although Reagan had spoken and worked for the Galveston improvements, his heavy involvement with the Interstate Commerce Act had been his first priority. With that bill now signed into law, the citizens of Galveston could only hope that his tremendous skills would be used as forcefully in the cause of deep water. In a poignant letter written in March, former senator Maxey expressed his postelection feelings: "In respect to the result of the last race, I have no regrets. . . . I would infinitely prefer defeat with my record to success by demagogy . . . I leave the Senate without a stain on a long, full and as I believe a valuable record."[18] In his practice of law at Paris between the end of the Civil War and his election to the senate in 1875, Maxey apparently had met Moody, possibly during his term in the Texas legislature, for he made reference to their friendship dating back to January, 1874. Maxey stated his belief that his greatest accomplishment was the legislation that gave the St. Louis and San Francisco Railroad the right-of-way through the Indian Territory, a bill that was also of great importance to Galveston since it served as the precedent for a similar bill later that gave the Gulf, Colorado and Santa Fe Railway its rights through the Territory. Maxey, who was often involved in steps to improve relations with the Indians, believed their future lay in the direction of individual farms rather than possession of territories.[19]

But of all the things that went wrong, or could have gone wrong in 1887, the death of Captain James Eads on March 8 was the worst. As Street explained, "The name of the lamented Eads was itself a tower of strength, and by the confidence it inspired both in the practicability of his engineering design and his ability to control the requisite capital, silenced opposition on those otherwise plausible grounds."[20] The Tehuantepec Ship-Railway occupied more and more of Eads's time and interest in his later years, as both Coke and Maxey had observed, and illness took its toll, but he always maintained his interest in the project at Galveston in spite of knowing the odds were heavily against his ever getting the job. In January of 1887 Eads was in Washington seeking congressional endorsement of the project when he became ill; on February 3 he sailed with his wife and daughter for Nassau in the Bahamas. In what may have been one of Eads's last letters, he wrote to Charles Fowler of the Seawall committee: "as my physician recommends absolute rest for me I cannot promise to answer any further professional questions which you may ask during my stay there. Please give my kindest regards to my numerous friends in Galveston and be assured that I will do all in my power to aid you in your laudable efforts for the protection of your city." He improved slowly and, becoming impatient, planned to return to Washington on a February 24 sailing. However, he died not ever knowing that the bill was never voted upon in the House of Representatives because of the opposition of Speaker Carlisle, who never permitted it to come up for a vote.[21]

Since the Army Engineers had adopted most of Eads's criticisms and everyone had accepted the fact that Eads, because of the hostile opposition of the Engineers, would never get the job at Galveston, his passing did not materially hurt Galveston's hopes for deep water. What Eads had done for Galveston was to convince a significant portion of the population of the possibilities of what could be done if only the people would persevere. At the time of his death it appeared that Judge Street and Colonel Moody were very determined that the possibilities would be realized—one way or the other.

Moody's Address to the Cotton Exchange

During 1887 Moody and Gresham, two of the prime movers in the deep water cause, were heavily involved in getting the new Airline railroad launched. Moody spent most the first half of the year in New York attempting to sell bonds to finance the road, and upon his return found himself pulled into the work of the seawall committee, along with Gresham. Perhaps a diversion from the frustration and intensity of the deep water activities was needed to refresh the combatants. Nevertheless, Moody returned to the wars in December when, as president, he addressed the sixteenth annual meeting of the Cotton Exchange. In this address he identified four obstacles to the increased cotton trade of the port: the disposition of cotton planters to sell their cotton in the interior; railroad discriminations; the lack of adequate banking facilities; and the lack of a good harbor.

Moody felt that the old system of cotton factors at the port benefited the planter because the factor could hold the cotton awaiting favorable prices instead of the planter selling it as if it were a perishable item. The factor was also in a position to obtain for the planters advances at the lowest possible interest rate and to buy his supplies at the lowest possible price. He hoped that planters were beginning to realize this and encouraged the members to promote this point of view. Regarding railroads, Moody said that they have become a law unto themselves, unhampered by the legislature, and that the solution was for the people to construct and operate a system of railroads for themselves.

In order to expand the banking facilities of the state and increase the availability of credit, he urged the passage by the legislature of a Factors Act, which England passed in 1823 and New York in 1830 and which many other states had enacted. Such an act would have enabled factors to use as security any bill of lading, custom-house permit, or warehouse keeper's receipt. Under the law not only the agricultural products of a country, but every kind of merchandise would be made available as a collateral security in whoever's hands they may lawfully be. He pointed out that no state had ever annulled this law, and that if it were repealed in New York, massive bankruptcies and disruption of the commercial system would result. According to Moody, money would become cheap and abundant, and no one would be compelled to force the sale of his products.

A good harbor was the fourth obstacle. Moody reviewed the logic and the rationale for a deep water harbor at Galveston and gave examples of the financial benefits to growers of cotton and wheat. While admitting that there were those who were satisfied with the depth of the present channel and those who did not wish further to antagonize the government engineers, he said that the people of Texas and the western states were becoming aware of these benefits and that Galveston should not weary in agitating until there was a full comprehension. At this point, he offered no specific plan for this agitation. Obviously the issue of deep water was not over and dead with him, and it would be interesting to know if there were specific plans in his mind at this time for carrying the battle beyond Galveston.[22]

The Campaign to Arouse the West

Before the month was over, Colonel Moody had launched his effort to agitate the people of Texas and the western states when he had a deep water resolution introduced at the Immigration Convention that convened in Dallas on December 20, 1887. This convention was the outgrowth of a meeting of the Dallas Merchants Exchange on December 3 to discuss means of increasing immigration and the influx of capital to Texas. At the time the northwestern states and California were making extensive efforts, with the cooperation of the railroads, to increase immigration, and doing so with great success. At the meeting the Dallas businessmen set December 20 as the date for a convention and invited cities across the state to send representatives authorized to act for the city. Chairman W. White named a committee consisting of J. S. Daughtery, Jules Schneider, Alex Sanger, J. F. Elliott, T. L. Marsalis, J. B. Simpson, and O. P. Bowser to carry out the convention.[23]

In response to the request from Dallas, Colonel Moody called a meeting at the Cotton Exchange on December 7. Mayor Roger L. Fulton served as chairman, and both he and Moody addressed the purpose of the meeting and its importance to Galveston. Mayor Fulton closed the meeting by naming Richard G. Lowe, William L. Moody, John D. Rogers, Morris Lasker, Henry M. Trueheart, John H. Focke, Edward T. Flint, and James D. Skinner to a delegation to attend the convention. From across the state came reports of other cities selecting their representatives and passing resolutions supporting the goals of the movement. When criticized for not being cooperative enough, one railroad official pointed out that Kansas and Nebraska had spent over $1 million each putting on exhibits and sending agents to the eastern states and to Europe. He said that when the state induced the immigrants to come, the railroads would be ready with the same cheap rates that they provided to Kansas and Nebraska.[24]

As the delegates began arriving in Dallas on December 19, there was talk of electing Colonel Moody permanent chairman of the convention. As proceedings got under way the next day, Henry Exall presided temporarily and the permanent chairmanship went to Moody's friend, former senator Maxey, a member of the Paris delegation. Moody may well have promoted this in order that his own freedom of action would not be restricted. The main business of the first day was the letter from William H. Newman, third vice president of the Missouri Pacific Railway and former passenger agent for the Gulf, Colorado and Santa Fe at Galveston. The letter was a response to one he received from Richard G. Lowe and expressed the willingness of the

Missouri Pacific and other railroads to cooperate with the convention. Newman went so far as to offer some suggestions regarding how to organize and proceed once the convention had defined its objectives. He specifically recommended that a small committee be designated to meet with the railroad representatives. Following the sessions, Moody's committee on resolutions met that evening and formulated a plan for a state central committee composed of one representative from each senatorial district, which would name a committee to meet with the railroad officials and choose a five-man executive committee to operate the organization. On the next day, Colonel Moody presented the resolution pertaining to the organization, which was unanimously approved. Next the central committee was established as each senatorial district selected its representative. Resolutions were then passed requesting the legislature to establish a state geological department and requesting each county to create an immigration bureau to cooperate with the state organization. Then a Mr. Browning, a member of the resolutions committee from the Panhandle, offered a resolution to urge the Texas delegation in Congress to seek a single deep water port on the Texas coast. The resolution expressed no preference for the site of the port, but it did state that the past method of scattering scarce funds over a number of port developments had not brought deep water to any of them. The resolution, probably written by Moody before leaving Galveston, was passed unanimously and the process of agitation had completed its first step.[25]

A meeting was held in Galveston on December 23 to hear a report on the proceedings at Dallas. The group approved forming a county organization and raising one thousand dollars to support the immigration activities. Another meeting was held on December 27, chaired by Richard S. Willis, with between 150 and 200 in attendance. At this meeting Walter Gresham offered a resolution indicating support of the Dallas resolutions and authorizing the chairman of the meeting to name a seven-man deep water executive committee to devise and carry out a plan for setting forth Galveston's superior claim to be that single Texas port. The resolution passed, and Chairman Willis said he would announce the committee at the meeting scheduled January 3, 1888, to organize the county immigration organization.[26] The meeting was postponed until January 10, at which time Willis announced his selections—Judge William P. Ballinger, Colonel

William L. Moody, Richard G. Lowe, George Sealy, Harris Kempner, and Walter Gresham. According to the resolution, Willis was an ex officio member. Henry M. Trueheart, who had been named the representative for the senatorial district, reported that the meeting of the central committee had been very harmonious and that the response of the railroads to better their excursion fare to California was all that could possibly be expected. He explained the purpose of the county organization and what was expected of it; however, choosing the officers was put off until a larger attendance could be achieved. Another meeting was held on January 12 and the following were chosen: president, Richard S. Willis; vice president, John D. Rogers; secretary, D. D. Bryan; and treasurer, J. P. Alvey. Willis then appointed the following to the executive and finance committee: John D. Rogers, Bertrand Adoue, John C. Wallis, John H. Focke, John S. Rogers, Julius Runge, and William F. Ladd.[27]

As Colonel Moody had perhaps intended, the deep water resolution introduced at Dallas had the effect of creating an alliance between the immigration organization and the Galveston Deep Water Committee. This alliance produced some quick results, sooner even than Moody had expected. In an executive committee meeting at Austin on January 24 and 25, 1888, two resolutions were passed. One authorized Major Barry Chilton and former mayor of Fort Worth John Peter Smith to confer with Colonel C. C. Gibbs at Houston to seek special excursion fares for Texans who wished to return home from California. The other resolution called for a delegation, made up of one representative from each congressional district, to go to Washington to meet with the Texas congressional delegation in support of the resolution passed at Dallas for a concentrated effort at one Texas seaport.

Galveston, confident of being selected for the deep water site, had now succeeded in marshaling statewide support of the movement, and the *Daily News* described it as "one of the most important steps that has ever been taken in behalf of a deep water seaport for Texas."[28]

Friends and Enemies

Before the delegation could go to Washington, however, cracks began to appear in the united front presented at the Dallas convention. The counties of southwestern Texas met at San Antonio on February 2 to organize in accordance with the Dallas resolution. However, their resolution pertaining to deep water varied from the Dallas version in that it called for increased appropriations for all of the potential sites on the Texas coast rather than the concentration of funds upon a single site. This convention also passed a resolution supporting a private effort to develop a pier into the gulf and an artificial harbor on Padre Island near Corpus Christi. In Beaumont a citizens committee had a survey of Sabine Pass made in preparation for a campaign to continue the work on deepening the channel there. In addition to these local activities, it was already known that Congressmen William H. Crain and Charles Stewart still supported the old system of "driblet" and "scatteration" through the rivers and harbors appropriation instead of any concentration of funds on a single port.[29]

Moody may have failed to capitalize on the support of another powerful group—the Farmers Alliance. The year-old organization, born out of the growing frustrations of the farmers, met in Dallas in early February to work on organizational matters. On February 4, the organization passed a resolution similar to the one passed by the immigration convention, calling for the concentration of funds at the most available port on the Texas coast.

The *Daily News* praised the organization's directors—A. J. Kessler, New Braunfels; W. E. Moore and T. Y. Collins, Paris; D. J. Eddleman, Denton; Ben Terrell, Seguin; R. J. Sledge, Kyle; and J. B. Reilly, Dallas—as men of clear views and practical sense. The fact that the organization numbered well over 200,000 was a matter that the Texas delegation in Congress could not be indifferent to, as the farmers could not be indifferent to the economic benefits to be realized when larger ships could carry their products at cheaper rates. In a series of letters to Moody in February and March, Sledge offered, "sub-rosa," to represent Galveston in the coming congressional battle for compensation. He pointed out the forces already aligned against the concentration of funds at Galveston. He also stated that many farmers held resentments against Galveston because of the wharf charges and high profits of the wholesale merchants that the farmers had long endured. He told Moody that relying upon the politicians and the ex-politicians Hancock and Giddings would not work, and that he was the kind of lobbyist that could bring Galveston success.[30]

Return to Washington

Hancock, Giddings, and Moody arrived in Washington on February 26, with Barry Chilton and John Peter Smith scheduled to arrive later. The first meeting was held in the rooms of Senator Coke on the night of Monday, February 27, with Senators Reagan and Coke and Representatives Constantine Kilgore, Joseph Sayers, William Martin, Samuel Lanham, Littleton Moore, Joseph Abbott, David B. Culberson, William H. Crain, and Charles Stewart present. Giddings opened the meeting by reviewing the resolutions that had been passed at the Dallas convention and at the Austin meeting of the executive committee. Hancock followed with an hour-long talk in support of the measure and added the recommendation that a commission of engineers determine the site on the Texas coast. Moody followed with a review of the Engineers' previous failures. As expected, Crain and Stewart objected. Crain said he could not understand why Moody opposed the current plan of the Engineers since they had adopted the Eads Plan. Crain also pointed out that Major Ernst, with $300,000 of prior year funds and $500,000 in the current bill, would be only $200,000 short of the $1 million that General J. C. Duane, the new chief of engineers, had said he could spend in the next year. Also, that would leave only $2.2 million to be appropriated before Galveston would reach twenty feet of water over the bar. However, Crain did not mention that the remaining appropriation could take four to ten years to obtain, based upon past experience. Stewart's objection was that Congress appropriated by project, not by state, and that the deletion of other Texas sites would not mean any more money for the one remaining. The congressional delegation supported Crain and Stewart, believing that a concentration of the appropriation was impractical and that it was too late in the session to attempt it anyway. The meeting adjourned until Thursday night for more discussion.[31]

In his report to Richard Willis, now chairman of the deep water committee at Galveston, Moody lamented the fact that the congressional delegation would not concur with the Dallas resolution for a single deep water port as soon as possible, regardless of where it was. He explained to Willis, however, that the delegation was not unanimous, as reported in the *Daily News*. The meeting had broken up, and some of the participants wandered into an adjoining room, the *Daily News* correspondent with them. Therefore, he did not hear Representative Moore state that he favored the concentration, or Senator Reagan state that he would introduce a bill to provide $5 million provided that Texas supplemented it with $2.5 million. Representative Abbott also voiced support of the concentration. Moody said the problem was with people like Representatives Silas Hare and Kilgore, who would leave the whole matter up to Representatives Crain and Stewart, in spite of the fact that only their districts benefit from the present system. Disappointed, Moody closed his report with this conclusion: "a united [immigration] committee, a divided [congressional] delegation. Texas is suffering."[32] In an interview before leaving Washington, Moody elaborated further: "We mean to prosecute the enterprise and make an issue of the subject, and let it become part of the election contest, and if possible elect gentlemen to congress who are in sympathy with the proposed deep water scheme. . . . The fight we propose to make in the state may relegate some of the present members of congress to private life, but that we cannot help."[33]

Representative Crain promptly wrote Moody a letter asking him if he had been quoted correctly.[34] The colonel replied that while he did not intend to give the *Daily News* correspondent an interview for publication, and was only expressing his personal view, nevertheless he meant to be frank and told Crain, "I have not faith in the gov't plan through the R&H system." He continued, "I am making no war on you. Others may, I may, but it will only be when I can see more clearly than I do now that you are an obstacle." He said he would rejoice to see both Crain and Stewart returned to Congress, working for deep water—not appropriations simply."[35]

The official report to the State Immigration Association by the committee sounded very much like Moody's report to Willis, except that it concluded with the following statement:

> We regret to add that the facts do not warrant that such action will be taken by our delegation in Congress as in our judgment will be calculated to secure for Texas her want, a deep-water port. We deem it proper that the facts should be known to all, rather than the public be left under a delusive hope, to be mislead and disappointed. We beg to submit for the consideration of the people of Texas, if it is not wiser for them to abandon all hope for relief, and themselves secure at least one first-class port on their coast![36]

Denver Awakens to Deep Water's Importance

While the results of the Washington visit and the reaction of the Texas congressional delegation were causing disappointment in Texas, far away in Denver events of far more importance were taking shape. No one was yet talking of a Denver Interstate Deep Water Convention, but the seeds were being planted. On March 27, 1888, the city of Denver staged a jubilee to celebrate the completion of the Denver–Fort Worth rail connection. At 2:40 A.M. on March 28, 1888, the Texas excursionists and the Denver welcoming committee who boarded at Pueblo pulled into the Denver station to join a celebration that had actually started the night before. Denver streets were ablaze with electric lights. Every business house and public building and many residences were decorated with flags and banners, and four blocks on Larimer Street and six on Sixteenth had arches bearing colored electric lights. Governor Evans delivered a speech to a packed house at the chamber of commerce and proclaimed that Denver had passed its third crisis.[37]

The *Rocky Mountain Daily News* that morning was a special edition describing the events, recounting the history of the Gulf-to-Rockies road, and containing biographies and pictures of the DT&FW officials, and Governor Evans's speech. The edition also contained an article regarding Denver's need for a better harbor on the gulf and a discussion of the situation at Galveston. Following the article was another that contained the report of the immigration association's delegation to Washington, calling to the attention of the citizens of Colorado the negative posture of the Texas congressional delegation regarding concentration and raising questions as to the next move.[38] This article was followed a few days later by another on the city of Galveston and its attributes, pointing out the economic significance of Galveston and its harbor to Denver and the western states. There was still no mention of a Denver convention, but the article made perfectly clear that Galveston and Denver shared a common destiny.[39]

Shortly after the Denver celebration, a group of Colorado editors traveled by special car over the new connection directly to Galveston to see for themselves the subject of so much attention. "We were not prepared to find at the end of our Texas journey such a remarkably fine city," said the president of the Colorado association, J. Dellenback. The visitors were given a trip to deep water on the first day and the second was devoted to entertainment, including an oyster roast for which Galveston was well known. William B. Denson, Robert H. Hawley, Garland B. Miller, Morris Lasker, James W. Moore, and other members of the Progressive Association saw to it that the visitors carried back only the most pleasant memories of the Island City. In the closing remarks to the editors, the importance of the new commercial relationship between Denver and Galveston as its natural port of entry was stressed in a speech by John H. Hawley.[40]

Doubtlessly, the excursion by such an influential group of newspaper editors played a very important part in the developing kinship between the two cities—Denver trying to establish itself as the commercial center of the Plains, and Galveston trying to establish itself as the port for all of the western states. But even more significant were meetings being held in north Texas by members of the Texas delegation that went to Denver to celebrate the opening of the Denver, Texas and Fort Worth railroad. Members of the Dallas Merchants Exchange had already corresponded with their counterparts in Denver and were proposing that a deep water convention be held in Denver, while Fort Worth was planning to hold one in that city. The *Daily News* favored a convention in Denver for the convenience of the western states; after all, it was the support of the western states for the deep water movement that the Texans were looking for. A convention in Fort Worth was too likely to turn into a squabble between the Texas ports as to which would be selected for the concentration of funds.

Competition from Aransas Pass

In fact, the *Daily News* may have suspected that very thing. This had probably been the case ever since the Southwestern Immigration Convention in San Antonio on February 2, 1888, had rejected concentration and passed a resolution favoring continued appropriations for all practicable harbor entrances. Another cause for suspicion appeared in the column next to the *Daily News* editorial. Reprinted was an announcement from the Aransas Pass Land Company that a regatta and town lot sale would be held July 5–9 and that all of the railroads were providing low excursion rates. The *Daily News* was quick to point out that the Fort Worth convention would start July 10, 1888, and that, one way or the other, the two events must be connected.

One motive attributed to the railroad, port, and land sale promoters at Aransas Pass was to attempt to break the favored position that Galveston seemed to have with the government engineers as a result of a report recently made by Major Ernst. The "report," in the form of a letter to George Sealy in response to an inquiry, stated that at depths of twenty-four, thirty, and fifty feet, Galveston had far more port capacity than any of the other four Texas sites. In taking aim at this potential objective of the Aransas supporters at Fort Worth, the *Daily News* concluded, "its projectors will hardly be successful, though they may be the means of defeating what may be a wise and prudent course on the part of the people of Texas by agitating and advocating an impracticable one which will never bear fruit. Such things have been done in the past, there is every reason to believe that the Aransas boomers contemplate something of the kind now."[41]

Development plans at Aransas Pass seemed to get into high gear in 1888, but they were nothing new. Lieutenant George McClellan included Aransas Pass in his survey of 1853 and was pessimistic about development. The citizens of Rockport built a six-hundred-foot dike on St. Joseph Island in 1868, but no trace remained two years later. The town of Corpus Christi had the Morris and Cummings Cut dredged in 1874 to provide a channel to Aransas Pass by going around Harbor Island and coming down Lydia Ann Channel, between Harbor Island and St. Joseph Island. A second survey by the Engineers produced a recommendation for parallel jetties extending from St. Joseph Island and Mustang Island, on either side of the Pass, and work on these was conducted between 1880 and 1885 by Major Mansfield. The jetties suffered the same problems as those at Galveston and were redesigned by Major Ernst. Initially, the funds available had to be used for a revetment to protect Mustang Island from erosion, and the jetty construction lagged. It was at this point that two private initiatives came forth. On January 25, 1888, the Corpus Christi and Padre Island company filed an application for a state charter to construct a harbor by building piers and breakwaters into the Gulf of Mexico off of Padre Island. On June 9, 1888, Representative Abbott introduced a bill in the House of Representatives to authorize the Aransas Improvement Company to dredge, construct piers, or otherwise provide a deep water port at Aransas Pass. The bill provided that the company could collect reasonable port fees and that the government would reimburse the company $1 million upon completion.[42]

The railroad connections into Corpus Christi, a town of only 3,000 in 1880 compared with Galveston's 22,000, were already in place. Uriah Lott, one of the state's most prominent railroad promoters, had built the Corpus Christi, San Diego, and Rio Grande to San Diego in 1878–79. After it became the Texas Mexican in 1881, it was extended from San Diego to Laredo. Then in 1884–85, he promoted the building of the San Antonio and Aransas Pass Railroad from San Antonio to Corpus Christi. Thus by 1887, Lott, the business community of Corpus Christi, and the developers of Aransas Pass and harbors were ready for deep water and their share of congressional attention.[43]

As the time for the Fort Worth convention approached, some of the fears in Galveston regarding the "Aransas boomers" began to materialize. Barnett Gibbs of Dallas, president of the Aransas Pass Land Company, showed up at a citizens meeting at the Dallas Merchants Exchange held to select delegates to the convention. Mayor W. C. Connor read the convention call from the Fort Worth Board of Trade in order to clarify the purpose of the meeting and then, as president of the Merchants Exchange, notified the meeting that the exchange had already selected delegates so there would not be any duplication with those to be selected by the citizens meeting. Then Gibbs introduced a resolution that concentration at a point be selected by three competent engineers, that private parties be allowed at their own expense to secure deep water, that the major part of the Texas coast should not be in one congressional district, and that government appropriation should be made only where there was state or federal control of wharf charges. After delegates were selected, including Gibbs, another resolution was introduced by him to the effect that the citizens of Texas could visit and invest their money without any advice or condemnation from the *Galveston Daily News,* but this resolution was ruled out of order by the chairman.[44]

The Fort Worth Convention

As the convention prepared to get under way, Major Ernst created something of a stir by including in his letter to the board of trade explaining his absence some comparative information on the ports indicating that Galveston had no rival as the principal port but that the best interest of the state required developing both Galveston and

Sabine Pass. Nevertheless, the resolution introduced on the second day of the meeting specifically requested that a board of competent engineers selected by the government select the site, and the convention steered clear of the divisive issue. The proposition to permit private development of ports was included in the resolution. Gibbs made another attempt to block Galveston by offering an amendment that would prohibit expenditures until the attorney-general of the United States gave an opinion as to whether wharf privileges were subject to government regulation. The Galveston delegation—Street, Leo N. Levi, Gresham, and Marcus C. McLemore—all answered that the Wharf Company did not control all of the wharf footage at Galveston, that its rates were the lowest to be found and that by its charter from the state it was subject to regulation.

The resolution passed by the resolutions committee had been the work of Gresham and Julius Runge. It was later revealed in the delegation's report at Galveston that in the resolutions committee deliberations Uriah Lott, also a member, had attempted to substitute "Aransas Pass" for the phrase "any point on the coast of Texas" where it occurred in the resolution, but it was voted down. Thus Galveston achieved its objective of unifying the state behind the idea of concentrating the appropriation and voting an amount adequate to do the job, knowing full well that any objective board would have to select Galveston as the most practical site. Aransas Pass was left with its private contractors free to do what they could, with a hope of being reimbursed if they reached twenty feet.[45]

Uriah Lott's Diplomacy

Late in July, perhaps to show what a good sport he was, Uriah Lott invited the business leaders of Galveston to visit Port Aransas, at his expense, and seventeen accepted. The *Daily News* carried an account of the trip from the *San Antonio Express* of July 31, 1888, evidently written by the staff humorist of the *Express,* who began his story as follows: "Galveston has seen Aransas Pass, has viewed it in all its length, breadth, and thickness, has sailed over it, sounded it, tested it, commented upon it and wept over it. Galveston has not changed its mind. Perhaps President Lott was only trying to make up for some of the rudeness and brashness of Barnett Gibbs of the Land Company, for it was known that 'Galveston's mind is tough. This truth has been in public possession for many years,' recounted the author. Surely Lott was not trying to buy Galveston's vote!"[46]

In the same style in which the Galvestonians were accustomed to treating excursionists to the island, President Lott and his folks gave a royal tour of the area. The *Express* reporter accompanied them every step of the way, recording for posterity this adventure to the "western country" and the responses and reactions of the adventurers. In spite of the trepidations they had about visiting the enemy, "To the great joy of their families they were returned in safety—slightly tired, slightly soiled, slightly sunburned, slightly thick of speech, but, thank God, safe." He called them the finest looking men that Galveston ever turned out, adding that in the aggregate they could draw a check for five million dollars. He then went so far as to apportion the five million among the seventeen visitors, starting with Richard Willis at two million. The best that he could say about the results that President Lott achieved was that "the spirit of the delegation which visited Aransas Pass is largely a spirit of compromise. They deprecate any war upon Aransas Pass. Almost to a man they express a recognition of the necessity of two deep water harbors for so large a state as Texas." Perhaps his assessment was somewhat optimistic.[47]

The Convention at Denver

No sooner had the Fort Worth convention ended than the Galveston deep water activists began moving into the new phase of their campaign—beyond the borders of Texas. When the strategy changed to making deep water at Galveston a national instead of a local issue, a convention such as the one coming in Denver was exactly what they dreamed of. The call would then be coming from the states that would benefit, not the local businessmen who also stood to benefit, but in a relatively small way compared to the farmers and merchants throughout the Midwest. Presumably, the issue of where to locate the single port had been settled at Fort Worth by leaving it to the government to decide. In addition to selecting Galveston delegates who were unified, the deep water committee also needed to do what it could to insure a unified Texas delegation that would leave the location issue at home when it went to Denver.

Events started rolling early, even before the Denver convention leaders had put out a call and established ground rules. The names of twenty-eight members of the delegation to Denver were announced at a meeting held on July 24. However, by August 4, Colorado governor Alva Adams had issued his proclamation and ground rules. Since alternates were also to be appointed, another meeting was held on August 10, at which Mayor Fulton named ten delegates and alternates to represent the city, and Thomas Gonzales, vice president of the Cotton Exchange, named five delegates and alternates to represent that organization. At the final meeting on August 23 when the list was made final, Walter Gresham was elected chairman of the delegation and presented a resolution, the one approved at Fort Worth, upon which the delegation voted to stand, sink or swim. Gresham also suggested that the convention should not be the end of the movement, since in fact it was only the beginning. He said a permanent committee should be appointed to go to Washington and impress upon the congressmen the actions taken at the convention.[48]

Gresham Becomes the Leader

With Colonel Moody stepping aside for the first time since 1884 as the leader of the deep water efforts, Gresham, who had supported Moody so strongly during those years, moved to the front with his election as chairman of the delegation. Perhaps it was a foregone conclusion that Gresham would do so, because he began to take an active role in shaping events before his election. As early as July 25, he had written to Judge John Hancock in Austin requesting his advice on the matter of introducing a constitutional amendment in the legislature that would authorize the state to make provisions for securing a deep water port. Hancock apparently approved and introduced a resolution to that effect at the State Democratic Convention in Dallas on August 13. In addition, Gresham kept busy writing letters to various parts of the state regarding preparations for the Denver proceedings. He wrote to Governor Sul Ross supporting the appointment of C. I. Battle of Wharton County as a delegate; to John Sayles [sic] of Abilene about obtaining proxies from western counties that might not send delegations; to General Maxey in Paris congratulating him on his appointment by Governor Ross and urging him to see that impartial delegates were selected from his area; again to Governor Ross requesting the appointment of W. Goodrich Jones, a Temple banker, to be a delegate from his senatorial district, and to name Marcus F. Mott and Joe A. Owens alternate delegates from the Galveston senatorial district; and to Judge N. A. Cravens of Willis, Texas, requesting a proxy to represent that county. As a result of Gresham's travels as a land agent for the Gulf, Colorado and Santa Fe, and of his term in the state legislature, it is very likely that he was acquainted with prominent people throughout the state and was now making use of these to Galveston's benefit.[49]

While the selection of delegates was proceeding in Texas, the citizens of Denver, already a city of 100,000, were in the process of making preparations for hosting the delegates and staging the convention. The arrangements were the responsibility of committees representing the chamber of commerce and the real estate exchange. Initially, the problem was estimating how many delegates would come, with W. G. Sprague saying three or four hundred and W. P. Caruthers and Frank L. Dana estimating it would be closer to one thousand. Entertainment, hotel rates, meeting facilities, and numerous other matters were discussed at this initial gathering.[50]

At the next meeting, plans were made for a mass meeting of Denver citizens, and several committees made their reports. Information was received that Mayor Connor of Dallas had reserved rooms at the Windsor Hotel for forty members of the Dallas delegation and that four hundred delegates were expected to come from the state of Texas alone. The same day the real estate exchange announced that its five delegates to the convention would be J. M. Berkey, Caruthers, Sprague, Dana, and J. C. Gallup. At the mass meeting, which filled the chamber of commerce hall, the audience was addressed by General R. A. Cameron, who was elected president of the meeting, and Sprague, J. T. Cornforth, Caruthers, and Governor Evans, all of whom addressed the significance of the coming convention and its importance to Denver and the West. Evans also spoke of Galveston and the natural outlet to the sea.[51]

In spite of the resolution passed at Fort Worth, it was becoming clear as the convention approached that the matter of location was far from settled. A dispatch from Galveston reported the delegation there as confirming its support of the Fort Worth resolution, "with the view of giving an official denial to a rumor which has gained more or less circulation to the effect that Galveston will indorse a compromise position for a deep water harbor both at Galveston and Aransas Pass."[52]

Apparently the Aransas boomers were doing their job well because the next day, in spite of the denial from Galveston, it was reported that a "very decided opinion has been developed in favor of two harbors on the coast."[53] The *Rocky Mountain Daily News* lent its editorial support to the two-harbor idea, raising the old issue of excessive port charges as a reason for not giving any one port a monopoly.[54] The *Daily News* also took exception to another Denver paper, the *Journal of Commerce,* when it maintained that the convention derived its authority from the Fort Worth convention and was thereby circumscribed.

The Denver convention would have a much broader base, argued the *Daily News,* and was not to be limited by previous actions. The point of this argument could have been a move by the convention committee to add the subject of storage reservoirs for irrigation to the agenda, or it could have been a successful move by the Aransas boomers to nullify the Fort Worth resolution.[55] As the early delegates began arriving and granting interviews, it became obvious that the merchants of San Antonio were out to challenge Galveston's position as the major distribution point for the state.[56]

While much attention focused on the rivalry between the Texas ports, there was evidence that the western states had the proper perspective on the broader objectives of the convention. For example, Cornforth and other Denver delegates praised an article from the Iowa *Homestead* as representative of this perspective.[57] An editorial in the *Rocky Mountain Daily News* was another example.[58] To the people of the western states, the issue was—pure and simple—the distance to the Atlantic ports and the cost of transportation even without the monopolistic grip that the east-west lines held. Recognizing that the eastern railroad interests had been successfully battling the previous attempts made for deep water on the Gulf of Mexico, both newspapers called for the producing interests in the Southwest and the West to stand together. The shorter distances—500 to 1,200 miles—and the cheaper costs of railroad construction across the sloping plains to the gulf would work to the benefit of the western farmers.

Three Ports Lobby

Maps of the three leading harbors—Galveston, Aransas Pass, and Sabine Pass—in the July 27 edition of the *Rocky Mountain Daily News* greeted the arriving delegates from thirteen states: Kansas, Nebraska, Dakota,

Wyoming, New Mexico, Utah, Arizona, Nevada, Idaho, Washington, Oregon, California, and Texas. The bulk of the delegates were to stay at the Windsor, which was the convention headquarters, the St. James, and the Albany hotels. Late in the day the Texas delegation met at the Windsor and elected Judge Carroll of Denton chairman. Sayles introduced the Fort Worth resolution, expressing no preference for the site, and the Lott forces introduced a substitute resolution requesting appropriations for both Aransas Pass and Galveston. A united stand against the substitute resolution by the Galveston delegation led to a rejection of the substitute and the Texas delegation went on record prior to the opening of the convention in favor of the government selecting the one site. As this meeting was going on, the advocates of the various other sites were busy in the lobby and public rooms of the Windsor buttonholing delegates, as banners strung from the balconies described the beauties of certain sections of the state, proclaimed the coming state fair, and advertised the other outstanding features of the "earthly Eden."[59]

The convention got under way at 2 P.M. on August 28 when L. B. Porter, chairman of the Denver Committee on Arrangements, called the convention to order and introduced Governor Alva Adams of Colorado for his welcoming speech. Then Barnett Gibbs moved and Judge Carroll seconded the nomination of ex-governor John Evans as temporary chairman. With no other nominations, Evans was elected by acclamation and escorted to the rostrum for his speech. The rousing speeches by these two popular proponents of deep water opened the proceedings in a very positive manner. But things became more complicated as they moved to the naming of the committee on credentials. Immediately basic problems began to arise as a result of the makeup of the delegations. There were even uncertainties as to what constituted credentials. If every state had selected all of the representatives requested in Governor Adams's convention call, there would have been a basis for representation reflecting population, although not based strictly upon it. However, every state responded differently. As it turned out, Texas had 341 delegates; Colorado, 159; Kansas, 47; Nebraska, 45; Missouri, 16; Iowa, 14; Wyoming, 6; New Mexico, 5; Arkansas, 3; Arizona, 2; and the Indian Territory, 1. One motion was to base representation on congressional seats, but not all states had that many delegates attending. After much debate and discussion, it was decided to have a committee made up of three representatives from each state and two from each territory. B. B. Paddock, W. R. Story, and William B. Denson of Galveston were selected as the Texas members, and the convention moved on to permanent organization. Again, more debate and discussion ensued, including the question of whether or not they could name the committee on permanent organization until the committee on credentials had reported on who belonged in the convention. Eventually, it was decided to follow the model of the credentials committee, three from each state and two from each territory. The Texans named were A. C. Kervin, J. T. Trezevant, and J. T. Brady. When the committee on resolutions came up, the same type of debate followed again and it was decided to postpone this committee until after the permanent organization was in place. Apparently in trying to conduct the convention in the manner of the political parties, the organizers failed to allow for the differences and to tailor the convention rules to suit the situation.[60]

The committee on permanent organization met after the convention adjourned and laid the groundwork for the next floor fight, again something not directly related to deep water. After electing Brady, a Houston delegate, chairman, the committee voted to nominate P. G. Noel of Kansas as permanent chairman. He was chosen over General John M. Thayer, the governor of Nebraska, by a vote of 14–13. The committee also nominated chairmen for each state and territory represented at the convention, Judge John Hancock being named for Texas.[61]

The Majority Report

The majority report passed by the convention on August 30, 1885, called for the appropriation of funds adequate to secure a port on the northwest Gulf of Mexico, west of the 93.5 degrees west longitude, capable of admitting the largest vessels and of being secured in the shortest possible time and maintained with the least possible cost. A minority report requested that two ports be built and that a committee of army and civilian engineers be named to make the selections. The resolutions were offered during the afternoon session, and debate continued until late in the evening at the third session of the day. Numerous resolutions were offered, and at one point Governor Evans presented a substitute for the majority report, trying to make the resolution as general as possible. During the debate Gresham had to take the floor in order to refute the charges that the Wharf Company's fees were outrageous and that Galveston should not be given a monopolistic position. Finally the question was called for and the majority report passed by a wide margin.[62]

The minority report was essentially the work of those pushing Aransas Pass, led by Uriah Lott and Barnett Gibbs. Congressman John Hancock led the support for the majority report, in opposition to his fellow Texans. The rancor among the Texans understandably did not sit well among the midwesterners, who were mainly interested in a port. This conflict undoubtedly led to Governor Evans's attempt to have all references to location removed. He made it clear that the overriding concern was the size of the appropriation, not the location.[63]

When the permanent committee was named, the Texas delegation consisted of Judge J. A. Carroll and G. W. O'Brien as well as Hancock, Gresham, and Lott. So it could be expected that further contention would occur. Governor Evans was elected chairman, and preliminary discussion was held regarding a follow-up convention at Topeka, Kansas.[64]

A Western Issue Arises

Just as Colonel Moody had seized the opportunity presented by the Dallas Immigration Convention to introduce the issue of a deep water harbor to a larger audience, so did the Coloradans take advantage of the deep water convention at Denver to introduce an issue of great import to them—the building of reservoirs for the storage of water. The matter first arose on August 30 when C. S. Thomas of Colorado introduced the following resolution: "Resolved, That is the sense of this convention that the Congress of the United States be memorialized to institute a system of reservoirs for the storage of water on the Western lands, to be constructed by the general government and to be used under state and federal control for purposes of irrigation."[65] With the involvement of the federal government in water usage in the West, another aspect of economic development was added to the list of "internal improvements" brought before Congress. On the final day, August 31, a modified resolution was unanimously passed requesting Congress to pass House Resolution 10540 "to provide for a line of surveys preliminary to the establishment of a system of reservoirs in the arid lands of the West."[66]

This turning to Washington for help by the western states may come as a surprise to those familiar with the stories of the self-reliance and independence of those who settled the Plains and pushed back the frontier. However, as pointed out by Frederick Jackson Turner, the historian who first analyzed the role of the frontier in American history, the magnitude of the West—the Great Lakes, the Prairies, the Great Plains, the Rocky Mountains, the Mississippi, and the Missouri—presented a new and vast scale. Demands for internal improvements had been made upon the government even during the democratic conquest of the wilderness. In this new West, "Individualism began to give way to cooperation and to governmental activity," according to Turner.[67]

As it became apparent that the methods of the pioneers were no longer adequate for coping with the problems of farming the Great Plains, there was a growing tendency to call for assistance from "the powerful arm of national authority." Now expensive irrigation works were required, cooperative activity in the utilization of water was demanded, and investment capital beyond the reach of the individual was necessary.[68]

It was also necessary for irrigation to evolve from a local issue to one of national importance, in the same manner as Galveston had elevated the issue of deep water to one of national importance. In order for the purposes of the Newlands Act to be accomplished, it was necessary to provide water with land. The movement toward irrigation began with the study made by Major John Wesley Powell, the explorer of the Colorado River. His *Report on the Lands of the Arid Regions of the United States* was published in 1878. He proposed storage of water in the upper regions and recognized the need for extensive labor and capital. Nevertheless, he did not propose national action, but instead proposed irrigation districts to cope with the problem. His efforts would lead to the passage by Congress in 1888, 1890, and 1891 of acts providing for the irrigation surveys by the U.S. Geological Survey and the selection of reservoir sites. The movement would continue to progress and evolve until Congress finally passed the Reclamation Act in 1902.[69] The Denver Deep Water Convention, at which the issues of irrigation and a deep water port for the western states came together, was therefore an important step in the economic development of the West. It may also be said that the convention marked a new degree of both economic and political sophistication on the part of western business and agricultural interests.

Focus on Washington

The Interstate Deep Water General (Executive) Committee was selected to present the resolution to Congress. It promptly met in Dallas on October 17, 1888, to commence its operations. The meeting was also the occasion for Walter Gresham to commence his operations on behalf of Galveston. Colonel William N. Mason of Nebraska suggested that the matter of visits to the several harbors should be the first item of business if the people of Texas desired such visits. Whereupon, Gresham promptly issued an invitation to the committeemen and their ladies to visit Galveston, stating that he was prepared with transportation to take them there and back to Dallas.

After considerable discussion, it was decided to visit the ports of Galveston, Aransas Pass and Sabine Pass as individuals and not as a committee, since they were going only to familiarize themselves with the harbors and not for the purpose of choosing the location. The committee also passed proposed legislation, drafted by Judge Hancock, requesting the president to appoint a commission of three Army Engineers and two engineers from civil life to select the most eligible point on the Texas coast for a deep water harbor able to accommodate the largest commercial and oceangoing vessels and that up to $10 million be appropriated to accomplish the task. The final action taken by the committee was to name a delegation of one member from each state and territory to go to Washington to put the bill through. Gresham was selected as the delegate from Texas.[70]

Gresham promptly notified the deep water committee members in Galveston that a party of twenty-seven would be arriving the next day to tour the harbor, and plans were laid to host the group on October 19, 1888. In addition to touring the harbor and the jetty work, the group had lunch at the Tremont Hotel followed by a carriage tour of the city and an oyster roast at Tildebeck's, down the island.[71] Initially, it was planned to keep the entertainment informal. However, after a day trip to Sabine Pass was added for October 20, a banquet for that evening was also added. The deep water committee was responsible for the harbor tour.[72]

The visitors were given a large dose of Galveston's typical hospitality, culminating with the banquet at the Tremont Hotel Saturday night. The preparations were described as follows: "Manager Gale, upon the short notice given, did himself great credit upon the excellent menu and the very artistic service which characterized the event. Everything that the season afforded was served according to the best style of the art [sic] cuisine, and the long table stretching the entire length of the dining hall was decorated with handsome floral designs and exotic plants." Seventy-five guests and citizens participated in the affair, which was closed well after midnight after appropriate toasts to all of the states represented and responses by the delegates. Marcus F. Mott acted as master of ceremonies and Marcus C. McLemore gave the welcoming address. In their responses, the guests commented upon the importance of their mission, as expected, and in addition also addressed the importance of such occasions in bringing together the people of the newly settled states in order that they could become acquainted and identify their common problems and interests. Colorado governor Alva Adams also took advantage of the opportunity to urge the businessmen of Galveston to support the building of reservoirs.[73]

The visitors departed for Aransas Pass and San Antonio, and Galveston turned to its normal affairs until Congress opened the winter session in December and affairs in Washington could move to center stage. Walter Gresham planned to leave for a two- or three-week stay there, but illness changed his plans and William B. Denson was chosen to take his place.[74] In Washington it was business as usual; the Chief of Engineers had recommended $1 million for Galveston, as previously announced. As it usually did, the House rivers and harbors committee cut the appropriations to one-third of the requested amount, and the bill carried $300,000 for Galveston. Among the Texas delegation there was no plan for what to do next. Senator Coke was waiting for a meeting of the delegation. Senator Reagan thought a $2 million surplus in the Texas treasury should be made available and that the government should appropriate $5 million. However, he thought that the selection of a site by a government board should be the first matter on the agenda. Representative Crain was ready to do everything possible; Representative Abbott believed that the old plan of small appropriations was the best that could be obtained; Representative Moore was opposed to the old plan; and the rest of the delegation was in disarray. Denson and the other members of the

Interstate Committee faced a formidable task as they gathered in Washington to support the Denver resolutions.[75]

Denson arrived in Washington on December 18, 1888, and it was announced that the other members of the interstate central committee would arrive subsequently. Denson brought some focus to the activity by stating that the objective during the current session would be to pass a bill providing for the commission of experts to examine the Texas coast and to select a site. With this objective in mind, his first act would be to hold a meeting of the Texas delegation. The meeting was held on December 21, and Representative Crain presented the delegation with copies of correspondence between General Thomas Lincoln Casey, the Chief of Engineers, and himself, in which Casey clarified his position that his estimate of $1 million was still the proper amount for the coming year.[76]

Competition Persists

By December 27 Gresham had arrived in Washington to lead the lobbying and, through the tireless efforts of himself and Denson, had succeeded in obtaining the unanimous support of the Texas delegation. It was decided that Senator Coke would introduce the measure in the Senate, where it would be referred to the commerce committee, of which Coke was a member. Senator Coke, said to be a favorite of President Cleveland, took Crain, Gresham, Denson, and George M. Courts to the White House for a tour and visit with the president. Cleveland was reported to be enthusiastic about the need for a deep water port in Texas, and felt that it should be accomplished by special legislation, which was interpreted as casting doubt upon the prospects for the rivers and harbors bill.[77]

Gresham, who at this time was a Galveston representative in the Texas legislature, returned home on Saturday, January 5, 1889, the day after Coke introduced the resolution to establish the Board of Engineers on Friday. As introduced, the resolution called for a board of three Army Engineers to examine the Texas coast, except for the mouth of the Brazos River, and to select "the most eligible point for a deep water harbor, to be of ample depth, width and capacity to accommodate the largest ocean-going vessels and the commercial necessities of the country." Gresham thought that the resolution would pass easily in the Senate but that it would take shrewd tactics in the

House to secure passage because the measure could be called up only by unanimous consent.[78]

At the same time all of Galveston's competitors were busy with their plans. The *Houston Post* announced that a group of investors had decided to move ahead with private plans for a deep water port at the mouth of the Brazos, the site excluded from Senator Coke's resolution. The group had hired Elmer L. Corthell, the eminent engineer who worked for James Eads, to do the job. The work on the jetties at Sabine Pass providing access to Beaumont and Orange was still being pushed by its supporters. In San Antonio, supporters of Aransas Pass were irate over rumors that several members of the Texas delegation, succumbing to Galveston money and influence, had conspired to have the entire appropriation designated for Galveston. Representative Crain had to make a public announcement pointing out that the Coke resolution provided that a board of government engineers would select the site and that the members of the congressional delegation were bound to abide by that recommendation.[79]

But this competition up and down the Texas coast was not looked upon with any particular foreboding at this time in Galveston. In its announcement of the Brazos plans, the *Post* declared: "Tell it not in Galveston . . . whisper it not at Aransas." To which the *Galveston Daily News* replied, "And why not tell it in Galveston? Deep water at the mouth of the Brazos makes a deep water port at Galveston all the more certain, both as to time and capacity." In fact, the *Daily News* went on to say, "Houston should be worried about the future impact of a port at the mouth of the Brazos." The *Daily News* then made a very prophetic statement: "Before many years have rolled around Buffalo Bayou will be a grand waterway from Houston to the open gulf at Galveston, and from this interior waterway Houston will reap innumerable benefits." The sale of land at the mouth of the Brazos and rise of a city there, perhaps claiming many Houston businessmen, was a threat to Houston's future that the *Post* should consider while providing free advertising to the project. But, in the eyes of the *Daily News,* neither port represented any threat to Galveston's future.[80]

The Site Selection Board

At the same time that competition from other Texas ports was presenting itself, cooperation in the form of support for the Denver resolution was coming from other sources, a direct result of the convention. The Arkansas General Assembly passed a concurrent resolution requesting its congressional delegation to support the Denver resolution. Kansas followed with a similar action shortly after.[81] In Washington Senator Coke obtained the approval of the Senate commerce committee on February 1, 1889, to propose the deep water resolution as an amendment to the sundry civil appropriation bill, and the Senate approved the incorporation on February 23, 1889. By March 21, the bill had passed both houses of Congress, and General Casey, the new Chief of Engineers, announced that Lieutenant-Colonels Henry A. Robert, Jared A. Smith, and George L. Gillespie would comprise the board to make the survey and select the site on the Texas coast.[82]

This trio, three of West Point's top graduates, would become three of the most important engineers in Galveston history when they submitted their report. Colonel Robert, who had already received some distinction for his *Pocket Manual of Rules of Order (Robert's Rules of Order)* first published in 1876, graduated fourth in the class of 1857. During the Civil War he was involved with the defenses of Washington, D.C., Philadelphia, and New Bedford Harbor, Massachusetts, before returning to West Point as an engineering instructor. Colonel Gillespie graduated second in the class of 1862, behind the famed Indian fighter Ranald S. Mackenzie. Colonel Smith graduated fifth in that same class. Both Gillespie and Smith saw service in the Civil War as military engineers in the Army of the Potomac, especially Gillespie, who saw continuous service in northern Virginia from the Battle of Antietam, September 17, 1862, to Chancellorsville in 1863 on to Cold Harbor and Petersburg in 1864 and finally to Appomattox Court House on April 9, 1865.[83]

As was the practice with the Army Engineers following the Civil War, each of these men became involved in civil engineering works, especially river and harbor projects, around the country. Although none received graduate education in engineering, each was immensely successful in his military career. Gillespie rose to the rank of major-general; Robert and Smith each reached the rank of brigadier-general and Robert was chief engineer when he retired. Among them they had been involved in the improvement of all of the major harbors in the United States, including Boston, New York, and Philadelphia, and had served on boards of engineers overseeing improvements at numerous sites.[84]

The board arrived in Galveston from Sabine Pass on May 8, 1889, to conduct their survey. They spent their first day conferring with Major Ernst and on the ninth were taken to see the site of the works. The board was accompanied on the trip over the jetty railroad by Major Ernst and a group of deep water committee members, including George Sealy, Colonel A. M. Shannon, the contractor, Bertrand Adoue, Julius Runge, A. J. Walker, James D. Skinner, and Robert Irvine. At this time the rock jetty extended almost 6,000 feet out into the gulf, 4,900 of which had been completed to a height of five feet above mean low tide. In addition, 9,500 feet of jetty had been built from Ninth Street across the flats to the point where the gulf jetty began to stop the erosion of the east end of the island. The work was described as having "an appearance of solidity about it that insures confidence as to its permanency."[85] After taking a trip aboard the tug *Cynthia* to the Outer Bar and taking depth soundings, the board held a public meeting to give the interested parties an opportunity to address the board. Whether or not the trip over open water was a factor or not, Colonel Robert was the only board member present, and the deep water committee was represented by Walter Gresham, Sealy, and Skinner. Drawing upon the numerous presentations that he had previously made, Gresham presented Galveston's case to Colonel Robert, reciting all of the facts regarding trade and commerce that had been assembled by the deep water committee. He also emphasized the fact that a vast railroad network, both in and beyond Texas, had been constructed, linking the region with the Gulf of Mexico at Galveston. Selection of another site, he pointed out, would also require the expansion of this railroad network, an additional burden upon the businesses of Texas. Additional presentations were made by Richard G. Lowe of the *Galveston Daily News,* George W. Kidd, secretary of the Houston Cotton Exchange, and S. K. Dick of the Inman company of Houston, on the commercial relationships between Galveston and Houston, and the importance of deep water to Houston. Colonel Robert concluded the session with a question period, and the following day the board left for Corpus Christi to continue its survey.[86]

The Convention at Topeka

Although a subsequent convention had not been called for by a resolution at the Denver convention, the subject had been discussed. However, the initiation of its planning did not take place until June, 1889, when Gresham suggested to Judge Carroll that he confer with Governor Evans regarding the idea of holding one. Gresham informed Howell Jones, a Kansas member of the central committee, of his action and told him that he may be hearing from Evans regarding the preferences of the committee members. He said to Jones, "I would rather it be held in your state, as your people are thoroughly alive as to the importance of the subject, and their enthusiasm would go a long way toward inspiring confidence in the weak-kneed ones from the far North-West." Gresham went on to tell Jones that, although he had no information as to what the board would decide, he had every confidence the decision would be in favor of Galveston. He revealed to Jones that General Casey does not hesitate to state his opinion that Galveston is the only point on the coast worthy of improvement as a first-class harbor, and that he had offered this opinion to Representative Crain and other members of the Texas congressional delegation.[87]

The wheels set in motion by Gresham turned rapidly, and in August Governor Lyman H. Humphrey of Kansas issued a proclamation calling for a deep water convention at Topeka on October 1, 1889, and establishing the basis for representation. The governor of each state and territory west of the Mississippi was named the appointing official of each state's delegation. The delegation would include four at-large members, two of whom would be senators; four members from each congressional district, one of whom would be the congressional representative; and presidents of chambers of commerce and boards of trade. The president of Mexico was also invited to send a delegation of five members. Harmony of views was also emphasized, since it was agreed upon to accept the decision of the Board of Engineers regarding the site and that the purpose of the Topeka convention was to marshall support for a large congressional appropriation that would provide for a deep water harbor to be obtained quickly.[88]

With the convention call issued, Gresham resumed his behind-the-scenes effort to insure success. He wrote to Judge Carroll regarding the appointment of "good men, who were not interested in Sabine

Pass or Aransas, to go as representatives from your section of the state" and said that he would try to obtain transportation for them. He also offered to draft a letter for Carroll to send to the cotton exchanges of the state urging them to appoint delegates in accordance with Governor Humphrey's call.[89] Gresham also suggested to Representative Crain, who was seeking nominees from his district, the names of Bertrand Adoue, George Sealy, and Leon Blum. After reminding Crain that he was already a member of the Texas delegation by virtue of his position on the central committee, Gresham offered that Adoue was "the best posted man in our city upon dockage and wharf charges" and that he was satisfied that any one of them, if chosen, would attend the convention. Gresham, however, had some reservations about his own attendance because of illness that had confined him to bed all summer.[90]

Apparently not all of the state was as enthusiastic about the convention as the Galveston interests, and concern was rising about the appointment of delegates by the congressmen to whom Governor Sul Ross had delegated the authority. Julius Runge, a delegate by virtue of his presidency of the Cotton Exchange, shared this concern and thought someone, perhaps the governor, should be determining the status of appointments.[91] Gresham, perhaps fearing a lack of interest by Governor Ross, again drafted letters and forwarded them to Judge J. A. Carroll to send to the congressmen to prod them to make appointments and to attend the convention themselves. Not overlooking any details, Gresham suggested to Carroll that since, like Gresham, he was a delegate by virtue of his position on the central committee, he should have Congressman Hare appoint another delegate from the district, thus adding another member to the delegation.[92]

In Kansas, as Gresham would have expected, it was a different matter. On September 4, Governor Humphrey announced his entire delegation and alternates. Senators John J. Ingalls of Atchison and Preston B. Plumb of Emporia and ex-governors Charles Robinson of Lawrence and George T. Anthony of Ottawa were named delegates at large. On the same day the governor also announced that he had received the names of the delegates from the governor of the Territory of New Mexico. News of the lack of action in Texas reached Kansas, and the press was very critical of the fact that the state that had the most to gain was lagging behind.[93] However, by convention time Senators Coke and Reagan were present along with Congressmen Crain, Stewart, Kilgore, Mills, Hare, Moore, Culberson, and Martin. Texas had one of the largest delegations.[94]

There was a sense about the convention that its significance extended beyond the bounds of its specific purpose—the securing of deep water. It was described as one of the finest bodies of men ever assembled in the West, consisting of governors, ex-governors, senators, congressmen, railroad presidents, bankers, and men from every important station in life. With the matter of the specific location of the port in the hands of the Board of Engineers, this body of delegates was free to unite and to build a sectional feeling of support behind the cause. This identification of western interests began with an opening speech by Congressman C. H. Mansur of Missouri, the temporary chairman, who pointed out that the central third of the country, represented by the delegates of the convention, was the part that was furnishing the country its agricultural wealth and had become the granary of the eastern third. Congressman Bishop W. Perkins followed in a similar vein in his welcoming address on behalf of the state of Kansas.[95] The *Topeka Daily Capital* said the convention was "composed of the most distinguished body of men that ever met in the west; it was the largest convention and it was the most harmonious convention that ever met in the west." Consequently, as it would go about achieving its goal in Congress, "the west is united as never before for this or any other subject."[96]

Chapter 9

Focused on Deep Water

The coming together of the western states on the matter of a deep water harbor on the Gulf of Mexico coincided with the rise of sentiment in those states on a number of political issues such as silver coinage, the tariff, and cheaper railroad rates. These issues would dominate national politics in the 1896 election when William Jennings Bryan carried all of the western states—with their low electoral votes. But these issues were mainly the issues of the farmers in those states, and farmers were not among the participants in the Topeka Deep Water Convention. Of course, the elected officials who participated were elected chiefly by farmers. Yet, the convention maintained a strict separation between the matter of deep water and the other political issues on the minds of the western states at that time. In fact, arguments made regarding the high costs of railroad transportation to the eastern ports attributed them to the greater distance in comparison to gulf ports, and did not attack the railroads for unreasonable rates.

The deep water issue was, in effect, a clash between competing commercial interests—competing merchants, bankers, railroads, and ports—in the new West versus those in the East, rather than a clash between farmers and railroads, or between Democrats and Republicans. An estimated $120 million in annual savings on transportation to eastern ports would remain in the West, to the benefit of the farmers and eventually to all of the commercial interests with whom the farmers would do business—merchants, bankers, and western railroads running south across the Plains toward the Gulf of Mexico. The western states came together on the issue of deep water, but the basis of the common concern was a relatively narrow commercial one in comparison to the broader political issues such as the coinage of silver and its economic implications. On this issue, it may be said, the interests of the conservatively oriented business community and the progressively oriented agricultural industry came together, and a deep water harbor became a great unifying cause. Nevertheless, it was the business community, represented at the Topeka convention as well as at the preceding gatherings, that carried on the lobbying effort.[1]

Each of the speakers rallied the Western states to the cause. Upon taking his place as permanent chairman of the convention, Senator Plumb of Kansas proclaimed: "I do not anticipate that if we act reasonably there will be any trouble in Congress. The power which is to speak the ultimate will of the American states resides West of the Mississippi River. What we decently and reasonably ask is certainly to be awarded to us." James F. Legate, a Kansas member of the central committee, exhorted the delegates: "The capitalization of railroads east of the Mississippi is estimated at seventy-five million dollars. . . . We must overcome that power by a route to the Gulf of Mexico. We can only secure it by having a determination so fixed and strong that nothing can drive us from our purpose. We must have it."[2]

The lack of contention between the competing Texas ports had given the proceedings an air of harmony that did not exist at Denver. Nevertheless, all was not perfect. The governor of Louisiana had sent a single delegate to represent that state, S. P. Watts, even though the state had not been specifically invited. He was accepted and, being the only delegate, placed on several committees. He surprised the convention when he submitted a minority report following the report of the resolutions committee. His report, which he did not bring up in committee deliberations, favored three ports on the Gulf of Mexico, not necessarily in Texas. Watts moved for its adoption as an amendment to the majority report. Louisiana, although a latecomer, was interested in having Calcasieu Pass, the outlet for the city of Lake Charles, developed. Several members of the resolutions committee rose to speak against the minority report, and it was defeated. In addition, the delegates were also presented with literature on three other proposed harbors—one ten miles east of New Orleans on the Mississippi coast, the Padre Island outer harbor, and the mouth of the Brazos River.[3]

At the call of Richard S. Willis, chairman of the deep water committee, a large group gathered at the Cotton Exchange on October 10 to hear a report from the Galveston delegation to the Topeka convention. Gresham gave a lengthy verbal report to the group, stating that everything had gone according to Galveston's desires. In comparing Topeka with Denver, Gresham said that not only were there more delegates at Topeka but the politicians were in greater attendance and more outspoken, reflecting the growing impact of the deep water movement upon their constituents. The farming element was now much more aware of the benefits, and the influence of public sentiment had evidently been at work in the West since the Denver meeting, reported Gresham. Noting that Kansas, Missouri, Iowa, and Nebraska had larger delegations than at Denver, he also pointed out the significance of the presence of Illinois: "We thought at first that these Chicagoans came simply in the interest of the world's fair, but we found them thoroughly alive to the needs of the deep water situation. . . . They desired particularly to bring about a competition for the South American trade through the opening of a gulf port."[4] Gresham praised both the Galveston and Texas delegations for their efforts at the convention, and pointed out that a number of delegates expressed a strong desire to visit Galveston. With this in mind, a committee of Bertrand Adoue, Marcus F. Mott, and George Sealy was appointed to confer with the railroads to inaugurate these excursions.

The Board Selects Galveston

For the next two months all of the parties to the conventions and the citizens of the three Texas ports anxiously waited while the Board of Engineers concluded its deliberations and prepared its report. Gresham had anticipated that the results of the report would be contained in President Benjamin Harrison's annual message to Congress to be delivered at the opening of the winter session in December.

The message was presented to the Senate on December 3 and read by the secretary of the Senate, Anson G. McCook. Although the decision from the Board of Engineers regarding the site of a port on the gulf was not included, the message did contain a very important statement in regard to federal projects. Urging that funding be provided only for works of general usage, President Harrison further stated: "I do not doubt that the end would be sooner and more economically reached if fewer separate works were under taken at the same time, and those selected for their greater general interest were more rapidly pushed to completion. A work once considerably begun should not be subjected to the risks and deterioration which interrupted or insufficient appropriations necessarily occasion."[5] At last, after almost a decade of protest and harangue about the bad effects of "scatteration" and the "driblet" system from Galveston, the arguments appeared in a major statement of administration policy. No doubt, General Casey, the latest Chief of Engineers, saw the waste of the rivers and harbors "pork barrel" system and persuaded the president to take a step his predecessors refused to do.

The Board of Engineers completed its report on December 11, 1889, and General Casey submitted his report to Secretary of War Redfield Proctor and the public on December 17. The conclusion was of no real surprise to anyone in Galveston: "The Board therefore deems Galveston Harbor the most eligible point on the northwest coast of the Gulf of Mexico west of the 93-degree, 30-minute west longitude for a deep harbor fulfilling all the requirements of the act under which it was constituted, this being the only point fulfilling these conditions."[6] After comparing the features of the potential harbors to satisfy the requirements of the board's charter, "for a deep harbor to be of ample depth, width, and capacity to accommodate the largest ocean going vessels and the commercial and naval necessities of the country, *which can be secured and maintained in the shortest time and at the least cost,*" the members found that only at the entrance to Galveston harbor could an entrance of ample width and depth be maintained without much if any dredging for maintenance. The natural advantage of the Bolivar gorge, 4,000 feet wide between the 18-foot curves with a maximum depth of 50 feet and a mean depth of 30 feet, provided a cross section of 120,000 square feet at its deepest part. The cross section of the entire gorge, over 8,000 feet wide, was 160,000 square feet, six times greater than the gorge at Sabine Pass and nine times greater than the gorge at Aransas Pass. The wider and deeper entrance at Galveston had allowed the scouring forces of nature to maintain a channel about 6,000 feet wider and more than 10 feet deeper than at either Sabine or Aransas Pass, and improvements such as jetties would also achieve greater results at Galveston. Given these facts, the board believed that only at Galveston could a continuous width of 2,000 feet be maintained with a channel over 30 feet deep over a width of not less than 600 feet, the minimum measurements established by the board to meet the requirement of accommodating the largest oceangoing vessels.[7]

The board recommended that an appropriation of $6.2 million be made at the earliest practical date to achieve deep water in the "least time," but granted that the work would not be delayed if the funds were spread equally over three years. Recognizing that an investment had already been made by the government in the jetties at Sabine and Aransas Passes, the board commended these harbors as worthy of consideration, noting that they would be excellent harbors if the present works were completed, even though they would not meet the requirements satisfied by Galveston.[8]

The deep water committee, of course, met the same day as the announcement was made in Washington to receive the news. Although there was great elation that this important milestone had been passed, the committee fully understood that the major task of securing the congressional appropriation was still ahead. Gresham informed the group that he had already wired Governor Evans requesting him to call a meeting of the central committee, as had been discussed at Topeka, and inviting him to hold the meeting in Galveston so that those chosen for the delegation to Washington could leave in a body from Galveston. Gresham explained that the tactics before the Congress, either pushing for a separate appropriation or including the appropriation in the rivers and harbors bill, would have to be decided upon by the central committee when it met. By getting an early start, he thought the independent route could be tried first. Then, if it failed, they could fall back upon the rivers and harbors bill since it traditionally was not voted upon until late in the session.[9]

The Central Committee Goes to Work

The central committee began the culminating year of the decade-long effort with a meeting in Galveston on January 4, 1890, to lay its plans. In the absence of Governor Evans, Judge J. S. Emery of Kansas was elected chairman. Other members of the committee also failed to attend, including the other Texas members—John Hancock and Uriah Lott. Lott, of course, may have lost interest after the selection of Galveston as the port site. However, Judge O'Brien of Beaumont and John T. Brady of Houston, advocates of deep water anywhere, were both present. After the usual greetings and trips to the jetties, the group got down to business. Subcommittees were appointed to estimate expenses and apportion the costs among the interested states. The central committee also met with the Galveston Deep Water Committee and had a harmonious exchange of views. They agreed that their unified support of Galveston would not be detrimental to any other Texas harbor that Congress might choose to improve.[10]

The second day of the meeting began with a discussion of strategies and tactics to be used before the Congress in support of the bill. James F. Legate and Gresham were named to lead the delegation to Washington and were authorized to call for whatever assistance they would need. Judge Emery, Gresham, and W. O. Kulp of Iowa were named to a finance and auditing committee, also fully authorized to do what it determined necessary in support of the bill. Gresham and Legate were to proceed to Washington, along with Frank L. Dana of Denver, the permanent secretary of the central committee, to set up a deep water headquarters.[11]

In spite of all that had gone before, it was announced that Congressman Charles Stewart of Houston would introduce a bill in the House of Representatives, taking advantage of the wording of the board's report, to provide appropriations for Galveston, Sabine Pass, and Aransas Pass. Since the board had deemed Sabine Pass and Aransas Pass as harbors worthy of development in the future, it was Stewart's intention to seek for them the full appropriation required for completion, a measure that the board had recommended only for Galveston. In other words, whereas the board had recommended $6.2 million for Galveston to be provided over three years, Stewart would ask for $1.8 million for Sabine Pass and $1.4 million for Aransas Pass in three years, in addition to Galveston's appropriation. The announcement immediately raised a question as to what had been accomplished at Denver and Topeka if the Texans had not made up their minds which site would be favored, and the Congress as a whole could be as confused as ever again. The implication of the board report was that

Sabine and Aransas deserved the same type of funding they had previously been receiving, and the central committee specifically positioned itself as not opposing such appropriations. Stewart's move, however, would seem to open the argument all over again.[12]

Some of the central committee members were surprised that there was not more of a "boom" atmosphere in Galveston. One member was quoted as saying, "If any city in the west had such advantages thrust upon it as Galveston has had by the recent report of the Engineers, it would be an incentive to an immense boom." Since the report was less than a month old, perhaps the boom-conscious westerners were being too hasty in expecting immediate results. However, signs of a boom did begin to appear in February. S. A. Cook announced plans for a townsite across the bay from Galveston and west of Virginia Point. The Gulf, Colorado, and Santa Fe railroad, whose tracks formed the eastern border of the new town, had built a switch connecting with the passenger depot already to receive prospective lot buyers. Cook proclaimed that he had already spent a great deal of his time in Colorado and Kansas booming up West Galveston and expected excursions of visitors from those states in March. He stated that a public sale of lots would be held March 4 and that trains would run out from Galveston as often as required to accommodate those who wished to attend the gala event.[13]

One delegation of Coloradoans had arrived by February 20, headed by L. B. Porter and a Mr. O'Donnell of Denver. The group was hosted by the Galveston Progressive Association. A trip down the island on the tracks of the Galveston and Western Railroad was arranged by Julius Runge, and visitors were shown the new cotton mill under construction and the fairgrounds where racing stock from the north and east had been quartered for the winter. The last stop was Laffite, the end of the line where the visitors proceeded to the suburban home of Julius Kaufman for the perennial oyster roast and speeches.[14]

The prospectors were apparently finding "gold" because considerable real estate activity and booming values were soon being reported. In addition to West Galveston, city lots and land in Arcadia, Dickinson, and Hitchcock were sharing in the boom. Down the island property was leading the activity. One transaction totaled $265,000, the largest single purchase at the time. Others involved thirty acres for

$10,000 and a fifteen-acre tract, one mile west of the city, at $150 per acre. It was reported that these properties ten years before could have been purchased at $3 to $5 per acre. On the mainland, Seybrook W. Sydnor reported that his sales for the current week totaled 12,800 acres at prices ranging from $4 to $7 per acre, up from $1.50 to $2.00 a year before. Hitchcock led the mainland in increasing values. Forty acres were sold by the Gulf, Colorado and Santa Fe Railroad for $60 per acre. This land had been purchased only two years before for only $15 per acre.[15]

Gresham, busy in Washington working for the passage of the bill, did not lose sight of the opportunity offered by the boom to seek additional support for the bill. Previously he had requested realtor John Adriance to provide him with the names and addresses of all purchasers living out of Texas so that he could write to them and urge them to write their congressman in support of the bill. However, Gresham found it necessary to remind Adriance in a jocular manner, "I suppose that you are so busy selling lots and 'booming the town' that you have forgotten my request."[16]

Dissident Voices Are Heard

Consideration of the Coke bill by the Senate commerce committee began on January 30, 1890, at which time a host of speakers for and against the measure made speeches. Strong presentations on behalf of Sabine Pass were made by a Mr. Koontz of New York, lumbermen William J. Lutcher of Orange and John H. Kirby of Woodville, and Captain Hyatt, who was in charge of the work on the Sabine jetties. It was reported that their information on the extent of the lumber industry in the area tributary to Sabine Pass made a deep impression on the commerce committee members. Uriah Lott was equally as impressive with his presentation of the case for Aransas Pass. Two other speakers, however, may have been more significant. Elmer Corthell, who of course had been Captain Eads's chief engineer, spoke, saying that he now favored development of all three ports to a depth of twenty feet, all that was needed, and that this could be accomplished for $2.5 million each. He also told the committee that he felt the jetties at Galveston in the current Engineers' plan were too far apart. Lewis M. Haupt, professor of civil engineering at the University of Pennsylvania, who had been in correspondence with Colonel Moody for two years about the project, criticized the report of the board and said that deep water could not be achieved at Galveston. He said he favored the Willett's Pier plan for Padre Island, which had been introduced in the House of Representatives by William H. Hatch of Missouri.[17] Of the two dissident voices, Haupt's was probably the most threatening to the successful passage of the appropriation for Galveston. Therefore, it may be beneficial to review Haupt's running conflict with the Army Engineers in the two years preceding 1890.

Haupt, another West Point–educated engineer, was well into a distinguished career, and his testimony regarding the technical feasibility of the jetty design could have had enormous impact upon the confidence of the Congress in proceeding with the project. He had become a factor in the Galveston picture in December of 1887 when he presented a paper to the American Philosophical Society entitled "The Physical Phenomena of Harbor Entrances," a paper that had earned him the society's Magellanic Premium award for his discoveries in physical hydrography. This paper dealt primarily with the Atlantic coast and its principal harbors, defining the currents and movements of the alluvial deposits and pointing out the defects in the current systems of improvement. His primary concern was maximizing the force of the ebb current without limiting the ingress of the flood tide into the tidal basin. His proposed solution for Galveston Harbor included the South Jetty extending from Galveston Island as contemplated by the Army Engineers. However, his design for the North Jetty on the Bolivar side of the channel was radically different. The North Jetty was offshore, permitting a beach channel between the jetty and the shore that would facilitate ingress of the flood tide. Half of the North Jetty was straight and almost parallel to the South Jetty, but the other half was concave to the channel-side.[18]

In February, 1888, a version of the paper directed to Galveston Harbor specifically was published. Haupt reviewed the design as proposed by the Engineers in their report of February 26, 1886, and the criticism of the design by Eads. At that time Eads maintained that a narrower channel between jetties rising above the surface was needed in order to produce the velocity in the ebb flow that would result in scouring of the deeper channel. Haupt disagreed with both parties, arguing that small inlets would not let the inflowing tide fill the inner bay to the level of the ocean, causing the ebb to occur between midtide and low water. The resulting lack of velocity would actually result in the inner channel filling up and closing the harbor. Haupt cited experience at Albermarle and Pamlico sounds as evidence of this phenomena. Thus, he concluded, "The problem is to discover a form and position of structure which will not seriously oppose the flood ingress, but which will utilize it for scouring over the bar."[19]

Haupt said that the fundamental phenomena affecting the sandy harbor entrances were a west and southwesterly drift of the shorelines year in and year out, and that the flood is the potent agent that lifts up the bars in front of the entrances that the superficial and enfeebled ebb is unable to cut down. He claimed that what was necessary was to barricade the sand by a breakwater of curved form, causing the flood to decompose and precipitate its burden of sand outside the channel, and to aid the tendency of the flood to cut a beach channel by a single line of works, half the length of the proposed high jetties. "Thus nature will be aided in her efforts to build up an island, or middle ground with a channel on either hand and a leeway for all conditions or storm or tide," he concluded.[20]

The appearance of the article in the *Galveston Daily News* probably was the work of Colonel Moody, who received two letters from Haupt in February and March of 1888. Haupt told him of an appearance before the House rivers and harbors committee "in behalf of your interests," and of a meeting with the Engineers' permanent board on his ideas. Initially, Haupt seemed optimistic about the reception his plans would receive. When Major Ernst informed him that he would have to report adversely if the plans were referred to him for comment, Haupt told Moody, "This I should expect if the desires to be consistent for the Corps [of Engineers] do not appear to recognize the existence of a resultant movement of the bar sands."[21]

In order to provide for a thorough examination of Haupt's designs, a five-man board of Army Engineers was appointed, consisting of Colonel Thomas Lincoln Casey, Colonel Henry L. Abbott, Lieutenant-Colonel Cyrus B. Comstock, Lieutenant-Colonel D. C. Houston, and Major W. R. King. The report of the board was submitted to the Chief of Engineers on March 16, 1888, in which the board members concluded that his views were "purely theoretical, are unconfirmed by experience, and contain nothing not already well known." They said the basic information regarding tidal currents contained in Haupt's paper had been presented by a Professor J. E. Hilgard to the American Institute seventeen years before, and that Haupt offered no data to support his contention that his tidal currents flowed with the velocity sufficient to move the material forming bars. His beach channel, they maintained, would also carry off part of the ebb tide needed to scour the main channel, leaving two bad channels instead of one good one.[22]

Haupt received a patent for his curved jetties on April 3, 1888. His application, which had been submitted on December 13, 1887, stated the general principles of hydraulics involved, explained his use of the principles, and including drawings of his plans for Charleston, Galveston, and the Delaware River. His plans utilized the existing South Jetty, placed a jetty with straight and curved sections on the Bolivar side of the channel, and supplemented these two with an "S" shaped jetty extended from Pelican Spit. In his explanation, he stated that "the breakwater is placed . . . so as to decompose and neutralize the flood energy and compress the flood on its passage through the shore channel. The Pelican jetty represents the reaction dike, in the form of a reverse curve, springing from Pelican Island, and co-operating with the [Bolivar] breakwater by conserving the energy of the inner forces for ebb effects." His drawing also indicates the shorelines of 1850 and 1867 to show erosion in those seventeen years and the position of the outer bar in 1850 and 1883 to show the movement of the bar seaward. He attributed this movement of the bar to the South Jetty, an effect Haupt desired to avoid.[23]

As did Captain Eads before him, Haupt refused to accept his rejection by the Corps of Engineers and told Moody that he would continue to dispute their views of his work. He told him that Major Ernst had been a contemporary of his at West Point, "an earnest man whom I very much respect," and while giving him "the credit of his convictions," expressed his doubts that "outsiders" would have a chance against the Army Engineers until the creation of the Department of Public Civil Works, as provided for in the Cullom-Breckinridge Bill.[24] It was January of 1890 before Moody again heard from Haupt, who still held the view that the plans envisioned by the Army Engineers ignored experience in the harbors of the world and would not produce deep water at Galveston with its one-foot tide.[25] In his testimony before the Senate committee on commerce on January 30, 1890, he challenged the Engineers very directly and emphatically. He began by quoting from the reports of the Engineers, who argued against the narrowly placed jetties advocated by Eads (2,000 feet or less) and giving 7,000 feet as a minimum distance to avoid jetty destruction and island erosion in storms. Consequently, a channel of 2,000-foot width and 30-foot depth over a width of 600 feet, involving a sectional area of 43,000 square feet, would have to be cut and maintained by jetties 7,000 feet apart. Given the fact that the tidal prism would be reduced by 30 percent as a result of the impact of the jetties upon the flood tide, Professor Haupt labeled as "absurd" the Engineers' claim that a channel could be maintained at the specified measurements.[26]

Haupt's Plan at Padre Island

In the two years that had passed since his previous submission to the Army Engineers in 1888, Haupt's own thinking on the subject of harbor improvement had moved forward because he now recommended to the Congress the plan of the Corpus Christi and Padre Island Harbor Company for an offshore harbor, the plan presented to Congress by John Willett, president of the company. Haupt said engineers around the world had begun to overcome the problems presented by sand bars and cited projects completed or under way at Madras, Colombo, Kingstown, Alderney, Dover, Ceara, and La Guayra, stating that they are safer, more capacious, cheaper, more accessible, and can be built in less time. He also mentioned a disaster at Samoa as an example of the dangers of inner harbors defended only by low sand spits. If the Congress thought it better to continue the work at Galveston, Haupt then offered his patented system of curved breakwaters as an alternative that would achieve the success the current Engineers' plan would never accomplish.[27] As presented to the House of Representatives in a bill introduced by Congressman Hatch of Missouri to authorize construction of the harbor at Padre Island, the plan called for the construction of a viaduct and then a seawall extending out to the 30-foot depth, then running southward parallel to the shoreline for 3,000 feet. The wall was to be erected upon a riprap or other suitable foundation and would rise 11 feet above mean low water. This seawall would be about 22 feet thick. Other breakwaters would be built to protect the shore end of the viaduct and entrance to the harbor. The bill authorized the Padre Island Company to issue $100,000 in bonds for every 1,000 lineal feet of viaduct completed, and after that as necessary up to an aggregate limit of $1.5 million. The only financial request of the federal government made was a guarantee of the 3 percent interest to the bondholders in the event of default by the company.[28]

Colonel Ernst Challenges Haupt

The reply to Haupt's charges for the Army Engineers was made by now Colonel Ernst, who had been transferred from the Texas district on November 2, 1889, but continued his involvement on matters pertaining to Galveston. Circumstances had finally forced Ernst, who graduated from West Point in 1864 ranked sixth in his class, to confront in person his erstwhile colleague, Haupt, who graduated seventh in the class of 1867. After reciting the facts pertaining to the physical description of the Galveston channel, Ernst went on to cite the harbor at Venice, Italy, as a comparable situation where a large bay with a very small tide had had its entrance (Malamocco) deepened from 10 to 30 feet deep. Ernst cited two factors that made the situation at Galveston even more favorable for improvement than the one at Venice. The area of Galveston Bay was 450 square miles versus the lagoon at Venice of only 58 square miles, with only two openings to the open sea at Galveston versus five at Venice. To give an idea of the strength of the ebb tide at Galveston Bay, Ernst compared it to the Mississippi River. The flow from Galveston Bay was estimated at 250,000 cubic feet per second, whereas the flow from the entire Mississippi River (through all passes) was 200,000 cubic feet per second and only 24,000 cubic feet per second through South Pass where Captain Eads had successfully built his jetties. Therefore, Ernst saw no problem with the enormous ebb tide from Galveston Bay being able to scour and maintain a 30-foot channel through the bar. As to the interval between the jetties, Ernst explained the 7,000-foot width as being the width of the Bolivar gorge, less shoal water less than 6 feet deep, at a point where the 30-foot channel is 1,600 feet wide with a maximum depth of 58 feet. Ernst reasoned that a depth of 30 feet could be maintained on the bar if the surface width were maintained at the same distance as at the gorge—7,000 feet. In addition, Ernst pointed out that during the great storms the equivalent of six

Mississippi Rivers stacked one upon the other would be flowing out through the channel and that jetties any closer together would simply be destroyed by the power of the current.[29]

Secretary Dana's Testimony

In spite of Professor Haupt's impressive professional and academic achievements and his support from the American Philosophical Society, it appears that his criticism never seriously impacted the members of Congress as the Galveston bill made its way through the tedious steps of the legislative process.[30] Perhaps more persuasive with the Congress was the impressive array of statistics presented by Secretary Frank L. Dana of the Interstate Deep Water Committee to the Senate commerce committee on February 18, 1890, when he translated into dollars and cents the economic impact that an adequate port at Galveston would have on the western states. Dana went on to present data on Kansas corn and wheat production and consumption, exports, and transportation costs, showing how transportation savings to be gained by shipping from Galveston instead of New York—a reduction of 560 miles—would have produced $25,391,871 in additional income to the producers. Adding in savings from other cereal products and livestock products, plus savings on imports, would double the figure, according to Dana. His table of information on corn, wheat, and cattle transportation savings for twenty-one western states totaled $170,630,106.[31]

Secretary Dana, claiming to speak on behalf of the fifteen million people represented at the Denver and Topeka conventions, went beyond merely presenting information to the Senate committee. He reminded the senators that upward of $600 million had been spent since the founding of the nation on public improvements, but that only $50 million of that had been spent west of the Mississippi River where almost a third of the population now lived. He told them the $6.2 million for the improvement of Galveston Harbor, which all of the western states believed was critical, was only a small step against what Congress would have to spend in the West to equalize treatment of both parts of the country, based upon population. In other words, the West was now demanding its share of the federal pie.[32]

With the Stewart bill pending in the House of Representatives, it was also necessary for Dana to review the resolutions passed at the

Denver and Topeka conventions whereby the participants agreed to abide by the decision of the Board of Engineers. He pointed out that the Stewart bill proposing to share the $6.2 million contained in the Coke bill was just the opposite of what the conventions had resolved to be in the best interest of the western states and their need for a major deep water port on the Gulf of Mexico. He apologized to the committee members that the battle between the Texas ports should have ever been brought before them, since it was a specific purpose of the two conventions to settle that issue. He said the fear expressed by supporters of Sabine Pass and Aransas Pass that their projects would not receive any appropriations if the Galveston bill passed did not justify their breach of honor and their attack upon Senator Coke's bill.[33]

But the Aransas boomers were going to continue firing until their ammunition was spent. When the commerce committee met on February 18, 1890, to take its final action on the bill, A. W. Houston of San Antonio was there trying to make a final plea on behalf of Aransas Pass. Senator William P. Frye, the committee chairman, asked if his remarks would be in reference to the inclusion of Aransas Pass in the bill under consideration, and, when answered in the affirmative, promptly told Houston that the committee did not wish to hear anymore on that subject and suggested that he carry his views to the House committee on rivers and harbors. The committee then approved a substitute for the Coke bill, which added the provision that "the amount so drawn from the treasury shall not exceed $1,000,000 in any one year," a change suggested by the Chief of Engineers and one that would not interfere with the progress of the work.[34]

The unanimous passage by the commerce committee constituted a major triumph for the supporters of the bill. Upon his return from Washington, Colonel A. M. Shannon, the contractor for the jetty work then currently under way, stated that the endorsement by the commerce committee was practically tantamount to its passage in the Senate. He praised the work on the interstate committee and reported that "Colonel Gresham, Colonel Legate and Mr. Dana are doing some excellent work in the cause, and the measure could not have been intrusted to better hands."[35] The *Galveston Daily News* correspondent reported that "Senator Coke . . . has been diligently and unceasingly at work to get it through the committee ever since the matter was submitted to it. . . . It is unnecessary to state how great his influence has been."[36] The *Houston Post* took editorial note of the committee action, proclaiming it "a triumph for Galveston, for Texas, and the entire southwest." Keenly aware of the implications for Houston, it observed that the passage would lead to "the early improvement of Buffalo Bayou and that Galveston and Houston will become the St. Paul and Minneapolis of the south."[37]

Quick Passage in the Senate

On March 29, 1890, Senator Coke was recognized on the Senate floor and asked that the Senate take up Order of Business 430, being Senate Bill 2716, to provide for the completion of the improvement of the entrance to Galveston Harbor, Texas. And the battle resumed! Immediately Senator Charles F. Manderson of Nebraska, who should have been in wholehearted support of the bill, raised the issue of the fate of Aransas and Sabine Passes and questioned whether the Senate should consider the bill. In response, first Senator Coke and then Chairman Frye, of Maine, went through a lengthy rehearsal of all the factors that had brought separate bills for Galveston and Sault Ste. Marie to the Senate floor and referred to President Harrison's remarks about the wastefulness of inadequate appropriations for those projects of national importance. Senator Frye was followed by Senator John H. Reagan, and between them they gave a quick summary of the reasons supporting Galveston's choice, and the process through which Galveston was selected.

In spite of the compelling logic, Senator Manderson followed their presentations with an amendment to the bill adding Aransas and Sabine Passes. Ignoring the fact that it was the Congress that earlier passed the resolution that a Board of Army Engineers would select the site, Manderson reopened the old arguments in favor of dividing the appropriation among the three locations. Senator Coke then resumed the defense of his bill against the amendment, adding to the information regarding Galveston that had already been presented and pointing out to Senator Manderson that his amendment was unnecessary because a private company had already been authorized to build a harbor at Padre Island and the jetties at Sabine Pass could be funded through the rivers and harbors bill. When questioned about his information by Senator Manderson, Coke politely referred him to the reports published in Senate Miscellaneous Document No. 89, of which the senator from Nebraska did not seem to be aware. When Coke's time expired, Senator Plumb of Kansas rose to the defense—only his supportive speech was partly a tirade against the Army Engineers. Since Senator Plumb was very familiar with the deep water movement and its evolution, it is surprising that he brought this subject up, and it was no doubt embarrassing to the managers of the bill—Coke, Gresham, and Legate—who were now working closely with the Engineers. However, at this point it appeared that the homework had been done and specious arguments were not to sidetrack the bill. In fact, after assurances from Senators Frye, Coke, and Plumb that Aransas Pass and Sabine Pass would not be neglected and that Texas would eventually have three harbors on the Gulf of Mexico, Senator Manderson withdrew his amendment and the Galveston bill passed the Senate unanimously.[38]

Another Struggle in the House

As the bill moved from the Senate to the House and began to make its way through the process there, Gresham became increasingly confident about its chances for passage. The lobbying effort created by the Denver and Topeka conventions was showing results as state legislatures sent memorials to Congress requesting the appropriation, and petitions from more than two hundred municipal corporations and commercial bodies poured in, according to Gresham. In addition, endorsements had been received from the National Grange and the Farmers Alliance, indicating the interest and support of the farmers for the deep water outlet. Gresham was glowing in his praise for Congressman Stewart, in order that his support for projects in his own district—Sabine Pass, Buffalo Bayou, and the Galveston Bay ship channel—not be misconstrued as opposition to the harbor improvements at Galveston. Gresham stated that "he is now working as zealously for the Galveston bill as he did for the first named places [in his district]. . . . I know whereof I speak when I assert that he is working actively and earnestly for the success of the bill."[39]

At this stage Gresham was completely confident that the bill would finally pass the House, and the influence of Congressman Stewart upon his colleagues on the rivers and harbors committee would be one of the principal factors. Stewart's impact was demonstrated at a banquet given for the committee by one of its members, Representative Isaac

Stephenson of Wisconsin, on April 16, 1890. Following remarks in support of the bill for the Sault Ste. Marie channel between Lakes Huron and Michigan, Stewart surprised the party by announcing that a greater value of goods and farm products passed over the Galveston bar than through the Sault Ste. Marie Canal, and went even further by quoting treasury department statistics that indicated greater business was done over the Galveston bar than through the Suez Canal. As reported, the information had a startling effect upon the committee, making them solid friends of the Galveston appropriation and providing persuasive information to be used in the hearings before the committee and the full House.[40]

For the next six months the Galveston backers were to go through a textbook case in the obstructions and delays that frequently occur in the legislative process. First, it was a congressional election year, and that obviously affected the behavior of the members. Second, President Harrison had set a ceiling on the rivers and harbors bill, making an additional $6.2 million for the Galveston bill even more of a target. Third, Speaker of the House Thomas P. Reed frequently resorted to high-handed methods to have his own way. Add to these factors the normal parliamentary maneuvering that took place, and the Galveston supporters faced a supreme test of their patience and resourcefulness.

On April 21, 1890, the House committee on rivers and harbors resumed business after the funeral for Congressman Sam Randall of Pennsylvania, one of the Democratic leaders, and heard Judge Legate present information on the Galveston bill similar to what Dana had already presented to the Senate commerce committee. Following a recess, the committee resumed the hearing that afternoon and unanimously approved the bill. Representative Stewart was instructed to prepare the report and present it to the House. Stewart's report was ready the next day but was not presented in order that it could go forward with the Sault Ste. Marie report. However, the plan for quick disposal of the bill hit an obstacle. The House agenda was revised, placing the tariff bill ahead of the rivers and harbors bill, thus setting the special appropriation bills back possibly three weeks.[41] A month later the rivers and harbors bill got its turn. Then another surprise occurred. Representative Burton of Ohio, without consulting the managers of either of the special bills, offered a resolution to set the date for the consideration of the Sault Ste. Marie bill. Consequently, Representative Stewart was forced to do the same with the Galveston bill. Both resolutions were referred to the rules committee for scheduling. Then two more interruptions took place. First, debate of the rivers and harbors bill was suspended while the legislation on the District of Columbia took its scheduled place before the floor. Then, Speaker of the House Reed's mother died, drawing him home. The rules committee was left without a chairman since Representative Reed had just been named to replace Representative James B. Beck, who had died. Thus, operations of the rules committee were suspended pending Reed's return and the appointment of a chairman. On May 28, the House concluded debate on the rivers and harbors bill, and Speaker Reed returned from his home in Maine. The delays were a natural part of the House operations and nothing ominous was seen in their occurrence.[42]

Conflicting Priorities in the House

Two weeks passed and Speaker Reed still had not taken any action to fill the vacancy on the rules committee. In the autocratic manner for which Reed became famous, he refused even to discuss the subject with the anxious supporters of both the Sault Ste. Marie and Galveston bills. Of some comfort to the supporters of Sault Ste. Marie was the fact that Speaker Reed had disclosed in a Republican caucus that the bill was one that must be passed. Supporters of the Galveston bill emphasized that the two bills had passed the rivers and harbors committee together and that they must not be divorced.[43] However, events were catching up with the Republicans. Representative Joseph G. Cannon of Illinois, Reed's first lieutenant in the House, warned of the increasing amounts being appropriated with the promises to the veterans for a generous pension bill still unsatisfied. By now President Harrison had joined those showing concern, and the $6.2 million contained in the Galveston bill began to look larger and larger as time passed. The more Reed was pressed to set a date, the more obstinate he became. In view of the problem arising, supporters of the bill drew up an amendment that would fix the obligation of the government to complete the work but provided for the annual appropriations to cover the work for the coming fiscal year. It also provided that these funds in future years would be contained in the civil sundry bill, which always passes, and would not go through the rivers and harbors committee. At this time Representative Crain advised Leo N. Levi in Galveston that the bill would be considered in the current session and that William J. McKinley, Benton McMillin, and James H. Blount on the rules committee would vote for consideration.

Bringing the bill to the floor, however, seemed to be a difficult matter. In order to encourage the Senate to pass the silver bill then before it, Representative William M. Harrison got Reed to move up the House consideration of their version. With Reed's attention focused on the issues that were going to help his party or himself, attempts to obtain a date for consideration simply met a stone wall. The best that could be hoped for at the time by the Galveston supporters was contained in a message from Senator Coke to Cotton Exchange president Julius Runge: "The Galveston bill is being pushed with judgment and ability by men who understand the situation thoroughly and who are most anxious for the passage. Its prospects for passage are good." It passed on June 17, 1890, after three days of debate.[44]

Party politics continued to interrupt the proceedings of the House. A meeting of the rules committee on June 24, 1890, was interrupted when the three Republican members withdrew to the lobby to argue over the order of the day as proponents of the federal elections, bankruptcy, and silver bills descended upon them, demanding priority for their interests. The silver men, feeling themselves being elbowed aside by their own party members, began cozying up to silver Democrats. Faced with this kind of internal party dissension, the backers of the elections bill became nervous about their timing. Therefore, the committee placed the silver bill first in order, to be followed by the bankruptcy bill, leaving the elections bill until party unity was restored. In this environment, there was no mention of either the Galveston or the Sault Ste. Marie bills.[45]

As the situation continued to deteriorate, the "Soo" backers reevaluated their strategy and introduced an amendment to the rivers and harbors bill, passed by the House and now awaiting action in the Senate, to include their project. Not wishing to have the Galveston bill alone as the only independent bill, Senator Coke immediately followed with another amendment to the rivers and harbors bill to include Galveston with the $1 million per year provision. The decision must have presented the managers of both bills with a difficult choice when rumors were already circulating that President Harrison might veto the rivers and harbors bill.[46]

Hopes Fade

As the month of June slipped away with no action being taken, the Senate commerce committee approved Senator Coke's amendment to the rivers and harbors bill, apparently now convinced that the chances of separate bills passing in the current Congress had evaporated. In the process the amounts for both projects were reduced to $500,000, the amounts contained in the last rivers and harbors bill.[47]

The dictatorial tactics of Speaker Reed, already nicknamed "Czar," extended to the halls of the Capitol as well as to the proceedings within the legislative chambers. Over time the halls outside the chambers had become thronged with souvenir and food stands catering to both those employed in the building as well as hoards of tourists. In the typical style for which he had become famous, Reed one day ordered all stands removed, and those who resisted returned to find that their property had been removed by the building staff. Those entrepreneurs and taxpayers found they had no more impact upon the "Czar" than the members of the House trying to obtain consideration for their legislation.[48]

As July began to pass and as August approached, another political consideration began to impact the rivers and harbors bill in the House. Congressional leaders, fearful of members departing early and concerned that they might fall short of the quorum needed to do business, began to move the bill backwards on the calendar. With almost every member having an interest in the bill, the leadership used it as a means of keeping them in Washington since they had to look after their districts' pet project. But the Republicans still had a dilemma. On the one hand, they wanted to have a quorum on hand when the elections bill came up; on the other hand, they did not wish to provide ammunition to the Democrats for the 1890 congressional elections by running up an immense appropriation. Consequently, there were also rumors that the bill would be held up until the winter session in December.[49]

At the end of July a new tactic was employed. The Senate scheduled the rivers and harbors bill for the eighth of August, while the tariff bill would still be on the floor. It would be passed and then sent to a Senate-House conference committee where it would remain until the end of the session, thus requiring members of both houses to stay around for the final vote on it. Not surprisingly, Reed's style eventually provoked opposition. While the House was acting as a committee of the whole on the general deficiency bill, the Democrats yielded most of their debate time to Representative John H. Rogers of Arkansas, who used it to make a speech very critical of the way Reed and the Republicans had conducted the session. He referred specifically to the Galveston bill, which he described as a matter of national interest that had been passed unanimously by committees in both houses, as a measure the speaker and his rules committee had suppressed. Meanwhile, a break in the dam at Sault Ste. Marie had brought attention to that project in both houses, and a delegation of interested members met with Reed to pressure him. They came away with his assurance that an appropriation would be approved, either in the special bill or in the rivers and harbors bill. Galveston supporters took this as an indication they would be treated the same way. Nevertheless, when the seventh of August arrived, Senator Frye announced that the Republican members of the committee had voted to postpone the bill for another week.[50]

With the Senate planning to adjourn on Saturday, August 16, the rivers and harbors bill came up for consideration on Friday, and Senator George F. Edmonds sought a postponement. Senator Frye and a majority of the Senate rose to do battle with Edmonds, who rallied only eight votes when the issue was put to the test. Frye quickly brought up the Galveston amendment, authorizing the government to contract for the completion of the jetties and providing $500,000 for the next fiscal year. The amendment was quickly approved. After the amendments, Frye announced that he would ask for a vote on Saturday, which would then send the measure to conference committee where it would be held until the final hours of the session. Reed, of course, was having his way. No separate bill and no large appropriation. Reed would preside over the conference committee, along with Senator John J. Ingalls, who was presiding over the Senate in the absence of Vice President Levi Morton. With Ingalls and Representative

Thomas J. Henderson of Illinois, chairman of the rivers and harbors committee, both supporters of Galveston, on the conference committee, the situation looked promising.

At this stage Representative Crain was so confident that the battle was won that he prematurely informed Richard G. Lowe of the deep water committee by telegram. With this news, the Galveston Artillery celebrated the occasion Friday night by firing a one-hundred-gun salute on the beach. Eighty-four guns were fired, one for each of the eighty-four senators, plus an extra round for Senator Coke, one each for Congressmen Crain and Stewart and Walter Gresham, and the balance "for general results."[51] On Saturday, August 16, the rivers and harbors bill was approved by the Senate with very little further discussion and sent on to the conference committee. Senators William P. Frye, Joseph N. Dolph, and Matt Ransom were appointed to the conference committee. Congress however, because of amendments and parliamentary wrangling over the controversial tariff and election bills, did not adjourn as planned. A week later, August 22, the bill came up in the House, and Chairman Thomas J. Henderson moved nonconcurrence and assignment to conference committee. Representative Daniel Kerr of Iowa succeeded in getting the bill to the committee of the whole, where he and four others quibbled over some amendments. The Texas delegation was ready with facts and figures to meet any argument, but the Galveston amendment was not attacked. Finally, on August 25, Henderson reintroduced his motion and the bill went to the conference committee. House members Thomas J. Henderson, Charles Grosvenor, and Newton C. Blanchard joined Senators Frye, Dolph, and Ransom on the committee. All of the members were known supporters of Galveston.

By the following Tuesday, September 2, the conference committee had completed its work and was preparing its reports for both houses. Now the total of the rivers and harbors bill with amendments had reached over $24 million, the largest amount ever appropriated but still under the $25 million limit that President Benjamin Harrison had placed on what he would sign. Besides breaking new grounds in terms of dollars, the bill also broke new ground by contracting for a complete job extending beyond the current fiscal year. After this was first accomplished in the Galveston amendment, backers of projects at Philadelphia, Baltimore, Sault Ste. Marie, and others succeeded in having the same technique applied.[52]

The Final Hurdles

But the war was not over yet. It seemed there was an endless list of items on the Republican-controlled agenda to be disposed of. One was the contested election case of Representative Clifton R. Breckinridge of Arkansas. A committee that had investigated the 1888 election, after which his Republican opponent had been murdered, submitted a report calling for the unseating of Breckinridge. This matter took over the floor on Tuesday, September 2, with no time limit on debate. In the middle of this Representative Joseph G. Cannon of Illinois made a twenty-five-minute speech defending the Republicans against charges of extravagance. Fearing that this speech might have too much effect on the president, supporters of the rivers and harbors and public buildings bills wished his speech had been delayed a few days. Chairman Henderson was able to introduce the conference report on the rivers and harbors bill, but he was not able to have it considered, the Breckinridge matter taking precedence. On Friday, September 5, the House voted overwhelmingly along party lines to unseat Representative Breckinridge, clearing that matter off the floor.

Henderson made another attempt for consideration of the conference report late Friday but backed down to allow Representative William S. Holman of Indiana the chance to have his say on Saturday.[53] Out of the $25 million in the bill, it was the $500,000 for Galveston that drew the fire on Saturday. Representative Holman and Representative Cannon of Illinois, later to become another famous speaker of the House ("Uncle Joe" Cannon), both attacked the technical feasibility of deep water at Galveston and expressed their doubts about it being achieved. Representative Kerr of Iowa joined the doubters, expressing his belief that deep water could be obtained only at Aransas Pass. Holman used his first thirty minutes attacking the Mississippi River appropriation, then used his extended time to question the method of appropriating for the work at Galveston by putting subsequent years in the civil sundry bill. Representatives Thomas J. Henderson, Charles Stewart, and Joseph Sayers of Texas, Newton Blanchard of Louisiana, and Bishop W. Perkins of Kansas spoke in defense of Galveston, reciting again the facts and arguments presented in committee and floor hearings. Finally, Holman's attempt for a roll call failed, and the bill passed overwhelmingly. The rivers and harbors bill immediately was sent to the Senate late Saturday, where only a dozen members were still present, and it was scheduled for a vote on Monday.[54]

President Harrison Signs the Bill

The bill passed the Senate immediately upon being presented on Monday and, presumably, was on its way to the president's desk for signature. But there appeared to be no end to the parliamentary and political snares awaiting this particular expression of "the will of the people." On September 14 Speaker Reed, again using the rivers and harbors bill as a weapon to insure a quorum, had not sent the bill to the president. Reed had not taken the final administrative step of signing the bill and "laying it before the House." In the final, hectic days of the session, patience exhausted and tempers flaring, Reed and Henderson had a sharp confrontation over the status of the bill. The president as well was unhappy with the situation in Congress. From Cresson Springs, Pennsylvania, came reports that he was considering an extra session for consideration of the federal elections bill, which still had not passed. Other legislation pending that also was of concern to him included the antilottery, labor, and Supreme Court bills. It was also reported that he had a copy of the rivers and harbors bill with him at Cresson Springs and was very familiar with its contents, and that special arrangements had been made to bring the bill to him when it was ready for signature.

At 5 P.M. on Wednesday, September 17, with debate on the contested elections not complete and time running out, Reed gave in and signed the bill. If the bill was signed by the Senate on Thursday and transmitted to the president on Friday, the ten days allowed the president to sign the bill would begin then. Of course, that assumed the Congress would be in session ten more days. If not, the president could either sign quickly or simply pocket, and thereby veto, the bill. As of September 17, the fate of the bill was still not assured. Vice President Morton signed the rivers and harbors bill on Thursday, September 18, and the bill was immediately signed for by a member of the president's staff, technically placing it in the president's hands and starting the ten-day period in which the he could sign or veto it. However, there was to be no more suspense and uncertainty surrounding the fate of the bill. President Harrison signed it immediately upon receiving it at Cresson Springs, and the bill became law.[55]

Whistles and Fireworks in Galveston

As soon as the information was received in Washington, the news was in turn relayed to Galveston by Senator Coke, Congressman Stewart, and Gresham, setting off an impromptu celebration that began with a long blast from a locomotive steam whistle. This was quickly joined by the whistles of all the ships in the harbor and the oil and flour mills in a chorus that lasted almost a half-hour. As people on the streets became aware of what had happened, the whistles were joined in the celebration by the cheers of the crowd. The people on the Strand and the wharves were quickly joined by others rushing to find the cause of the excitement and were greeted by dignified businessmen throwing their hats in the air and shouting the news. Mayor Fulton immediately issued a proclamation authorizing the citizens of the city to fire cannons, small arms, and firecrackers, and to blow whistles of every variety that night and the following night to celebrate the passage. Later Friday night the mayor issued a longer proclamation declaring Saturday to be a public holiday, and called a meeting on Saturday morning at the Cotton Exchange to plan the activities for Saturday night's celebration. In addition, he invited the mayors of Houston, Dallas, Fort Worth, Waco, and San Antonio to come to Galveston and join the festivities.[56]

Friday night's activities were described as rivaling Galveston's Mardi Gras celebrations. Citizens of all ages abandoned their usual decorum to join in the noisemaking, stripping the stores of fireworks and horns stocked for Christmas. People took advantage of the mayor's proclamation and were firing all types of guns and pistols. A band was eventually assembled that toured the business district on a wagon while other groups marched among the crowds. "Hurrah for Galveston and Deep Water!" was the cry heard everywhere. Bonfires dotted the city, and flags and bunting were displayed from buildings and houses. The Beach Hotel was illuminated, and neighboring establishments put on fireworks displays, bringing the beach front into the celebration. As the *Daily News* summed up its description, "it was a night which will go upon the pages of Galveston's history."[57]

In its Saturday morning edition, a *Daily News* editorial reminded its readers of the twenty-five years of hope and despair, partial triumphs and defeats that led to the passing of the appropriation. It summarized the long struggle, in which, of course, Colonel Belo and the *Daily News* played a very active role, and reviewed once again the benefits to accrue to the western states, Texas, and Galveston once deep water was available. The report of the *Daily News* Washington correspondent was full of praise for the indispensable effort in Washington by Senator Richard Coke, Congressman Charles Stewart, and Gresham. It was clear that without the tireless work of these men for the past nine months in the halls of Congress there would not have been an appropriation for Galveston insuring the completion of the jetties.[58]

While the squabbling continued Saturday in Washington over another of the contested seats, Gresham met with General Casey, who informed him that the Engineers would proceed as expeditiously as possible to get the work under way. General Casey immediately appointed a commission composed of Colonel Ernst, Major Adams, and Major Allen, all of whom were thoroughly familiar with the works at Galveston, to draw up the specifications on which bids could be taken. The commission was to meet in a day or two to begin defining the work required to complete both the North and South Jetties, as provided for in the legislation. Meanwhile, in Galveston Saturday began with a continuation of Friday night's festivities. Prior to the meeting called at 10 A.M. to plan the celebration, the deep water committee met to prepare a report for the general meeting. Their first action was to send a telegram to Senator Coke thanking him and the entire Texas delegation in Congress for their accomplishment, not only for Galveston but for the entire state of Texas and the states of the West that would benefit.[59]

The arrangements committee shortly after announced the plans for a torchlight parade Saturday night from the Strand to the Beach Hotel, led by Janke's Military Band. The parade was placed under the direction of Marshal A. M. Shannon, and assistants A. B. Homer and Hawley. All military companies and civic societies were invited to join the march. Activities at the Beach Hotel would include a cannon salute by the Artillery Company, speeches, and a fireworks display.[60]

At 6 P.M. the city's whistles and church bells set off the night's activities, the first being a fireworks display all along the parade route on Tremont Street. The parade units began forming, and at 7 P.M. the Santa Fe train coming from Houston with guests from around the state appeared. It was greeted with a twenty-five-gun salute by the Artillery Company, and the arriving guests responded with fireworks from each of the eight passenger cars. Upon embarking, all of the Houston and Galveston bands and military units, public officials, committee members, and approximately five hundred marchers proceeded down Tremont to the Beach Hotel, where they were greeted again by whistles and bells, fireworks, and a fifty-gun salute from the Artillery Company. The bands, Herb's Military Band from Houston and Professor Voight's Band of Galveston, serenaded a crowd estimated at fifteen thousand while the participants took their place upon the elevated platform to begin the program. Taking their places were Mayor Fulton, Denson, Mott, deep water committee members George Sealy and Leon Blum, Aldermen John Reymershoffer, Ullman, Levine, and Clark, Major Charles J. Allen of the Army Engineers, Robert G. Street, former governor Frank R. Lubbock, Mayor John McDonald of Austin, Mayor Henry Scherffius of Houston, and George Kidd, secretary of the Houston Cotton Exchange.[61]

First on the evening's program was the reading by Mott of the resolution prepared by the committee. Reviewing the importance of deep water to Texas and all of the western states, the resolution thanked all of those in Congress who had supported the bill and all of those in various capacities who had worked on behalf of the bill during the past several years. The first speech of the evening was made by Major Marcus C. McLemore. Calling Colonel Ernst one of Galveston's best and strongest friends, McLemore emphasized the vital role he played and expressed Galveston's gratitude to him. He also singled out the efforts of Senator Coke, Representative Stewart, and Walter Gresham, stating, "The work performed by these gentlemen would be inscribed on that monument of memory that would last forever."

McLemore was followed on the rostrum by Robert G. Street, a longtime and strong advocate of deep water at Galveston. He reminded those gathered that a deep water port was only an opportunity for Galveston; that "what she will do with it must largely depend upon her own people." He urged that every public improvement within the limits of reasonable taxation should be undertaken and that all new business enterprises should be encouraged. Street also recognized Houston for its support of Galveston's bid. He spoke of the partnership between the two cities—Houston as the railroad center of Texas and Galveston as the only deep water port between Vera Cruz and the Mississippi River. Though fifty miles from the coast, he believed Houston would remain a great railroad center because it was the nearest practicable point to a great seaport for this purpose. He pointed out Houston's solid support for Galveston at Fort Worth, Denver, and Topeka, and said Galveston had no greater friend than Houston's gifted son, Charley Stewart. Short speeches by the visiting dignitaries concluded the evening's program, amid the firecrackers and Roman candles.[62]

Provision for Houston

While they celebrated the provision in the Rivers and Harbors Act of 1890 that authorized the completion of the jetties at Galveston harbor, another provision that was much on the mind of the Houstonians attending the festivities was overlooked. That clause authorized a commission of the Army Engineers to estimate the value of improvements made over the years by the Charles Morgan interests to the Houston Ship Channel. This estimate would permit the completion of a plan finally to turn over the improvements to the federal government that were first accepted by Congress on March 3, 1879. The final acceptance by the government was delayed until the ship channel up Galveston Bay to Morgan's Cut was completed. Since the channel in the bay suffered the same lack of appropriations that the entrance to Galveston Harbor did, it was not completed until July, 1889, but the canal through Morgan's Point, known as Morgan's Cut, remained closed by a huge chain. The commission of engineers would be the first step in effecting the transfer of the canal and making further improvements to deepen the ship channel. Although Galveston was receiving all of the attention, there were those at that time dreaming of oceangoing vessels going up the channel. John T. Brady, who had attended the deep water conventions and dreamed of a railroad from the head of navigation to Houston as early as the sixties, founded the Houston Belt and Magnolia Park Railway in April, 1889, in anticipation of the day when navigation would reach Bray's Bayou. Eber W. Cave, a longtime associate of Morgan and treasurer of the Houston and Texas Central Railroad, was another strong advocate of the channel, who kept the idea alive after Morgan died. Cotton Exchange secretary Kidd, who spoke to the crowd that night at Galveston, would be another strong advocate, who would gather data and statistics in the years ahead to support the project. But the celebration that night at the Beach Hotel was entirely focused on Galveston's future, not Houston's.[63]

Planning a Jubilee

No sooner was the "spontaneous" celebration over than work started on the "planned" celebration, the Deep Water Jubilee. On Tuesday, September 23, Mayor Roger Fulton, following up on the motion made the previous Saturday by William H. Sinclair, appointed the planning committee.[64] Mayor Fulton offered some grand ideas for the nature of the jubilee. He called for the grandest trade display in the state's history. The Texas senators and congressmen should be the honored guests, and those invited should include every city in Texas and the governors of the states and mayors of each city west of the Mississippi. Sinclair agreed with the mayor and expanded upon his ideas. He suggested that the entire Congress should be invited, especially those who aided in the passage of the bill. He went on to propose a three-day celebration with a flotilla on the gulf the first day, a Mardi Gras–type parade on the second day, and the trades display on the third. He forecasted twenty to thirty thousand visitors being drawn to the island for the festivities. The committee met on Wednesday and selected Sinclair as chairman and D. D. Bryan secretary. After discussing the pros and cons of different proposals, it was decided to have the Deep Water Jubilee on November 18, 19, and 20, a trades display and Mardi Gras in February, and a Saengerfest in April. "This will keep Galveston humming for the next six months," commented one member.[65]

Gresham Returns

Gresham, the conquering hero, returned to Galveston on Friday, September 26, to the congratulations of the deep water committee and his friends, and to the praises of the *Daily News*. Said the *Daily News:*

"Colonel Gresham's work at Washington has been of such a character as to prevent his receiving through the press that credit and recognition of which his service has been preeminently deserving. But those of Galveston's citizens who have visited Washington during the interim of his successful lobby are fully appreciative of the value of his able generalship."

Gresham carefully explained to the *Daily News* reporter the exact provisions of the legislation. The $500,000 in the new rivers and harbors bill would fund the contract for work on the jetties until exhausted. Thereafter, he explained that appropriations would be made from time to time in the sundry civil service bill to carry on the work to completion. The appropriations of this bill fund the ongoing expenses of the government, such as the army and navy, the mail contracts, and the Library of Congress, which was being built under exactly the same type of contract as the jetties. "In other words," said Gresham, "the government is now pledged to the work just as it is to carrying out the mail contracts."[66]

The members of Congress who worked hard for the Galveston appropriation drew praise from Gresham, starting with Senator Coke and Representative Stewart. He was also full of praise for the Kansas delegation—Senators Preston B. Plumb and John J. Ingalls and Representatives Bishop W. Perkins, Samuel R. Peters, and E. N. Morrill. Although they were not from western states, Gresham also cited the efforts of Representatives Newton C. Blanchard of Louisiana, John H. Bankhead of Alabama, and Senator William E. Chandler of New Hampshire. Shortly after this, the Interstate Deep Water Committee, meeting in Des Moines, Iowa, passed resolutions thanking both houses of Congress on behalf of the people of the Great West for their support of deep water at Galveston.[67]

Even before the work could begin on deepening the channel to Galveston's wharves, there were indications of the new directions to come in the city's business dealings. A shipment of twenty carloads of goods, described as the first imports of any magnitude through the port, arrived destined for points in Colorado. Coincidentally, the shipment arrived upon the Mallory steamship *Colorado*. Doubtlessly, the attention drawn to Galveston by the deep water conventions was already bringing results.

Galveston Holds a Jubilee

Galveston ended the period 1887–90 with the festival of all festivals—the Deep Water Jubilee. By the time of the scheduled date of the affair, Tuesday, November 18, 1890, all of the fifteen committees had completed their planning and the activities began. The opening event was a harbor excursion for visitors to the city aboard the elegant Mallory steamer, the *Comal*. The boarding was to be accompanied by a band concert and a salute from the Galveston Artillery Company. The three-hour excursion was to proceed to the Outer Bar and to return, with the *Comal* accompanied by the tug *Cynthia* and the revenue cutter *Dix*. The 10 A.M. excursion was to be followed by an oyster roast and fish chowder party at the beach park (a baseball field) and an 8 P.M. reception at Garten Verein.[68]

Some seven hundred passengers took the trip on the *Comal*, described as a "floating palace" and lighter ships were provided to accommodate another eight hundred visitors the next day who also wanted to make the trip. More than one thousand attended the oyster roast and listened to the music and the speeches. Former Texas governor Francis R. Lubbock was awarded the Champion Oyster Eater prize (as a means of introducing him) and gave the major address to the crowd. A veteran of the Texas scene, he recalled the tremendous progress made in the state and spoke of the great future ahead. He was followed by Senator John Reagan, Congressman Charles Stewart, Mayor William Gardner of Cleveland, Ohio, and Mayor G. W. Clements of Wichita, Kansas. Senator Richard Coke arrived too late for the oyster roast, but he was in time for the reception that evening at the Garten Verein.[69]

Wednesday's banquet was preceded by two parades in the afternoon and a fireworks display that night. The first included all of the military units—the Washington Guards, the Sealy Rifles, the Galveston Artillery, and others—followed by the various fire companies and their steamers. The second was a military dress parade staged at the beach lawn, which featured the Brenham Rifles.

The banquet that night was held in Harmony Hall, and the *Daily News* reported that "never before has there been given in Galveston such a banquet as the one last night complimentary to the specially invited guests." The banquet was held on the second floor, "which seemed for the occasion transformed by fairy hands into regular sylvan grotto." The entire hall and its entrance had been decorated with rare tropical plants, palms, ferns, banana plants, and boughs of orange and lemon trees laden with ripe and ripening fruit. The French menu was as elegant as the decorations were beautiful.[70]

The following toasts were offered at the dinner: to the president, with a response by Senator Richard Coke; to the United States Senate, response by Senator John Reagan; to the House of Representatives, response by Representative Charles Stewart; to Army Corps of Engineers, response by Major Charles J. Allen; to the Interstate Deep Water Committee, response by Judge J. A. Carroll of Denton; to Galveston and the Great West, responses: for the Great West, G. W. Clements, mayor of Wichita, Kansas; for Galveston, attorney Robert G. Street. All of the speakers spoke eloquently of the benefits to be received by the millions of Americans now living in the western states and the millions to come.

Judge Carroll had high praise for the citizens of Galveston and their long fight for deep water. He also had high praise for Governor Evans of Colorado, chairman of the Denver convention and the interstate committee, for his leadership and contributions. Also coming in for high praise was Walter Gresham, who probably did more than anyone to create and steer the entire lobbying effort.[71] If anything brought lumps to anyone's throats on that gala occasion, it might have been the final toast to "Galveston and the Great West." There must have been more than a few in the audience that night who remembered the editorial title by that name that appeared in the *Galveston Daily News* back in 1866 and that started the thinking and planning process that led to this very night.

Everything was now harmonious between the citizens and the Congress and the Corps of Engineers. With the death of James Eads and the retirement of General John Newton, that conflict no longer hampered progress. With two Army Engineers' reports favorable to Galveston, the deep water committee was no longer at odds with the corps. Consequently, the banquet was not the occasion for reminding everyone that it was Colonel Moody who had shaken the system to its roots, that it was Moody who attacked Congress head-on for its wasteful ways in appropriating inadequate amounts (the "driblet" system) that prevented the Engineers from working efficiently, and that it was

Moody who attacked the Engineers head-on for pursuing bad designs and not listening to Eads's ideas on the design and placement of the jetties. But everyone knew it was the tall, forceful, impressive Virginian who had had the courage to challenge the system and shake it out of its ways.

Of course, the Engineers still faced the job of constructing the jetties—only the funding problem was solved. But there seemed to be no doubt now that new corps leadership and management with a new design would succeed. And, once the twenty-five-foot depth had been achieved, there seemed to be no doubt that Collis P. Huntington would bring his Southern Pacific Railroad to Galveston and make the port his terminal on the gulf.

Chapter 10

 Triumph

The 1890s would be a decade for Galveston the likes of which it might never see again. It was a decade of continued accomplishments as well as a decade of celebrations. The banks and commercial houses on the Strand and the castles on Broadway would stand permanently as evidence from the period, but other markers and signposts of Galveston's economic development are less obvious.

The first meeting of the Conference of the Western States was held in Galveston February 6–12, 1891. This conference was an obvious outgrowth of the Denver and Topeka deep water conventions where the western states first began to develop their consciousness of their shared interests. In fact, Mayor G. W. Clements of Wichita, Kansas, a prominent figure at the recent jubilee, was elected permanent chairman of the conference. When the conference convened again in Topeka, September 30, 1895, a full range of economic and commercial topics vital to the western states was on the agenda. There is no doubt that these conferences played a part in coming national politics as the various movements in the West came together in the William Jennings Bryan presidential campaigns. The role of the Galveston Deep Water Committee, Walter Gresham in particular, in fostering this cohesion among the western states in pursuit of economic goals was a significant contribution to American history.[1]

The benefits of Galveston's railroad connections and opportunities for importing and expanding trade with Central and South America became a matter of national attention in 1894 when a Santa Fe train carrying fresh bananas made the 1,400-mile trip to Chicago in a little over fifty hours, the fastest time ever recorded in the United States. On the leg from Galveston to Purcell, Oklahoma (the GC&SF portion), the running time was 17 hours and 15 minutes, an average speed of 29.45 mph. On March 2, the Santa Fe broke its own record by reaching Chicago in 42 hours and 45 minutes, an average of 32.98 mph over the 1,410 miles. The trips were not isolated stunts, however, but were part of a campaign to expand trade with all of the countries to the south. The increase of exports and imports with Latin American was also a goal of the Conference of Western States.[2]

With the jetty construction proceeding on schedule and the depth over the bar appearing certain to reach the 25-foot level, President A. C. Hutchinson of the Southern Pacific's Atlantic division came back to Galveston to open the negotiations for the long-talked-about terminal facilities in Galveston. Hutchinson spent May 12, 1896, in Galveston with George Sealy and left the next day with a proposal from the Wharf Company to present to Huntington.[3] Sealy remarked that the terms of the proposal were very liberal and that he felt sure Huntington would accept. Hutchinson also agreed as to the favorableness of the terms but said a thorough analysis by the Southern Pacific staff would be required to be sure. He said land was available at either end of the Wharf Company's docks but that the western end would be more suitable because of its central location. On the same day, the *Daily News* noted, "Verily, Galveston's cup of felicity should be overflowing," because the Galveston, La Porte and Houston railroad, "the Bay route express," had sent its first train to the island.[4]

The impact to Galveston would not only involve grain shipments from California headed by ship to the East Coast; a dispatch from New Orleans made it clear that cotton shipments formerly made out of Houston and New Orleans on Morgan Line steamers would now go out of Galveston, a large blow to the trade of New Orleans.[5] While not reveling in the Crescent City's misfortune, the *Daily News* summed up the significance of the occasion this way:

The entrance of the Southern Pacific system into Galveston will mark the greatest step yet made toward a realization of the benefits to come to this city, Texas and the west through deep water. Victory only awaits an agreement as to details to crown the efforts of twenty years of ceaseless energy. . . . The Southern Pacific system, with its vast marine and railroad traffic covering the Great West and Mexico, is the crowning event. Its coming places Galveston in command of an increased traffic large enough to insure prosperity.[6]

The new terminal was not built overnight, however. Because of state ownership of the tidal flats on the north side of the island, it was again necessary to seek legislative action to approve the city ordinance closing the streets involved and for the state to cede its rights over the tidal flats. The negotiations over the next three years could be the subject of a book of their own, but to summarize the action: the Southern Pacific signed a contract to purchase from the City Company city blocks 701–710, or the waterfront from 41st Street to 51st Street, on January 12, 1899; legislation was introduced and a supporting memorial to the legislature was submitted on March 9, 1899; the "Southern Pacific Bill" was passed on May 1, 1899. Construction began soon after on Pier B, said to be one of the largest in the world, and Pier A, which would have an adjoining grain elevator and be devoted to handling the loading of grain.[7]

The visit of President Benjamin Harrison to Galveston on April 18, 1891, gave the officials and citizens a chance to thank the president for his supportive role in the passage of Galveston's appropriation. There was considerable appreciation for the fact that Harrison, in his annual message to Congress given at the opening of the December sessions in 1889, had first recommended full funding of important projects. Then, of course, in September, 1890, he signed the bill making harbor improvement at Galveston one of those projects. Governor James Stephen Hogg, who took a great interest in the importance of gulf ports to the economic future of Texas, was responsible for bringing the president to Texas. He had met the president the year before, finding him to be "personally charming and unassuming."[8] When he heard of Harrison's planned western tour for the spring of 1891, Hogg invited him to visit Galveston on his way west.

Senator Reagan and Governor Hogg met the presidential party, which included Postmaster General John A. Wanamaker and Secretary of Agriculture Jeremiah Rusk, at Palestine on April 18. The party stopped briefly at Houston and arrived in Galveston promptly at 3:30 P.M. The welcoming committee, which met the train at Houston, consisted of Leo N. Levi, George Sealy, Alderman C. M. Mason, Julius Runge, William F. Ladd, Richard G. Lowe, J. W. Burson, J. N. Sawyer, Mr. and Mrs. R. B. Hawley, D. D. Bryan, Major and Mrs. Charles J. Allen, Mrs. William F. Ladd, Mrs. Roger L. Fulton, and Mrs. Aaron Blum. By the time the train arrived, the streets from the depot to the Tremont Hotel were packed with thousands cheering the visitors.[9]

Later the party, the reception committee, and one hundred or more guests boarded the Mallory ship *Lampasas* for an excursion to the jetties and the Outer Bar, at which time Major Allen, the district engineer took charge of the president and explained how the government's money would be spent. Walter Gresham did the same for Governor Hogg. During the trip, the party posed for the photograph published later in the *Daily News.* Following the harbor cruise, the dignitaries proceeded in a parade of carriages to the Beach Hotel. Behind the carriages followed the military units, the bands and about twenty-five varied organizations. Governor Hogg was reported to have been overjoyed at the tremendous outpouring of emotion by the citizens for this Republican president. Banners and decorations were everywhere along the route out Tremont Street and at the Beach Hotel.

The banquet that evening displayed Galveston at its best, surpassing the elegance brought forth for earlier affairs honoring former President Grant and celebrating the Deep Water Jubilee. In his introduction General Thomas N. Waul praised the president's foresight in looking after the economic interests of the nation as a whole, proclaiming that the new outlet to the ocean at Galveston would have the same impact on the West that DeWitt Clinton had upon New York when the Erie Canal connected the Great Lakes to the Atlantic Ocean. In his speech President Harrison reiterated the policies regarding government projects defined in his messages to Congress, and related events at Galveston to his overall views on world trade and the expansion of America's foreign commerce. He specifically referred to his policies to rebuild the nation's maritime fleets by granting liberal mail contracts to American carriers, saying we must adopt competitive measures to stay alive in international trade. The president ended the long day by standing on the balcony of the hotel and shaking hands for nearly an hour with well-wishers who filed by in a long line.[10]

The city's next opportunity to display its prowess at hospitality, honor a benefactor, and celebrate its civic success came when the chamber of commerce recognized Governor Evans of Colorado on March 2, 1894, for his long interest in deep water and his vital support in obtaining the passage of the bill. Evans and his party received the usual warm welcome, carriage tour of the city, and excursion to the outer harbor. In addition, they were able to witness the unveiling of monuments dedicated to Texas heroes David G. Burnet and Sidney Sherman at Lakeview Cemetery by the Daughters of the Republic of Texas.[11]

The banquet took place in the Beach Hotel's spacious dining hall. The tables were arranged in a large semicircle with the distinguished guest and the speakers placed at the apex of the curve. Governor Evans was seated in the center with chamber president William F. Ladd on one side of him and Colonel William L. Moody on the other. In his response to the toast on Galveston and the Far West, Evans, by then eighty years old, first read from a letter he had written when he was afraid he could not make the trip. These remarks pertained mainly to railroad routes in the West and the need for more connections in addition to Denver–Fort Worth line. Following his prepared statement, he made additional remarks pointedly aimed at Galveston. On the subject of equal access to the wharves, he made the following recommendation: "The only way, it occurs to me, to remedy this impediment to commerce is the construction of a circle around Houston, connecting on equal and liberal terms with all her other railroads, and those yet to be built, and extending it to your docks, to be used by all that may desire business relations with the city and easy access to cheap transportation by water."[12] His other remark pertained to the ultimate depth of the channel through the outer bar, and he offered this advice: "It is trifling with us of the Rocky Mountains to talk of less than thirty feet as a deep water harbor. It is trifling with us when you are talking of being several years yet in getting the harbor opened, that ought to have been opened before this time."[13] In other words, it was not yet time for Galveston to rest on its laurels.

Among those who had to wire their regrets at being unable to attend the banquet were Governor Hogg and Senator Coke; Walter Gresham, now the congressman from Galveston's district; Colonel Oswald H. Ernst, the former Galveston district engineer and now the superintendent of West Point; Senator Roger Q. Mills, the former congressman who had replaced John H. Reagan in the Senate; and Collis P. Huntington and A. C. Hutchinson of the Southern Pacific. These absences were regrettable, but fortunately, there would be other occasions coming.

The next celebration, on a smaller scale, was a luncheon on February 28, 1895, to mark the reception of the 1,500,000th bale of cotton at the port of Galveston, the first time that much had been handled in a single season. The main room of the Cotton Exchange building was converted into a banquet hall by placing boards over the "bull pen" so that it could serve as a lunch counter and placing two large tables and smaller ones for six or seven guests each around the room. In addition to the members of the Cotton Exchange, the guests included public officials, consuls, and representatives of railroad and shipping companies. Cotton was mixed with the greenery decorating the hall, and the flags of all nations doing business with the port were hung from the railing of the gallery. Exchange president Julius Runge, Mayor A. W. Fly, and chamber of commerce president William F. Ladd occupied the center table along with the consuls.[14]

In his remarks President Runge reviewed the history of the cotton business in Galveston, pointing out that it was only in 1891 that Galveston had reached 1 million bales in a season and that that number had increased by 50 percent in four years. Customs collector George Finlay offered some interesting information on Galveston's prosperity. His comments were reported as follows: "Galveston has become the principal Texas port and has grown to be the great money center of the entire western country. There are few banks in the state of Texas that did not have their origins with Galveston men. Of the conditions of the people of Galveston he said that they are in better shape than in any other city and the working people are paid higher wages. In closing he said Texas is a great state and Galveston is bound to be a great city." Following Runge, Jens Moller remarked that one dollar per bale is left in Galveston for stevedores, wharfage, and other expenses, and that with the Wharf Company having increased capacity by 40 percent two years ago, the port could handle 2 million bales the next year. His prediction was three years too soon.[15]

The Army Corps of Engineers was the honoree of the next celebration held September 9, 1897, the year that the jetties were considered finished. The corps had moved out promptly after the September, 1890, legislation. Bids were opened on Saturday, December 27, 1890. On April 24, 1891, a contract was awarded to the Dallas firm of O'Connor, Laing and Smoot. One Galveston company, the Southern Construction Company (W. H. Ricker, president), had bid. The other bidders were from Kansas, Boston, and New York City. By 1895, the depth had reached 20 feet, and it was 23 feet, six inches by May, 1896. The *Belgian King,* drawing 24 feet, 7 inches, crossed the bar a year later on May 16, 1897. Although work continued, the project was considered finished. Major Alexander Macomb Miller, the district engineer at the time, received the honors just before he was transferred in September. The project stood at 61,500 feet for both North and South Jetties, almost twice the aggregate length of the next longest.[16]

Major Miller represented a long line of distinguished engineers trained at West Point who had served at Galveston since 1865, in both military and civilian capacities. They worked on railroads and public works in addition to the jetties. All of them graduated at or near the top of their class, many of them became generals, and some rose to Chief of Engineers. An honor roll of those men and their graduation dates reads as follows: Albert M. Lea, 1831; John G. Barnard, 1833; George B. McClellan, 1836; Braxton Bragg, 1837; P. G. T. Beauregard, 1838; Horatio G. Wright, 1841; Zebulon B. Tower, 1841; John Newton, 1842; Samuel B. Maxey, 1846; James C. Duane, 1848; Walter H. Stevens, 1848; Quincy A. Gillmore, 1849; Thomas Lincoln Casey, 1852; Henry L. Abbott, 1854; Cyrus B. Comstock, 1855; Miles D. McAlester, 1856; Henry M. Robert, 1857; William E. Merrill, 1859; Samuel M. Mansfield, 1862; George Gillespie, 1862; Jared Smith, 1862; Charles Howell, 1863; Oswald H. Ernst, 1864; Charles J. Allen, 1864; A. Macomb Miller, 1865; Charles E. L. B. Davis, 1866; James B. Quinn, 1866; and Henry M. Adams, 1866. Galveston and Texas owe much to these outstanding men, who should never be forgotten.[17]

The important civilian engineers who helped Galveston, of course, should not be overlooked: Caleb G. Forshey, who did attend West Point for three years; Lewis Haupt, who graduated from West Point in 1867 and who resigned from the army to become a professor of engineering at the University of Pennsylvania; Henry C. Ripley, a graduate of the University of Michigan who worked in the Corps of Engineers office at Galveston; and perhaps the greatest of them all, James Buchanan Eads, self-educated.

The last, but certainly not the least, of the celebrations occurred when Collis P. Huntington accepted the invitation of the chamber of commerce to be the honored guest at its seventh annual banquet on March 16, 1900. The occasion was without the parades and fireworks that marked the visits of Grant and Harrison, but the banquet at the Tremont Hotel must have equaled those previous festivities. Huntington was accompanied by many of the top Southern Pacific executives, and Aldace F. Walker, chairman of the board of the Atchison, Topeka and Santa Fe, was also present. By the time of his visit to Galveston, Huntington, president of the Southern Pacific of Kentucky, commanded twenty-six railway and steamship lines and employed thirty thousand people. In addition he was also the president of Pacific Mail and owned shipyards and dry docks at Newport News, Virginia, a city he created. He was certainly one of America's industrial giants.[18]

In his speech Huntington devoted the first part to a review of the march of progress that had taken place in the field of transportation, pointing out the changes wrought by new methods. Even the Erie Canal, which had meant so much to New York, had now been made obsolete by the trains.[19]

In addition he also expressed his views in opposition to the proposed Nicaraguan and Panama canals, discussing at length why they would be commercial failures and the reasons for the superiority of railroads. But perhaps for the businessmen of Galveston, his most relevant remarks were those made in an interview before the banquet, as reported by the *Daily News:*

> *"The cities of the gulf coast have paid entirely too much attention to the water," Mr. Huntington continued. "They have attached too much importance to the commerce of the ports and have neglected their opportunities for manufacturing. The commerce is all right enough; it is a good thing and should be promoted, but it is manufacturing, in the making of something, that there is the best opportunity for these cities to grow. There has been too much shipping in of goods from the north, too much sending away of raw material to be returned in manufactured form. Cotton ought to be made into fabrics here."*[20]

Actually the business community had been aware of this problem, and a concerted effort had been made throughout the 1890s to create new manufacturing companies. The principal results of this effort were the Texas Star Flour Mills and several cottonseed oil plants. Apparently Huntington thought more needed to be done.

Early the next morning Huntington and Walker, the two "octupi," as Walker termed them in his remarks the night before, made a rail tour of Santa Fe facilities in the area. Before leaving the city, Huntington purchased Blocks 449, 450, and 451, located between Twenty-ninth and Thirty-second Streets, and Post Office and Church Streets. The Southern Compress Company occupied two blocks and one was unimproved. His visit to the city and his purchases attracted a lot of favorable attention to Galveston, which, according to a special dispatch from New York, served "to make the city of Galveston more talked about in railroad and financial circles than anything that has happened recently."[21] Copies of the *Daily News* were sold out in New York as interested parties sought to know more about what was transpiring in the gulf city. It was understood that Huntington and the Southern Pacific had additional plans in the city, and, concluded the dispatch, "it would seem that some of the eastern people with money are beginning to watch the columns of *The Galveston News* for good real estate investments, either at Galveston or in the vicinity of Galveston."[22]

A Period of Partnership

As reflected in the celebrations that took place, events in Galveston since the end of the Civil War were the result of both private and governmental initiatives. History generally has represented this period as one in which the laissez-faire economic theory was totally prevalent. The events in Galveston indicate the opposite; it was a period in which government and private capital cooperated to achieve great goals, such as the land-sea transportation network to serve the western states by way of the Gulf of Mexico. Later railroads were built with private capital, but in another example of this early cooperation, many received federal and state land grants. Port developments around the country were financed with federal appropriations and managed by the Army Corps of Engineers. In this arena the competition was not between government and private enterprise; the competition was among local entrepreneurs and politicians trying to get the largest congressional appropriations for projects in their states and cities.

In the first half of the century, beginning with the Gallatin Plan of 1808, such involvement of the federal government in economic development was almost taken for granted. In his in-depth study of that era, historian Frank Bourgin, while recognizing the limited role for the federal government expressed in the Constitution, points out that analysis of the writings of Alexander Hamilton, James Madison, and Thomas Jefferson leaves no doubt as to their intentions regarding that role in promoting commerce. He states, "during the early period of affirmative government, it seems to have been assumed by a number of persons in high political authority that powers such as those over roads and canals, granting charters of incorporation, encouraging agricultures and manufactures, and establishing seminaries and schools were well within the scope of federal authority."[23]

When arguing for the adoption of the Constitution, Madison proclaimed the following benefits to be derived from the document: "Roads will everywhere be shortened, and be kept in better order . . . an interior navigation on our eastern side will be opened throughout, or nearly throughout, the whole extent of the thirteen States . . . the communication between the Western and Atlantic districts, and between different parts of each, will be rendered more easy by those numerous canals with which the beneficence of nature has intersected our country."[24]

Jefferson's views on the matter are made clear in this passage from one of this letters, quoted by Bourgin:

> the greater part of their public revenue may, and probably will, be applied to public improvements of various kinds, such as facilitating the intercourse through all parts of their dominion by roads, bridges, and canals; such as making more exact surveys and forming maps and charts of the interior country, and of the coasts, bays, harbors, and perfecting the system of lights, buoys, and other nautical aids; such as encouraging new branches of industry, so far as may be advantageous to the public, either by offering premiums for discoveries, or by purchasing from their proprietors such inventions as shall appear to be of immediate and general utility, and rendering them free to citizens at large.[25]

Histories of the post–Civil War period tend to focus on the rise of the large corporations and their monopolistic practices. Toward the end of the century, as a result of the Progressive movement and the Bryan campaigns, an adversarial relationship between industry and government is frequently presented. However, before that a total of 131,350,534 acres of public lands were contributed to the railroads by the federal government and another 48,883,372 acres by the states. Historians Samuel S. Morison and Henry S. Commager concluded that the western railroads probably would have never been built in the nineteenth century without these grants, and point out that subsidies to transportation were "as old as the Republic and as recent as the last session of Congress."[26]

The money spent on rivers and harbors has not received the attention that the railroad subsidies have, but the amount has been very significant. Through September, 1890, when the appropriation for Galveston was passed, a total of $207,415,380.69 had been appropriated by Congress. Starting with $22,700 in 1822, the annual amounts had progressively increased until reaching a peak of $25,307,124 in September, 1890. The House rivers and harbors committee was faced with the task of paring down a "worthy" list of projects that would have required $140 million to complete. First, money had to be set aside for the projects under way. Then the remaining funds had to be dispersed across the new projects to be started that year. In all, 435 projects received funding in the 1890 appropriation.[27]

Thus, Republican administrations in the late nineteenth century revitalized the internal improvements program of the early Republic. In commenting upon this Republican effort to correct the damage to national development caused by the Jackson administration, historian H. Wayne Morgan stated:

> *Only a strong, expert central government could have avoided unequal economic development, but the United States did not have the tradition, the machinery, or the public desire for central direction. Republican spokesmen had to run the risk of uneven development and poor supervision inherent in indirect methods while enacting the greatest program of economic nationalism since Hamilton. While William Graham Sumner taught the virtues of laissez faire, politicians funded every major sector of a mixed economy, and Herbert Spencer's facile*

ideas of automatic progress appealed more to the intellectuals than to businessmen accustomed to pursuing the main chance.[28]

Emory Johnson, writing in 1892, offers the following reasons for the strong federal government role in river and harbor development:

1. *The constitutionality of the river and harbor bill is now seldom questioned. When public utility has been recognized, a measure will not long be regarded as unconstitutional. The declaration that the ultimate basis of legislative action is public utility would have seemed, even to a loose constructionist, a broad statement fifty years ago, but I think it correctly expresses the present attitude of the American people toward the Constitution. . . .*

2. *A second reason for the improvement of rivers and harbors by the general government is that such work, when inter-state commerce is aided thereby, is of general benefit.*

3. *Water routes for freight and passengers serve as a check on railroad tariffs.*

4. *The best argument for the aid to river and harbor improvement at the expense of the United States government is that all great nations pursue such a policy.*[29]

Another who has made an intensive study of the affirmative government and mixed economy of the nineteenth century is Carter Goodrich. His observations, made about railroad and canal development, in the early part of the century would seem to apply equally to the river and harbor developments in the latter part. He wrote:

what appears is a set of characteristics long familiar to students of American history. Among them are a decentralized structure of government, a distrust of centralized national plans, and pragmatic attitude in the choice of means. Students from other countries might find two aspects of the movement extraordinary: One is the degree of authority exercised by local governments and the strength of community or "booster" spirit in the promotion of improvement; the second is the importance of voluntary civic organizations both as pressure groups influencing government decisions and as agencies of direct collective action. Finally, the preference for mixed as against purely public enterprise, the empha-

sis on private leadership in the joint undertakings, and the reliance upon
private interests to exploit the opportunities offered by the improvements,
show the degree to which this use of the public powers conformed to the
traditions, and served the purposes, of individualistic free enterprise.[30]

The events at Galveston and the activities of the Galveston Deep Water Committee and the Interstate Deep Water Committee created at the Denver convention all conformed to the descriptions of the role of the federal government cited in the preceding passages. Questions of constitutionality were never raised; public benefit was the only criteria recognized. In that era often cited as the Golden Hour of Free Enterprise, there was clearly an accepted role and function for the federal government to play in the economic development of the nation.

Galveston's Pride

The optimism and jubilation in Galveston was not without foundation. Foreign exports of cotton had climbed from 296,035 bales in 1879–80 to 453,151 bales in 1888–90 to 491,883 in 1899–1900. In cotton receipts, Galveston had climbed from 480,352 bales in 1879–80 (fourth place) to 1,701,243 bales in 1899–1900 (second to New Orleans after having been first the previous year). Galveston's total exports for 1899–1900 were valued at $86,376,486, compared with $78,994,652 for 1898–99. Of these amounts, cotton accounted for only 75 percent, as the volume of other products increased. Galveston also had advanced to third place in wheat exports, seventh place in corn exports, and sixth place in cattle exports. In terms of increased business with Galveston, exports to Japan had increased fourfold in the past year.[31]

Unfortunately, there are no existing accounts of the conversations in the offices, restaurants, and saloons where the occupants of the Strand gathered daily in the weeks after Huntington's visit to chat about current events, cotton prices, and other miscellany. One can only imagine what kind of deep pride and satisfaction they were experiencing in those days as the result of what had been accomplished by the city. The port was full of ships from many places. The people of Galveston could board trains to carry them anywhere in the country, and people from Boston and New York could take those same trains to come to Galveston to invest their money. They could visit Broadway with its castles and gardens and see an avenue as beautiful as one anywhere.

Feelings of pride and accomplishment must have been especially strong in those who were in Galveston in 1866 and participated in the laying out of the future: George Sealy, John H. Hutchings, Colonel Alfred H. Belo, Colonel William L. Moody, Walter Gresham, Robert G. Street, Waters Davis, Albert Somerville, Leon Blum, Charles W. Hayes (journalist, historian, and statistician), and others; there were those who arrived later and made their contributions to the harbor and railroad developments: Richard S. Willis, John C. Wallis, John D. Rogers, Harris Kempner, William D. Skinner, Bertrand Adoue, and others; and there were those who saw the beginnings but did not survive to see the final triumph: Caleb G. Forshey, Willard Richardson, George Ball, John Sealy, Henry Rosenberg, Judge William P. Ballinger, Moritz Kopperl, Colonel Alfred M. Hobby, Mayor Charles W. Hurley, and others.

The spring and summer of 1900 must have been a wonderful time to have lived and been in business in Galveston. They knew what it was like to be sitting on top of the world!

Epilogue

As readers of Galveston history know, the excitement and joy of that summer of 1900 were short-lived. On September 8, a devastating hurricane struck the Island City, killing an estimated six thousand people and destroying or damaging all of its buildings. Instead of abandoning the island and starting over on the mainland, the residents of Galveston, with outstanding leadership, set about the job of rebuilding. A seawall was built to protect the city against future hurricanes, and the grade level of the city behind the seawall was raised to provide additional safety. The port resumed its leadership position and was handling as many as 4 million bales of cotton in the peak years, 1912–13 and 1915–16.

Notes

Chapter 1. Richardson Points the Way—West

1. Material in this chapter was drawn from the following sources: Morison and Commager, *Growth of the American Republic*, vol. 2, ch. 8; Cochran and Miller, *Age of Enterprise*, chs. 7–10; Richmond and Mardock, *Nation Moving West*, chs. 7, 10; Cashman, *America in the Gilded Age*, pt. 1; Webb, *Great Frontier*, chs. 1, 4, 5; Billington, *Westward Expansion*, sect. 3, chs. 31, 34, 35, 37; Spratt, *Road to Spindletop*.

2. McComb, *Galveston*, 2.

3. Randal Joy Thompson, review of *A Theory of Technology: Continuity and Change in Human Development* by Thomas De Gregori, *Houston Post*, Nov. 3, 1985.

4. Fornell, *Galveston Era*, ix.

5. *Galveston Daily News*, June 13, 1865.

6. Ibid., Aug. 27, 1865. Biographical information on Richardson and historical information on the *Galveston Daily News* can be found in Acheson, *35,000 Days in Texas*.

7. *Galveston Daily News*, June 13, 1865.

8. Ibid., Aug. 27, 1865. Journalist/historian Charles W. Hayes, writing in 1879, had the following to say about this period: "The supineness and indifference manifested by so many of the Southern cities at the close of the civil war was not imitated here. The citizens of Galveston [who] returned to find their city in the hands of a conqueror, their commerce destroyed, and their beautiful houses dilapidated and in a state of decay, were undaunted, still having an abiding faith in their city, bravely and energetically went to work to regain and re-establish connections, restore the commercial relations, and for the rebuilding and advancement of Galveston to a more prominent position than she had attained before the war." *Galveston*, 670–71.

9. Ibid., Mar. 25, 1866.

10. Ibid., May 3, 1866. Hayes, *Galveston*, 800–810.

11. Ibid.

Chapter 2. The Struggle for National Attention

1. *Galveston Daily News,* Aug. 16; Sept. 5; Oct. 3; Nov. 18, 1866.
2. Ibid., Jan. 1, 8, 15, 24, 30, 1867.
3. Ibid., Aug. 16, 1890. This issue carried a very good summary of the deep water history.
4. Alperin, *Custodians,* 23.
5. *Galveston Daily News,* Dec. 22, 1867. Alperin, *Custodians,* 23.
6. *Galveston Daily News,* Mar. 4, 1868.
7. Ibid., Mar. 21; Apr. 25; June 21; Oct. 24, 1868.
8. Ibid., Jan. 27, 1869. *Flake's Bulletin,* Jan. 27, 1869.
9. Bishop appears to have misspelled the French word "Essayons," which is also the motto of the U.S. Army Corps of Engineers. It means "We will try." The source of this fact is the *Quadrangle,* the class annual for the author's class at the Engineer Officer Candidate School (1953).
10. *Galveston Daily News,* Mar. 11, 1869.
11. Ibid., Apr. 17, 1869.
12. Ibid., June 26; July 7, 8, 20, 1869.
13. Ibid., July 21, 22, 1869.
14. Ibid., July 20, 30, 1869.
15. Ibid., Sept. 7; Nov. 2, 11, 20, 1869. *Flake's Bulletin,* Nov. 21, 1869.
16. The first bonds were purchased by the following: George Ball and Henry Rosenberg, each $1,000; Joseph J. Hendley, $600; J. H. Hutchings, John Sealy, Thomas W. Peirce, Frank H. Merriman, Julius Kaufman and Co., Gustave Ranger, Union Marine and Fire Insurance Co., J. S. LeClere, A. P. Lufkin, Merchants Insurance Co., and T. J. League, each $500; Edward T. Austin, C. E. Richards, John P. Davie, Emily Labatt, each $300; Theo. Wagner, F. A. Anderson, Greenleve, Block and Co., Ballinger and Jack, Botts and Dean, John S. Thrasher, M. Kopperl, J. L. Sleight, T. B. Stubbs and Co., C. L. Barton, L. and H. Blum, F. Haiff and Co., Wolston, Wells and Vidor, V. J. Baulard, C. W. Hurley and Co., W. Jockusch and Co., Hohorst, Frauenfeld and Co., S. Jacobs and Co., Willard Richardson, each $200; Somerville and Davis, John D. Rogers and Co., Edward Webster, C. W. Hurley, T. M. Joseph, Andrew Baldinger, J. M. Brown, Joseph W. Rice, H. M. Trueheart, William L. Moody, Barstow and Morris, W. E. Hertford, Julius Frederich, S. Heidenheimer and Co., Von Harten and Nichols, George Schneider and Co., C. H. Jordan, B. R. Davis and Bro., J. B. Woodyard and Co., each $100.
17. *Galveston Daily News,* Nov. 20, 1869. *Flake's Bulletin,* Nov. 21, 1869.
18. *Galveston Daily News,* Nov. 23, 1869.
19. In closing the convention, President Filley announced the committee members who were to continue to investigate their subjects and report on them at the next commercial convention at Louisville, Kentucky, on Oct. 10, 1869, and Mr. Rudd of Kentucky presented an invitation to all of the delegates to attend. Ibid., May 25, 27, 28, 29; June 1, 1869. *New Orleans Daily Picayune,* May 23, 25, 26, 27, 28, 30, 1869. *New York Times,* May 26, 27, 28, 29, 1869.
20. William Watson Davis, "Ante-Bellum Southern Commercial Conventions," *Studies in Southern and Alabama History* 5 (1904): 53–102.
21. *Memphis Daily Appeal,* May 22, 1869. *New Orleans Daily Picayune,* May 21, 22, 23, 1869. *Galveston Daily News,* Sept. 12, 1869.
22. *Galveston Daily News,* Oct. 13, 14, 15, 16, 1869. *New Orleans Daily Picayune,* Oct. 13, 14, 15, 16, 1869.

23. *Galveston Daily News,* Dec. 15, 1869.

24. "Memorial of the Galveston Chamber of Commerce to the Congress of the United States," Feb. 8, 1870, Barker Texas History Center, University of Texas, Austin.

25. *Galveston Daily News,* Apr. 23, 1870.

26. Alperin, *Custodians,* 23. A photograph of the pile jetty and the Army Engineers quarters at Fort Point appears on p. 26.

27. *Galveston Daily News,* Dec. 29, 1870.

28. Emory Johnson, "River and Harbor Bills," *Annals of the American Academy of Political and Social Science* 2 (May 1892): 782–88. Hull and Hull, *Origins and Development,* 9–10. Goodrich, *Government Promotion,* 19–48.

29. *Galveston Daily News,* Apr. 30, 1870.

30. Ibid., May 10, 12, 18; June 17, 1870.

31. Ibid., Dec. 29, 1870; Jan. 15; July 14, 1871. Alperin, *Custodians,* 25.

32. *Galveston Daily News,* July 12, 28; Aug. 9, 1870; Jan. 19, 1871.

33. *Proceedings of the Southern Commercial Convention,* at Cincinnati, Ohio, Oct., 1870. Caleb G. Forshey Collection.

34. *Galveston Daily News,* Aug. 5, 27; Sept. 1, 1871.

35. *Annual Report of the Chief of Engineers to the Secretary of War, 1871,* 516–23. Alperin, *Custodians,* 25. *Galveston Daily News,* Feb. 6, 1872.

36. *Annual Report of the Chief of Engineers to the Secretary of War, 1871,* 554–55. Alperin, *Custodians,* 26.

37. *Galveston Daily News,* Mar. 20, 30, 1872.

38. Ibid., May 19, 1872.

39. Ibid.

40. Ibid., June 27, 1872.

41. Ibid.

42. Ibid., July 16; Dec. 11, 1872; Mar. 13, 1873.

43. Ibid., Mar. 16; Apr. 24; May 3; June 20, 1872.

44. Reed, *History of the Texas Railroads,* 376–77.

45. Mar. 19, 1870.

46. L. Tuffly Ellis, "The Revolutionizing of the Texas Cotton Trade, 1865–1885," *Southwestern Historical Quarterly* 73 (Apr. 1970): 478–80, 486. J. L. Waller, "The Overland Movement of Cotton, 1866–1886," *Southwestern Historical Quarterly* 35 (Oct. 1931): 137–45.

47. McComb, *Galveston,* 52.

48. S. H. Gilman, *The Relations of Railroads to the Commerce of Galveston,* 1871. Rosenberg Library, 23-5209. The map is designated 71-0098.

Chapter 3. Galveston's "Kansas City Movement"

1. Glaab, *Kansas City and the Railroads,* 27–28. Bernard DeVoto, "Geopolitics with the Dew on It," *Harper's,* Mar., 1944, pp. 313–23. This article is a critique of the theories of Gilpin and other geopoliticians by an eminent historian.

2. Glaab, *Kansas City,* 29–33.

3. Ibid., 175.

4. Ibid., 179–87.

5. Ibid., 188. *Galveston Daily News,* Apr. 25, 27; May 1, 2, 1873.

6. Glaab, *Kansas City,* 189. *Galveston Daily News,* Jan. 31, 1874.

7. Glaab, *Kansas City,* 190–91. *Galveston Daily News,* Feb. 11, 1874.

8. Accompanying Van Horn were Edward Dunscomb, chairman of Kansas City Bag Manufacturing Company; James E. Marsh, president of the Water Commission; Thomas J. Bigger, a beef and pork packer; J. G. Pangburn, superintendent of Kansas City *Times* Publishing Company; W. A. M. Vaughan, grain elevator owner; B. A. Finneman, wholesale liquor dealer; M. Dively, commission merchant; J. A. Dewar, proprietor of Diamond Flouring Mills; J. W. Branham, proprietor of Advance Hominy Mills; and T. P. Cook, superintendent of Western Union Telegraph Company.
9. *Galveston Daily News,* May 16, 1874.
10. Ibid., May 16, 1874.
11. Ibid., May 26, 1874.
12. Ibid., June 7, 1874.
13. Ibid., June 5, 1874.
14. Ibid., May 26; June 2, 10, 12, 1874.
15. Ibid., June 14, 16, 18, 19, 1874.
16. Ibid., June 28, 30, 1874.
17. *Kansas City Times,* July, 1, 2, 3, 1874.
18. Later ads also appeared for William Hendley and Company; Brown and Lang; Bering and McNeil; A. C. Crawford and Sons; Walthew and Company; Charles Nichols; the First National Bank; H. Seeligson and Company; Leon and H. Blum; Hobby and Post; C. W. Adams and Company; P. H. Hennessy and Brothers; Charles W. Hurley and Company; J. Reymershoffer's Sons; L. Desforges and Company; G. B. Miller and Company; William Windmeyer; J. S. McKeen; and Kaufman and Runge. Houston was represented by many of its leading businesses, including T. W. House; William Brady; Milby, Porter and Company; William D. Cleveland; City Bank of Houston; and the Houston Direct Navigation Company. *Kansas City Times,* July 19, 21, 1874.
19. *Galveston Daily News,* Dec. 22, 1874.
20. Ibid., Dec. 22, 1874.
21. Ibid., Jan. 3, 1875.
22. Members were named to the various committees. From the board of aldermen: Mayor Charles W. Hurley, George Sealy, Charles Fowler, Patrick H. Hennessey, F. B. Mosebach, J. H. F. Chapman, and City Attorney Walter L. Mann. From the chamber of commerce: President Alfred M. Hobby, James M. Walthew, James Sorley, R. J. Hughes, and R. R. Lawther. From the Cotton Exchange: Moritz Kopperl, C. M. Todd, William K. McAlpin, John D. Braman, D. C. Stone, John Woolston, Julius Runge, George P. Alford, Julius Frederich, Noah N. John, Leander Cannon, Elbert S. Jemison, Alex H. Ladd, Joseph H. Metcalf, W. A. Oliphint, and W. E. Wilmerding. From General Mercantile interests: James Moreau Brown, John D. Rogers, Bevin R. Davis, Leon Blum, Richard S. Willis, William H. Willis, Sampson Heidenheimer, D. Theodore Ayres, L. LeGierse, Marks Marx, J. N. Sawyer, Ed Webster, George Flournoy, Thomas M. Jack, Thomas N. Waul, John S. Thrasher, Garland B. Miller, George M. Steirer, Alfred H. Belo, Michael Quin, Willard Richardson, Henry Rosenberg, T. W. Foltz, L. D. Michel, L. Kloppman, Thomas A. Gary, Theodore K. Thompson, Alexander C. Crawford, R. F. George, and Henry Seeligson. *Galveston Daily News,* Jan. 6, 1875.
23. Ibid., Jan. 8, 1875.

Chapter 4. The Army Engineers Try—and Fail
1. *Galveston Daily News,* Jan. 11, 1873.
2. Ibid., Mar. 18, 1873.

3. President Rosenberg reported that $165,000 of discounted bonds had been sold, providing $149,940.70 of operating funds. A balance of $4,000 in unsold bonds remained. Expenditures had totaled $147,933.81, leaving a balance of $2,006.89 on hand.

4. *Galveston Daily News,* Apr. 15, 25; May 8, 1873.

5. Aldermen Joseph C. Ogle and F. B. Mosebach, James Moreau Brown, Peter J. Willis, John Sealy, Charles Vidor, D. Theodore Ayres, Isadore Dyer, John S. Sellers, James Sorley, W. H. Sorley, Leon Blum, William H. Jack, Judge William P. Ballinger, Marcus F. Mott, William L. Mann, R. J. Hughes, Captain Charles Fowler, Dr. William R. Smith, Robert G. Street, and others joined Mayor Hurley and Colonel Hobby in welcoming the visitors. *Galveston Daily News,* Apr. 27, 1873. This visit preceded the visit of 1874 described in ch. 3.

6. Ibid., Apr. 27, 1873.

7. Ibid., May 22, 1873.

8. Ibid. General Thomas N. Waul, at this time a prominent attorney in Galveston, was the commanding officer of "Waul's Legion" in the Confederate Army and one of Texas's greatest Civil War figures.

9. Ibid., Aug. 29, 1873.

10. Ibid. Oct. 7; Apr. 5, 1873; Feb. 27, 1874.

11. Ibid., Jan. 11; Mar. 4, 1874. House, *Exec. Doc. No. 136,* 43rd Cong., 1st sess., 14–16. Alperin, *Custodians,* 26–28.

12. House, *Exec. Doc. No. 136,* p. 11.

13. Ibid., 10–14.

14. In the latter half of the twentieth century such experimental engineering efforts were called "research and development projects." Examples were the Intercontinental Ballistic Missile Program (ICBM) and the Manned Lunar Landing Program, also called Apollo.

15. House, *Exec. Doc. No. 136,* 43rd Cong., 1st sess., 1–2, 17–21. Alperin, *Custodians,* 27–28.

16. House, *Exec. Doc. No. 136,* 43rd Cong., 1st sess., 18–21.

17. *Galveston Daily News,* Jan. 29, 1874.

18. Ibid., June 21; Feb. 18; Mar. 17; Apr. 8, 1874.

19. Ibid., Apr. 23, 1874. Representative A. H. Willie's speech probably drew heavily upon the data prepared by Colonel Hobby and James Sorley of the chamber of commerce.

20. Ibid., Apr. 23, 1874.

21. Ibid.

22. Ibid., Oct. 8; Dec. 6, 12, 1874. Alperin, *Custodians,* 28–29.

23. The archives at Rosenberg Library has two copies of a photograph album containing excellent pictures of the facilities at Fort Point. One was probably collected by the Galveston Historical Association in the nineteenth century. The other was found in the city dump in the twentieth century and donated to the library. See U.S. Army Corps of Engineers Album, 1875, Rosenberg Library, Galveston.

24. House, *Exec. Doc. No. 115,* 43rd Cong., 2nd sess., 2–3; *Galveston Daily News,* Dec. 12, 1874.

25. *Galveston Daily News,* Oct. 8; Dec. 6, 12, 1874. House, *Exec. Doc. No. 115,* 43rd Cong., 2nd sess., 8.

26. *Galveston Daily News,* Dec. 20, 22, 1874; Jan. 5, 13, 14, 1875. House, *Exec. Doc. No. 115,* 43rd Cong., 2nd sess., 1–2.

27. *Galveston Daily News,* Feb. 20, 26, 1875.

28. Senator Maxey was joined by Governor Richard Coke and several members of the Texas Press Association, including B. B. Paddock of Fort Worth, G. H. Cutler of Dallas, John W. Callahan of Navasota, Tom R. Burnett of Bonham, W. L. Andrews of Ennis, A. L. Darnell and T. J. Crookes of Sherman, B. C. Murray of Denison, J. B. Dale of Bryan, J. S. Leachmem of Dallas, and Jesse Shain of McKinney. *Galveston Daily News,* May 14, 15, 1875.

29. Ibid.

30. Ibid., Sept. 16, 17, 18, 1875. "The Recent Cyclone in Texas," *Frank Leslie's Illustrated Newspaper,* Oct. 16, 1875. Bennett, "Church and the Hurricane," nos. 12–16. Alperin, *Custodians,* 29–30.

31. "The Jetty Works at Galveston Harbor," *Scientific American Supplement* 1, no. 16 (Apr. 15, 1876).

32. Alperin, *Custodians,* 32–33.

33. Fleming, *West Point,* 16. Ambrose, *Duty, Honor, Country,* 18. Dupuy, *Men of West Point,* 8–9. Goetzmann, *Army Exploration,* 12–14.

34. Goetzmann, *Army Exploration,* 17.

Chapter 5. Gould and Huntington Seek A Gulf Port

1. *Galveston Daily News,* Mar. 8, 1881.

2. Ibid. *St. Louis Globe Democrat,* Mar. 16, 1881.

3. *Galveston Daily News,* Mar. 8, 1881.

4. Ibid.

5. Robert L. Peterson, "Jay Gould and the Railroad Commission of Texas," *Southwestern Historical Quarterly* 58, no. 3 (Jan. 1955): 423. Charles S. Potts, *Railroad Transportation in Texas,* 117. Reed, *Texas Railroads,* 574–75.

6. *St. Louis Globe Democrat,* Mar. 16, 1881.

7. *Galveston Daily News,* Mar. 29, 1881.

8. Ibid., May 5, 1883.

9. Yenne, *Southern Pacific,* 23, 31, 42, 51.

10. *Galveston Daily News,* June 3, 17, 23; July 8, 12, 20, 1881. *Railroad Gazette,* June 24; July 22, 1881.

11. *Railroad Gazette,* Oct. 21, 1881.

12. Ibid.

13. *Galveston Daily News,* Mar. 22, 1882.

14. Ibid., July 28, 1882.

15. Yenne, *Southern Pacific,* 51. *Galveston Daily News,* Feb. 25; May 5; June 3, 1883.

16. *Galveston Daily News,* Sept. 2; Oct. 1, 13, 1883.

17. Ibid., Mar. 11, 1884.

18. Ibid., Sept. 26, 1884.

19. Ibid., Aug. 26, 1884.

Chapter 6. The Deep Water Committee Attacks

1. *Galveston Daily News,* Jan. 9, 13, 1880.

2. Ibid., Nov. 16, 1880.

3. Alperin, *Custodians,* 41–51. Dorsey, *Road to the Sea,* 275–81.

4. Alperin, *Custodians,* 41–47.

5. *Galveston Daily News,* Feb. 1, 1880.
6. Ibid., Oct. 7, 1880.
7. Ibid., Dec. 3, 5, 21, 26, 1880.
8. Ibid., Dec. 15, 16, 25, 29, 1880.
9. Ibid., Nov. 16, 27; Dec. 21, 1881.
10. Ibid., Dec. 4, 11, 1881.
11. Ibid., Aug. 15; Oct. 10, 24, 1882.
12. Ibid., Jan. 16, 1883.
13. Ibid., Feb. 6, 1883.
14. Ibid., Oct. 30; Nov. 6, 9, 15, 1883.
15. Ibid., Dec. 28, 1883.
16. Ibid., Jan. 2, 9, 13, 1884.
17. Charles Fowler to Col. A. H. Belo, Feb, 1, 1884, William L. Moody Collection.
18. Charles Fowler to Col. A. H. Belo, Feb. 2, 1884, Moody Collection.
19. John C. Brown to Col. A. H. Belo, Feb. 4, 1884, Moody Collection.
20. *Galveston Daily News,* Jan. 11; Feb. 4, 1884.
21. Ibid, Feb. 18, 19, 21, 1884. Claude H. Hall, "The Fabulous Tom Ochiltree," *South-western Historical Quarterly* 71, no. 3 (1968): 365. Hall suggests that Rep. Ochiltree may have played a broader role in organizing Galveston's lobbying effort. At any rate, this is an article everyone interested in Texas and Galveston history must read. Ochiltree's life was nothing short of fabulous.
22. *Galveston Daily News,* Feb. 28: Mar. 23, 1884.
23. Ibid., Mar. 19, 1884.
24. Ibid., Mar. 20, 1884.
25. Ibid., Apr. 1, 3, 1884.
26. Ibid., Apr. 8, 14; May 3, 6, 7, 1884.
27. Moody to Alex G. Cochrane, May 9, 1884, and Moody to Sen. Samuel B. Maxey, May 9, 1884, Moody Collection. *Galveston Daily News,* May 10, 1884.
28. *Galveston Daily News,* May 11, 15, 16, 18, 1884.
29. Ibid., May 18, 1884.
30. Gen. John Newton to Hon. Albert S. Willis, May 20, 1884, Moody Collection (copy).
31. Ibid., May 9, 1884.
32. Ibid., May 23, 1884.
33. Ibid., June 2, 1884. The entire testimony of Capt. Eads on May 22, 1884, was printed in the *Daily News,* taking over two full pages. Verbatim proceedings were taken by reporters using shorthand. The testimony also appeared in the *Congressional Record.*
34. Eads to Moody, May 24 and 25, 1884, Moody Collection. *Galveston Daily News,* May 24, 1884.
35. *Galveston Daily News,* May 28, 31; June 12, 1884.
36. Eads to Moody, June 3, 1884, Moody Collection.
37. *Galveston Daily News,* June 4, 1884.
38. Ibid., June 8, 1884. Reflecting his legal training at the University of Virginia, Moody moved point by point through his well-documented presentation to his conclusions. On this and other occasions he demonstrated that he had versed himself well in the technical aspects of achieving deep water. As early as 1879, historian Charles W. Hayes had noted Moody's mental traits. He wrote: "Colonel Moody, in a rare degree,

possesses the element of success. Calmly and dispassionately weighing all matters of trade or finance that come under his consideration, he acts with decision, and rarely ever makes a mistake. A close observer of persons and events, with clear reasoning faculties, he carefully digests his line of policy, and pursues it boldly and undeviatingly." Hayes, *Galveston,* 964. This book is excellent for biographical material.

39. *Congressional Record,* June 10, 1884, pp. 4960–64. *Galveston Daily News,* June 11, 17, 1884.

40. *Miscellaneous Document No. 111,* Senate, 45th Cong., 1st sess., *Report in Regard to the Proposed Improvement of the Harbor at Galveston, Texas,* prepared by Joseph Nimmo Jr., chief of the bureau of statistics.

41. *Galveston Daily News,* July 1, 1884.

42. Ibid, Nov. 18, 1884. The *Daily News* also contained a biography of Eads that said that the ironclad ships built by Eads that were used by the Union forces in the capture of Forts Donelson and Henry were still the property of Eads at the time of this early Civil War battle. Ironically, at this battle Confederate Captain William L. Moody was captured and imprisoned.

43. Ibid., Dec. 3, 16, 19, 1884.

44. Ibid., Dec. 30, 31, 1884.

45. Ibid., Jan. 4, 5, 7, 11, 15, 1885.

46. Ibid., Jan. 23, 1885.

47. Ibid., Jan. 25, 1885.

48. John H. Hutchings to Moody, Jan. 20, 1885, Moody Collection.

49. Ibid., Jan. 8, 9, 10, 11, 1885.

50. Ibid., Jan. 12, 16, 18, 29, 1885. *New York Times,* Jan. 19, 1885.

51. Eads to Moody, Jan. 21, 1885, Moody Collection.

52. *Galveston Daily News,* Jan. 23, 1885.

53. Ibid., Jan. 25, 27, 1885. *New York Times,* Jan. 26, 27, 1885.

54. Ibid., Jan. 28, 29, 1885. *New York Times,* Jan. 28, 1885.

55. Ibid., Jan. 29, 30; Feb. 4, 1885. *New York Times,* Jan. 31; Feb. 1, 2, 3, 4, 1885.

56. Ibid., Feb. 6, 9, 10, 11, 12, 1885. *New York Times,* Feb. 5, 6, 8, 1885.

57. Ibid., Feb. 11, 18, 19, 24, 27, 28, 1885.

58. Ibid., Mar. 1, 2, 6, 7, 29, 1885.

59. Ibid., Mar. 29, 1885.

60. Ibid.

61. Ibid.

62. House, *Exec. Doc. No. 85,* 49th Cong., 1st sess., Feb. 25, 1886. *Galveston Daily News,* Feb. 26, 1886.

63. *Galveston Daily News,* June 4, 1886. Reprint.

64. *Congressional Record,* Jan. 31, 1885, pp. 1142–43.

65. *Galveston Daily News,* Mar. 13, 1885. Reprint.

66. Speech by James B. Eads to American Society of Civil Engineers, May 6, 1885, Moody Collection. (Reprinted in *Galveston Daily News,* Dec. 7, 1885). *Galveston Daily News,* Apr. 8, 18, 1885.

67. *Galveston Daily News,* Oct. 30, 31, 1885. In regard to the New York papers, I counted twenty-six articles in the *New York Times* pertaining to the rivers and harbors bill and Galveston.

68. *Galveston Daily News,* Feb. 17, 18, 1886.

Chapter 7. Denver Needs a Port

1. *Galveston Daily News,* Apr. 17, 1886.
2. Ibid.
3. Bernard Axelrod, "Galveston: Denver's Deep Water Port," *Southwestern Historical Quarterly* 70 (Oct. 1966): 217–19. In this chapter I am indebted to Axelrod's article.
4. Overton, *Gulf to the Rockies,* 40–41. Axelrod, "Galveston," 219. *Denver Daily News,* Oct. 14, 1881.
5. Overton, *Gulf to the Rockies,* 41–43, 46. Evans's predecessor as governor of Colorado was William Gilpin, another man interested in broad objectives and long-run goals, who later became very well known at Kansas City. Also see *The National Cyclopedia of American Biography,* 1896, vol. 6, p. 445, s.v. "John Evans."
6. Speech by John Evans to the Denver Board of Trade, June 28, 1883, John Evans Collection, Colorado Historical Society, Denver, p. 9.
7. Ibid.
8. *Denver Daily News,* Dec. 23, 1883. Overton provides a very detailed account of Evans's conflict with the other railroads in *Gulf to the Rockies.*
9. *Denver Tribune,* Mar. 29, 1884. *Denver Daily News,* Mar. 29, 1884. Overton, *Gulf to the Rockies.* 142–43.
10. *Galveston Daily News,* Apr. 17, 1886.
11. Ibid., Jan. 11, 1884. Rep. James B. Belford to Evans, Mar. 8, 1884; Sen. Nathaniel P. Hill to Evans, Mar. 5, 1884; Sen. Thomas Bowen to Evans, Mar. 5, 1884, Evans Collection.
12. "The Denver, Texas and Gulf Railroad," speech by John Evans to the Denver Chamber of Commerce and Board of Trade, Aug. 12, 1886, pp. 3–4, Evans Collection.
13. *Rocky Mountain Daily News* (Denver), Apr. 10, 1887. Overton, *Gulf to the Rockies,* 148–51.
14. *Rocky Mountain Daily News* (Denver), Mar. 28, 1888.
15. *Galveston Daily News,* Apr. 10, 1888. Overton, *Gulf to the Rockies,* 196–200.

Chapter 8. The Western States Are Aroused

1. *Galveston Daily News,* June 24; July 3, 20; Aug. 6, 1886.
2. Ibid., July 7, 11, 13, 1886.
3. Ibid., Feb. 8, 10, 1887.
4. Andrew Onderdonk to Moody, Jan. 24, 1887, Moody Collection. William M. Douglas to Moody, Mar. 31, 1885, Moody Collection. *Galveston Daily News,* Feb. 8, 1887.
5. Douglas to Moody, Apr. 2, 1885, Moody Collection.
6. Douglas to Moody, May 5, 1885, Moody Collection.
7. Douglas to Moody, May 6, 1885, Moody Collection.
8. Douglas to Moody, June 2, 1885, Moody Collection.
9. Ibid.
10. Elmer Corthell to Moody, July 10, 1886, Moody Collection.
11. Douglas to Moody, Oct. 6, 1886, Moody Collection.
12. Among those attending who had previously been involved were Judge William P. Ballinger, George Sealy, B. R. Davis, Henry Rosenberg, Richard S. Willis, Judge Robert M. Franklin, Jens Moller, A. M. Shannon, James Sorley, Judge Robert Street, J. D. Skinner, William H. Sinclair, Morris Lasker, John D. Rogers, and Julius Runge. Prominent among the newcomers were Thomas J. Groce, John H. Focke, William F. Ladd,

John Reymershoffer, William K. McAlpine, John C. S. Spencer, William F. Beers, Edward D. Garrett, Andrew G. Mills, Henry M. Trueheart, John Adriance, and Marcus F. Mott. In spite of the fact that many of those attending had already endorsed the Douglas proposal, it was not discussed at the meeting. *Galveston Daily News,* Feb. 11, 1887.

13. Ibid.
14. Ibid., Apr. 1, 1887. Walter Gresham to Robert G. Street, Feb. 12, 1887, Walter Gresham Collection, Rosenberg Library.
15. Ibid., Mar. 1, 13, 1887.
16. Douglas to Moody, Apr. 22, 1887, Moody Collection.
17. *Galveston Daily News,* Mar. 5, 6, 1887.
18. Samuel Maxey to Moody, Mar. 10, 1887, Moody Collection.
19. Ibid.
20. *Galveston Daily News,* Apr. 1, 1887.
21. James B. Eads to Charles Fowler, Feb. 2, 1887, Robert M. Franklin Collection. Franklin had been appointed to a committee in 1886 to investigate the possibility of a seawall on the island to stop beach erosion and to provide storm protection.
22. *Galveston Daily News,* Dec. 1, 1887.
23. Ibid., Dec. 4, 1887.
24. Ibid., Dec. 10, 12, 13, 1887.
25. Ibid., Dec. 20, 21, 22, 1887.
26. Ibid., Dec. 24, 28, 1887.
27. Ibid., Jan. 10, 11, 13, 1888.
28. Named to the delegation were General Maxey, Paris; James W. Throckmorton, McKinney; B. H. Davis, El Paso; William D. Cleveland, Houston; John Peter Smith, Fort Worth; John Hancock, Austin; B. T. Barry, Corsicana; James F. Miller, Gonzales; D. A. Nunn, Crockett; James H. Jones, Henderson; Colonel DeWitt C. Giddings, Brenham; and Colonel Moody. Quote from *Galveston Daily News,* Jan. 26, 1888.
29. Ibid., Feb. 2, 3, 26, 1888.
30. Robert J. Sledge to Moody, Feb. 9, 20, 24, 28; Mar. 5, 1888, Moody Collection.
31. *Galveston Daily News,* Feb. 28, 1888. General J. C. Duane was a member of the Engineers Board that made the Feb. 26, 1886, report on the situation at Galveston and thus could be expected to support its conclusions.
32. Moody to Richard S. Willis, Feb. 28, 1888, Moody Collection.
33. *Galveston Daily News,* Mar. 1, 1888.
34. Rep. William J. Crain to Moody, Mar. 5, 1888, Moody Collection.
35. Moody to Crain, Mar. 12, 1888, Moody Collection.
36. *Galveston Daily News,* Mar. 14, 1888.
37. Ibid., Apr. 17, 1886. *Rocky Mountain Daily News* (Denver), Apr. 10, 1887; Mar. 28, 1888. Overton, *Gulf to the Rockies,* 185–87.
38. *Rocky Mountain Daily News,* Mar. 28, 1888.
39. Ibid., Mar. 31; Apr. 10, 1888.
40. *Galveston Daily News,* May 22, 1888.
41. Ibid., Feb. 3; May 15; June 22, 1888.
42. Alperin, *Custodians,* 126–29. *Galveston Daily News,* Jan. 26; June 10, 1888.
43. Zlatkovich, *Texas Railroads,* 65, 85, 89.
44. *Galveston Daily News,* June 24, 1888.
45. Ibid., July 10, 12, 19, 20, 1888.

46. Ibid., Aug. 2, 1888.

47. Ibid.

48. Those named by Mayor Fulton were Leon Blum, Charles L. Cleveland, Bertrand Adoue, Robert G. Street, Henry M. Trueheart, Richard G. Lowe, A. M. Shannon, William H. Sinclair, Marcus C. McLemore, Albert Weis. Alternates were William B. Denson, Thomas Sweeney, John Reymershoffer, Charles H. Moore, Thomas E. Thompson, James McDonald, Morris Lasker, J. A. McCormick, A. J. Walker, and Valery E. Austin. Those named by Gonzales were Richard S. Willis, John D. Rogers, James D. Skinner, William L. Moody, and Julius Runge. Alternates were John Adriance, William F. Beers, Charles Fowler Jr., John S. Rogers, and Garland B. Miller. In addition to these, Walter Gresham and Powhatan S. Wren were appointed by Governor Sul Ross to represent the senatorial district, and Mayor Fulton was named to represent Galveston County. Further action was required when Moody, McLemore, Shannon, and others indicated they would not be able to attend. Robert V. Davidson, Charles C. Sweeney, Daniel Buckley, Dr. Carey H. Wilkinson, Dr. Thomas McClanahan, and Marks Marx were added to those previously named. *Galveston Daily News,* July 24; Aug. 4, 10, 21, 24, 1888.

49. Walter Gresham to Gov. Sul Ross, Aug. 8, 1888; Gresham to Judge John Sayles, Aug. 8, 1888; Gresham to Gov. Ross, Aug. 10, 1888, Gresham Collection.

50. The members were, from the chamber of commerce, chairman L. B. Porter, J. T. Cornforth, D. K. Wall, Lucious Moore, E. M. Ashley, E. F. Hallack, Phil Feldhauser, William Wilson, Senator John Poole, Wolfe Londoner, C. A. Roberts, and E. L. Scholtz, and from the real estate exchange, chairman W. P. Caruthers, T. W. Herr, J. C. Gallup, George A. Bushnell, W. G. Sprague, J. C. Montgomery, Frank L. Dana, James A. Jones, R. A. Gurley, F. G. Patterson, J. M. Berkey, A. C. Fisk, and O. J. Frost. *Rocky Mountain Daily News,* Aug. 4, 1888.

51. Ibid., Aug. 9, 11, 1888.

52. Ibid., Aug. 13, 1888.

53. Ibid., Aug. 14, 1888.

54. Ibid.

55. Ibid., Aug. 14, 22, 1888.

56. Ibid., Aug. 24, 1888.

57. Ibid., Aug. 25, 1888. Reprint.

58. Ibid., Aug. 26, 1888.

59. Ibid., Aug. 27, 28, 1888.

60. Ibid., Aug. 29, 1888.

61. Ibid., Aug. 30, 1888.

62. Ibid., Aug. 31, 1888.

63. Ibid.

64. Ibid., Sept. 1, 1888.

65. Ibid., Aug. 31, 1888.

66. Ibid., Sept. 1, 1888.

67. Turner, *Frontier in American History,* 257.

68. Ibid., 258.

69. Webb, *Great Frontier,* 250–59. Webb, *Great Plains,* 252–361. Reissner, *Cadillac Desert,* 47.

70. *Galveston Daily News,* Oct. 18, 1888.

71. Ibid., Oct. 19, 1888.

72. Ibid. The following citizens were named to the entertainment committee: Albert Weiss, chairman; Leon Blum, Garland B. Miller, Frank Lee, Ed Ketchum, Samuel M. Penland, Charles H. Moore, W. E. Gregory, Charles Fowler, George Dobson, Fenelon Cannon, D. D. Bryan, George Seeligson, N. H. Rucker, Moses Freiberg, Herman C. Lange, Joseph A. Robinson, Joseph G. Goldwaithe, E. H. Fordtran, Leo N. Levi, Barney Tiernan, and T. B. Gale.

73. Ibid., Oct. 21, 1888.

74. Gresham to Senator Richard Coke, Dec. 13, 1888, Gresham Collection. *Galveston Daily News,* Dec. 12, 1888.

75. Ibid., Dec. 13, 18, 1888.

76. Ibid., Dec. 19, 22, 1888.

77. Ibid., Dec. 27, 1888.

78. Ibid., Jan. 5, 6, 1889.

79. Ibid., Jan. 7, 11, 12, 13, 1889.

80. Ibid., Jan. 18, 1889.

81. Ibid., Jan. 26; Feb. 10, 1889.

82. Ibid., Feb. 2, 23; Mar. 22, 1889. Alperin, *Custodians,* 52.

83. Cullum, *Biographical Register of Officers and Graduates of the U.S. Military Academy at West Point,* s.v. Robert, 676; Gillespie, 844; Smith, 848.

84. Ibid.

85. *Galveston Daily News,* May 9, 10, 1889.

86. Ibid., May 11, 1889. Alperin, *Custodians,* 52.

87. Gresham to Howell Jones, June 27, 1889, Gresham Collection.

88. *Galveston Daily News,* Aug. 20, 1889.

89. Gresham to Judge J. A. Carroll, Aug. 22, 1889, Gresham Collection.

90. Gresham to Rep. William Crain, Aug. 29, 1889, Gresham Collection.

91. *Galveston Daily News,* Aug. 31, 1889.

92. Gresham to Carroll, Sept. 5, 1889, Gresham Collection.

93. *Topeka Daily Capital,* Sept. 5, 14, 1889.

94. Ibid., Oct. 1, 1889. The Galveston delegation included, in addition to Gresham and Runge, Leon Blum, Peter J. Willis, attorney Marcus F. Mott, G. H. Mensing, Colonel William H. Sinclair (president of the Galveston City Railway), Colonel A. M. Shannon, John Reymershoffer, Mayor Roger L. Fulton, Robert B. Hawley, Frank L. Lee, Thomas W. Jackson, Frank M. Spencer, J. W. Terry, William F. Beers, William Parr, A. B. Homer, John Adriance, J. Wineberger, J. M. Calloway, representing the Texas State Grange, James D. Skinner, B. C. Adoue (son of Bertrand Adoue), and Captain W. M. Andrews, harbor pilot. Colonel Moody, president of the National Bank of Texas, and Nick Weeks, president of the Island City Savings Bank, arrived after going to the bankers convention at Kansas City. Also accompanying the Galveston delegation were Congressman William H. Crain; State Comptroller J. D. McCall, L. L. Foster, commissioner of insurance, statistics, and history, and D. D. Bryan, city editor of the *Galveston Daily News.*

95. Ibid., Oct. 2, 3, 1889.

96. Ibid., Oct. 4, 1889.

Chapter 9. Focused on Deep Water

1. Brown, *America,* 849–62. *Topeka Daily Capital,* Oct. 4, 9, 1889.

2. *Topeka Daily Capital,* Oct. 4, 1889.

3. Ibid.

4. *Galveston Daily News,* Oct. 11, 1889.

5. *Congressional Record,* Dec. 31, 1889, 84.

6. House, *Exec. Doc. No. 56,* 51st Cong., 1st sess., 17. *Galveston Daily News,* Dec. 17, 1889. Alperin, *Custodians,* 53.

7. House, *Exec. Doc. No. 56,* 51st Cong., 1st sess., 14–17.

8. Ibid., 17–18.

9. *Galveston Daily News,* Dec. 19, 1889.

10. Ibid., Jan. 5, 1890.

11. Ibid., Jan. 6, 1890.

12. Ibid.

13. Ibid., Feb. 21, 1890.

14. Ibid., Feb. 26 and Mar. 1, 1890. The original group from Colorado was soon expanded by the arrival of an additional party headed by J. T. Cornforth, the prominent Denver merchant who had attended the Fort Worth Deep Water Convention and chaired the first citizens' meeting that led to the Denver convention. Accompanying him were Dirks Cornforth, a member of the family wholesale firm, W. J. Wilson, a Denver capitalist, W. J. Kenzie, president of the Kenzie Implement Company, J. M. Milson, president of the German National Bank of Denver, and M. S. Bailey, proprietor of the Manitou and Mansion Hotels at Manitou Springs. These gentlemen were accompanied by their families and were reported to be in Galveston for pleasure and prospecting.

15. Ibid.

16. Gresham to John Adriance, May 27, 1890, Gresham Collection.

17. *Galveston Daily News,* Jan. 31, 1890.

18. Lewis M. Haupt, "Physical Phenomena of Harbor Entrances," presented to the American Philosophical Society, Philadelphia, Dec. 16, 1887, Moody Collection. Haupt, who graduated seventh in his class from West Point in 1867, left the army in 1869 and was professor of civil engineering at the University of Pennsylvania during this period. Many early engineering schools were either founded by or staffed by West Point graduates.

19. *Galveston Daily News,* Feb. 5, 1888.

20. Ibid.

21. Haupt to Moody, Feb. 25; Mar. 10, 1888.

22. Senate, *Miscellaneous Doc. No. 89,* 1st Cong., 1st sess., *Report of the Board of Engineers,* Mar. 16, 1888, pp. 16–17. This is the Engineers' reply to Haupt.

23. United States Patent Office, Patent No. 380,569, issued to Lewis M. Haupt, Moody Collection.

24. Haupt to Moody, Apr. 25; May 8, 1888, Moody Collection.

25. Haupt to Moody, Jan. 19, 1890, Moody Collection.

26. Senate, *Miscellaneous Doc. No. 89,* 51st Cong., 1st sess. Lewis M. Haupt, "How to Obtain a Deep Water Port on the Gulf," Jan. 30, 1890, pp. 11–13.

27. Ibid., 15–16.

28. *Galveston Daily News,* Jan. 31, 1890.

29. Ibid., Feb. 15, 1890. Colonel Ernst's testimony to Congress of January 31, 1890.

30. Alperin, *Custodians,* 129–31. Alperin also relates the history of the Haupt project at Padre Island, its eventual failure, and its rescue by the Corps of Engineers.

31. *Galveston Daily News,* Feb. 19, 1890.

32. Ibid.
33. Ibid.
34. Ibid.
35. Ibid., Mar. 7, 1890.
36. Ibid., Feb. 19, 1890.
37. Ibid., Feb. 21, 1890. Reprint.
38. *Congressional Record,* Mar. 29, 1890, pp. 2792–97. *Galveston Daily News,* Mar. 30; Apr. 4, 1890.
39. *Galveston Daily News,* Apr. 17, 1890.
40. Ibid.
41. Ibid., Apr. 23, 24, 1890.
42. Ibid., May 25, 27, 29, 1890.
43. Ibid., June 10, 12, 13, 1890.
44. Ibid., June 15, 17, 18, 22, 24, 1890.
45. Ibid., June 25, 1890.
46. Ibid., June 25, 27, 1890.
47. Ibid., July 1, 1890.
48. Ibid., July 8, 1890.
49. Ibid., July 13, 26, 1890.
50. Ibid., July 30; Aug. 5, 6, 8, 1890.
51. Ibid., Aug. 16, 1890.
52. Ibid., Aug. 23, 26; Sept. 2, 1890.
53. Ibid., Sept. 3, 4, 6, 1890.
54. Ibid., Sept. 7, 1890.
55. Ibid., Sept. 18, 1890.
56. Ibid., Sept. 19, 20, 1890.
57. Ibid., Sept. 20, 1890.
58. Ibid.
59. Ibid., Sept. 21, 1890.
60. Ibid. The general meeting began with Mayor Fulton being chosen as chairman and D. D. Bryan as secretary. Bryan immediately proceeded to read telegrams of congratulations from Governor Sul Ross of Texas, Mayor W. C. Connor of Dallas, Bryan Callaghan of San Antonio, Mayor C. C. McCulloch of Waco, Mayor John McDonald of Austin, and Mayor A. P. Chamberlain of Des Moines on behalf of the Iowa state committee. Committees were appointed to plan Saturday's activities and another celebration when the members of Congress returned to Texas. On the arrangements committee were Colonel William B. Denson, Colonel William H. Sinclair, Thomas W. Jackson, W. F. Turnley, and Thomas H. Sweeney. On the finance committee were James Moore, A. B. Homer, and J. N. Stowe. On the transportation committee were L. S. McKinney, Charles League, and J. S. Montgomery. On the resolutions committee were Marcus F. Mott, Richard S. Willis, George Sealy, Richard G. Lowe, and Robert B. Hawley.
61. Ibid.
62. Ibid.
63. Marilyn McAdams Sibley, *The Port of Houston,* 108–12.
64. *Galveston Daily News,* Sept. 24, 25, 1890.
65. Those appointed were Julius Runge, Thomas Goggan, Benjamin O. Hamilton, George Dobson, Thomas W. Jackson, James W. Moore, Thomas H. Sweeney, N. Weekes,

Robert G. Street, Charles Moore, Barney Tiernan, Frank L. Lee, H. A. Chandler, Robert H. Hawley, J. G. Goldwaithe, Arthur Bornefeld, Isaac Lovenberg, Joseph Lobit, Thomas Ratto, and Leon Blum.

66. Ibid., Sept. 27, 1890.
67. Ibid., Sept. 27; Oct. 10, 1890.
68. Ibid., Nov. 18, 1890.
69. Ibid., Nov. 19, 1890.
70. Ibid., Nov. 20, 1890
71. Ibid.

Chapter 10. Triumph

1. *Galveston Daily News,* Feb. 6–12, 1891; Sept. 30; Oct. 2, 3, 1895. Cotner, *James Stephen Hogg,* 358. Also see: Hofstadter, *Age of Reform,* 46–59.
2. *Galveston Daily News,* Feb. 2, 5, 25, 26, 28; Mar. 1, 2, 3, 4, 1894.
3. "A Brief History of the Galveston Wharf Company," published by the company, 1927, Rosenberg Library. Leon Blum was president of the company at this time. George Sealy would become president Feb. 1, 1898.
4. *Galveston Daily News,* May 12, 13, 1896.
5. Huntington's Southern Pacific empire acquired the Morgan steamships lines at the same time that it acquired the railroads. The new SP Docks at Galveston would also be referred to as the Morgan Line Docks.
6. *Galveston Daily News,* May 16, 17, 1896.
7. Galveston City Co. Records 46-0002, Rosenberg Library. City Co. Records include a copy of the memorial that was printed in the *Galveston Daily News.*
8. Cotner, *Hogg,* 358–59. *New York Times,* Apr. 19, 1891. *Galveston Daily News,* Apr. 19, 1891.
9. *Galveston Daily News,* Apr. 19, 1891.
10. Ibid.
11. Ibid., Mar. 3, 1894.
12. Ibid.
13. Ibid.
14. Ibid., Mar. 1, 1895.
15. Ibid., Mar. 1, 1895; Apr. 11, 1942.
16. Alperin, *Custodians,* 53–55. *Galveston Daily News,* Dec. 28, 1890; Apr. 25, 1891; Sept. 29, 1895; May 17, 1896; Sept. 5, 10, 1897.
17. Cullum, *Biographical Register,* vols. 2 and 3.
18. *Galveston Daily News,* Mar. 16, 1900.
19. Ibid., Mar. 17, 1900.
20. Ibid., Mar. 16, 1900.
21. Ibid., Mar. 18, 27, 1900.
22. Ibid., Mar. 27, 1900.
23. Bourgin, *Great Challenge,* 45.
24. Ibid., 44.
25. Ibid., 141.
26. Morison and Commager, *Growth of the American Republic,* 176. Also see 173–76.
27. Emory Johnson, "River and Harbor Bills," *Annals of American Academy of Political Science* 2 (May 1892): 787, 791–92.
28. Morgan, *Gilded Age,* 5. William H. Goetzmann points out that exploration was never

questioned as a proper function of the federal government. He states that "one of the ironies of the history of American exploration is the fact that our most memorable expeditions—those by Lewis and Clark, Zebulon Pike, Stephen H. Long, and John C. Fremont, and even the great Pacific Railroad Survey of 1853—were all launched by strict-constructionist Democrats. Jackson was no exception. He responded very positively to the stream of petitions from maritime interests, which reached a crescendo just as he was taking office in 1828." *New Lands, New Men,* 270.

29. Johnson, "River and Harbor Bills," 785.
30. Goodrich, *Government Promotion,* 294.
31. *Galveston Daily News,* Jan. 1, 1900; Sept. 1, 1900.

Bibliography

Published Sources

Acheson, Sam. *35,000 Days in Texas*. New York: Macmillan, 1938.

Alperin, Lynn. *Custodians of the Coast: History of the United States Army Engineers at Galveston*. Galveston: Galveston District, United States Army Engineers, 1977.

Ambrose, Stephen E. *Duty, Honor and Country: A History of West Point*. Baltimore: Johns Hopkins Press, 1966.

Axelrod, Bernard. "Galveston: Denver's Deep Water Port," *Southwestern Historical Quarterly* 70 (Oct. 1966): 217–28.

Baugham, James P. *Charles Morgan and the Development of Southern Transportation*. Nashville: Vanderbilt University Press, 1968.

———. *The Mallorys of Mystic*. Middletown, Conn.: Published for Maritime Historical Association by Wesleyan University Press, 1972.

Billington, Ray Allen. *Westward Expansion*. New York: Macmillan, 1960.

Bourgin, Frank. *The Great Challenge: The Myth of Laissez-Faire in the Early Republic*. New York: George Braziller, 1989.

Brown, George Tindall. *America: A Narrative History*. New York: Norton, 1984.

Cartwright, Gary. *Galveston: A History of the Island*. New York: Atheneum, 1991.

Cashman, Sean Dennis. *America in the Gilded Age*. New York: New York University Press, 1988.

Cochran, Thomas C., and William Miller. *The Age of Enterprise*. New York: Harper and Row, 1961.

Cotner, Robert C. *James Stephen Hogg*. Austin: University of Texas Press, 1959.

Cullum, George W. *Biographical Register of Officers and Graduates of the U.S. Military Academy at West Point*. Boston: Houghton Mifflin, 1891.

Davis, William Watson. "Ante-Bellum Southern Commercial Conventions." *Studies in Southern and Alabama History* 5 (1904): 53–102.

DeVoto, Bernard. "Geopolitics with the Dew on It." *Harper's*, Mar. 1944, pp. 313–23.

Dorsey, Florence. *Road to the Sea.* New York: Rinehart and Company, 1947.

Dupuy, R. Ernest. *Men of West Point: The First 150 Years of the United States Military Academy.* New York: William Sloane Associates, 1951.

Ellis, L. Tuffly. "The Revolutionizing of the Texas Cotton Trade, 1865–1885." *Southwestern Historical Quarterly* 73 (Apr. 1970): 478–86.

Fleming, Thomas J. *West Point: The Men and Times of the United States Military Academy.* New York: William Morrow and Company, 1969.

Fornell, Earl Wesley. *The Galveston Era: The Texas Crescent on the Eve of Secession.* Austin: University of Texas Press, 1961.

Glaab, Charles. *Kansas City and the Railroads.* Madison: State Historical Society of Wisconsin, 1962.

Goetzmann, William H. *Army Exploration in the American West, 1803–1863.* New Haven: Yale University Press, 1959.

——. *New Lands, New Men.* New York: Viking Penguin, 1986.

Goodrich, Carter. *Government Promotion of American Canals and Railroads.* New York: Columbia University Press, 1960.

Hall, Claude H. "The Fabulous Tom Ochiltree," *Southwestern Historical Quarterly* 71, no. 3 (1968).

Hayes, Charles W. *Galveston: A History of the Island and the City.* Austin: Jenkins Garrett Press, 1974. (The original manuscript was completed by Hayes in 1879 but never published.)

Henson, Margaret Swett. *Samuel May Williams: Early Texas Entrepreneur.* College Station: Texas A&M University Press, 1976.

Hofstadter, Richard. *The Age of Reform.* New York: Knopf, 1955.

Hull, William J., and Robert W. Hull. *The Origins and Development of the Waterways Policy of the United States.* Washington: National Waterways Conference, 1967.

"The Jetty Works at Galveston Harbor." *Scientific American Supplement* 1, no. 16 (Apr. 15, 1876).

Johnson, Emory. "River and Harbor Bills." *Annals of the American Academy of Political and Social Science* 2 (May 1892): 782–812.

McComb, David G. *Galveston: A History.* Austin: University of Texas Press, 1986.

Morgan, H. Wayne, ed. *The Gilded Age.* 1963; rpt., Syracuse: Syracuse University Press, 1970.

Morison, Samuel Eliot, and Henry Steele Commager. *The Growth of the American Republic.* New York: Oxford University Press, 1962.

National Cyclopedia of American Biography. New York: James T. White, 1896.

Overton, Richard. *Gulf to the Rockies.* Austin: University of Texas Press, 1953.

Peebles, Robert H. "The Galveston Harbor Controversy of the Gilded Age," *Texana* 12, no. 1.

Peterson, Robert L. "Jay Gould and the Railroad Commission of Texas," *Southwestern Historical Quarterly* 58 (Jan. 1955): 422–32.

Potts, Charles S. *Railroad Transportation in Texas.* Austin: University of Texas Press, 1909.

"The Recent Cyclone in Texas." *Frank Leslie's Illustrated Newspaper.* Oct. 16, 1875.

Reed, St. Clair G. *A History of Texas Railroads.* Houston: St. Clair Publishing, 1941.

Reissner, Marc. *Cadillac Desert.* New York: Viking, 1986.

Richmond, Robert W., and Robert W. Mardock. *A Nation Moving West.* Lincoln: University of Nebraska Press, 1966.

Sibley, Marilyn McAdams. *The Port of Houston.* Austin: University of Texas Press, 1968.

Spratt, John Stricklin. *The Road to Spindletop: Economic Change in Texas, 1875–1901.* Austin: University of Texas Press, 1955.

Thompson, Randal Joy. Review of *A Theory of Technology: Continuity and Change in Human Development* by Thomas De Gregori. *Houston Post,* Nov. 3, 1985.

Turner, Frederick Jackson. *The Frontier in American History.* 1920; rpt., New York: Hold, Rinehart and Winston, 1967.

Waller, J. L. "The Overland Movement of Cotton, 1866–1886." *Southwestern Historical Quarterly* 35 (Oct. 1931): 137–45.

Webb, Walter Prescott. *The Great Frontier.* Boston: Houghton Mifflin, 1952.

———. *The Great Plains.* Waltham, Mass.: Blaisdell, 1959.

Yenne, Bill. *Southern Pacific.* New York: Bonanza, 1985.

Zlatkovich, Charles P. *Texas Railroads: A Record of Construction and Abandonment.* Austin: University of Texas Press and Texas State Historical Association, 1981.

Unpublished Sources

Bennett, Vernon. "The Church and the Hurricane." Subject File: "Storm of 1875," Rosenberg Library, Galveston.

"A Brief History of the Galveston Wharf Company." 1927. Rosenberg Library, Galveston.

Evans, John, Collection. Colorado Historical Society, Denver.

Forshey, Caleb G., Collection. Rosenberg Library, Galveston.

Franklin, Robert M., Collection. Rosenberg Library, Galveston.

Galveston City Co. Records. 46-0002. Rosenberg Library, Galveston.

Gresham, Walter, Collection. Rosenberg Library, Galveston.

Kelly, Ruth Evelyn. "'Twixt Failure and Success: The Port of Galveston in the Nineteenth Century." Master's thesis, University of Houston, 1975.

"Memorial of the Galveston Chamber of Commerce to the Congress of the United States," Feb. 8, 1870. Barker Texas History Center, University of Texas, Austin.

Moody, William L., Collection. Rosenberg Library, Galveston.

U.S. Army Corps of Engineers. Album 1875. Rosenberg Library, Galveston.

Government Documents

Annual Report of the Chief of Engineers to the Secretary of War. Washington, D.C.: Government Printing Office, 1871.

Annual Report of the Chief of Engineers to the Secretary of War. Washington, D.C.: Government Printing Office, 1872.

Congressional Record, 1884. Washington, D.C.

Congressional Record, 1886. Washington, D.C.

Congressional Record, 1890. Washington, D.C.

U.S. Congress. House. *Executive Document No. 136.* 43rd Cong., 1st sess.

U.S. Congress. House. *Executive Document No. 115.* 43rd Cong., 2nd sess.

U.S. Congress. Senate. *Miscellaneous Document No. 111.* 45th Cong., 1st sess. *Report in Regard to the Proposed Improvement of the Harbor at Galveston.*

U.S. Congress. House. *Executive Document No. 85.* 49th Cong., 1st sess.

U.S. Congress. House. *Executive Document No. 56.* 51st Cong., 1st sess.

U.S. Congress. Senate. *Miscellaneous Document No. 89.* 51st Cong., 1st sess. *Report of the Board of Engineers,* Mar. 16, 1888.

Index

221

Clay, Henry, 23
Clements, G. W., 181, 184
Cleveland, Charles L., 89–90, 92, 94, 104
Cleveland, Grover, 114, 118, 143
Clinton, DeWitt, 187
Clinton, Tex., 76–77
Cochrane, Alex C., 86, 94
Coke, Richard: and Eads bill debate, 94; and federal lobbying effort, 81–83, 95, 98, 101, 126, 165, 169; Jubilee activities, 181; press praise for, 164–65; and sundry civil appropriations bill, 145; and Topeka Deep Water Convention, 149; and western states' lobbying effort, 142, 143
Cole, James P., 28
Collins, T. Y., 125
Colorado Traffic Association, 113
commerce, lines of. *See* deep water development; railroad development
commercial conventions, role in publicity for Galveston, 17–21, 24, 27
commercial development, post–Civil War return of, 3, 6–8
Comstock, Col. Cyrus B., 103–104, 159, 190
Conference of Western States, 184–85
Congress. *See* federal government
Connor, W. C., 131
Cook, S. A., 156
Cornforth, J. T., 135
corporations, regulation of, 72
Corpus Christi, Tex., 125, 130
Corthell, Elmer J., 104, 116, 144, 157
Cotton Exchange, Galveston, importance of harbor improvements to, 120–21
cotton industry: diversification from, 42–43; expansion of, 189, 196, 199; Galveston's role in, 3–4, 6, 61
Courts, George M., 143
Crain, William H.: and federal lobbying effort, 95, 104, 105, 126, 142, 143, 169, 172; support for "driblet" funding system, 125; and Topeka Deep Water Convention, 149
Crocker, Charles, 73
Culberson, David B., 126, 149
Cuney, Wright, 85
Custodians of the Coast (Alperin), 80

dams, and harbor improvement design, 57, 58
Dana, Frank L., 135, 155, 163–64
Darragh, John L., 89–90
Darton, Capt. M. W., 14
Daugherty, J. S., 122
Davis, B. R., 45
Davis, Lt. Charles E. L. B., 67, 190
Davis, Edmund J., 25
Dean, John, 17
DeBray, Gen. X. B., 68
Deep Water Committee, 89–90, 134, 155, 180
deep water development: celebration of, 175–83; and defeat of Maxey, 118–20; delay of, 41; economic impact of, 51–53, 72, 74, 75, 84, 120–21, 163, 184–97; engineering proposals for, 10–17, 24–33, 79–80, 91, 157–63; Engineers' progress with, 55–60, 63–69, 81–82, 103–104, 117–18, 150, 153; federal lobbying effort for, 53–56, 61–63, 79–88, 88–106, 125–27, 154–75; federal role in, 12, 21–24, 26, 28, 30, 33–34, 51–56, 61–63, 194; intrastate competition for, 124–25, 129–33, 135–39, 144, 153–56, 157–64; local proposals for, 114–17; necessity of, 9; and rail connections to Galveston, 70–78; regional publicity for, 17–21; state government role, 23, 26–27, 114, 116–17, 134, 142; western states' support of, 108, 111, 121–24, 128–29, 133–52
Deep Water Jubilee, 179–83
DeGregori, Thomas, 5
Dellenback, J., 128
demographics: and development of the West, 4–5, 7, 36, 37; in Galveston area, 3
Denson, William B., 129, 138, 142–43, 176
Denver, Colo.: and campaign for deep water, 128–29; economic development in, 9; need for closer port, 107–13; trade talks with, 45
Denver, Texas and Fort Worth (DT&FW) Railway, 112, 129
Denver and New Orleans (D&NO) Railway, 107, 108, 110
Denver and Rio Grande Railway, 109–10

Denver Deep Water Convention of 1888, 133–41

Denver Texas and Gulf (DT&G) Railway, 107–108, 111

Dick, S. K., 146

Dodge, Gen. Grenville M., 70, 82, 113

Dolph, Joseph N., 172

Dorsey, Florence, 80

Douglas, William M., 115–16, 118

dredging plans, 12–15, 26–27, 28

Duane, Gen. James C., 103, 126, 190

Dunham, M., 48

Dunscomb, Edward, 44

Eads, Capt. James B.: criticism of Engineers, 89, 91–92; death of, 119–20; and federal lobbying effort, 88–89, 94, 95, 101–102; honoring of, 191; impatience with legislative delay, 97; importance of private contract, 84–85; political astuteness of, 92; position on Eads bill, 98–99; proposal for deep water, 79–80; Southwest Pass project, 56; vindication of technical expertise, 103–104, 105

Eads bill, 77, 87, 89–106

Eastern commercial interests, vs. Western, 38, 40, 99–101, 136, 150–51

Eckert, Gen. Thomas T., 71

Eddleman, D. J., 125

Eddy, Col. J. M., 72

Edgerley, Samuel A., 21

Edmonds, George F., 171

Elliott, J. F., 122

Ellis, L. Tuffly, 35

Emery, J. S., 154–55

English, T. William, 104

Enterprise, 39

Ernst, Maj. Oswald H.: celebration of federal funding, 176, 177; challenge to Haupt's designs, 159, 162–63; honoring of, 190; initial plans for jetty project, 117; support for Galveston, 130, 131–32, 146

Europe, Southern regional trade with, 18–19

Evans, Charles, 45

Evans, John, 128; on Deep Water Jubilee, 181–82; at Denver Deep Water Convention, 135, 137, 138–39; and railroad development in Denver, 108–109; role in Galveston development, 45; visit to Galveston, 188

Evans, T. J., 49

Exall, Henry, 122

Factors Act, 121

Falkenthal, Louis, 85

Farmers Alliance, 125, 166

federal government: harbor improvement role, 12, 21–24, 26, 28, 30, 33–34, 51–56, 61–63; influence on economic development, 41–42, 139–40, 192–96; and lobbying effort for deep water, 79–88, 108, 126–27, 141–49, 154–75; regulatory authority of, 110; reluctance to support rivers and harbors, 67, 87–106, 118; technology's effect on need for support from, 6

Felkner, William B., 110

Fillmore, Millard, 20

Finlay, George, 189

First National Bank, 8

Fisher, Lorenzo C., 80, 82, 89–90

Flanagan, James W., 54, 60

Flint, Edward T., 122

Flournoy, George, 25, 45, 46

Fly, A. W., 189

Focke, John H., 122, 124

Fornell, Earl Wesley, 6

Forshey, Caleb G.: commercial convention role, 17–18; and dredging alternative, 13; honoring of, 190; and marketing of Galveston, 20–21, 27; and railroad development, 38, 68

Fort Point, 58, 67

Fort Worth and Denver City (FW&DC) Railway, 111, 112

Fort Worth Convention of 1888, 129, 131–33

Fowler, Capt. Charles: and board of harbor improvement, 15, 16; and dredging vs. jetty, 12, 13–14; and federal lobbying effort, 94, 105; and Huntington, 86; jetty progress, 26

Fox, Henry S., 45

Frederich, Julius, 45

Frye, William P., 164, 165, 171, 172

Fulton, Roger L.: and celebration of federal funding, 176, 179; and Denver Deep Water convention, 134; and Eads plan, 85; and federal lobbying effort, 89–90, 94, 100; at Immigration Convention, 122; and local improvement efforts, 115

gabion jetty design, 57–60, 63–65, 67, 68, 80

Gallatin, Albert, 23

Gallup, J. C., 135

Galveston: advantages of, 7–9; celebration of deep water funding, 175–83; Civil War damage to, 6–7; development plan for, xi; economic impact of transportation development, 156–57, 184–97, 199; economic role of, 3–4, 6, 43, 46, 49, 61, 62, 66–67, 128; Engineers' relations with, 4, 52, 79–81, 88, 115–16, 117, 182–83; Latin American trade role, 19, 52, 71, 152, 185; national importance of, 18, 61–63, 81–82, 93; national publicity campaign for, 17–24, 33–36; post–Civil War era of transformation, 4–5; press relations, 96, 99–101, 128–29; regional importance of, 51–53; reliance on technology for growth, 5–6. See also deep water development; railroad development

Galveston, Harrisburg and San Antonio (GH&SA) Railroad, 74, 76, 105

Galveston: A History (McComb), 5

Galveston Daily News: as city booster, 9; on Congressional interest in Galveston, 53–54; criticism of Engineers, 88; in defense of harbor improvement board, 16; on expansion of Midwest trade, 46–47; on Farmers Alliance, 125; on funding for deep water, 22, 26, 27–28, 56; on Gresham, 179–80; on post–Civil War amnesty, 7; on railroad developments, 34–35; on relationship with Denver, 107; on Sen. Coke, 164–65; on superiority of Galveston as port, 130; on Texas' internal competition for port facilities, 144; on triumph of deep water movement, 176, 181–82, 185–86

Galveston Era, The (Fornell), 6

Galveston Flats, railroad interest in, 77

Galveston Houston and Henderson (GH&H) Railroad, 4, 105

Galveston Progressive Association, 156

Gardner, William, 181

geographical determinism, 39, 40

Gibbs, Barnett, 131, 132, 137, 139

Gibbs, Col. C. C., 124

Gibson, Eustace, 92, 98

Giddings, DeWitt C., 60, 114, 126

Gillespie, Lt. Col. George, 145, 190

Gillmore, Gen. Quincy A., 79, 190

Gilman, Capt. S. H., 35–36

Gilpin, William, 38–39

Glaab, Charles N., 40

Goetzman, William H., xi–xii, 69

Gonzales, Thomas, 134

Goodrich, Carter, 195

Gould, Jay, 3, 70–73

Gowan, Col. J. E., 24, 25

Goyne, T. B., 17

grain trade. See agricultural trade

Grant, Ulysses S., 20

Great Northern Railroad, 21, 105

Great Plains, The (Webb), 5

Gresham, Walter: and celebration of federal funding, 176, 179–80; at Denver Deep Water Convention, 139; and Engineers' survey of Galveston, 146; and federal lobbying effort, 86, 89–90, 94, 95, 104, 124, 155; and intrastate competition for port facilities, 132; as leader of deep water movement, 134; praise for, 181–82; and real estate investment support, 157; state lobbying effort, 117; and Stewart's influence, 166–67; and Topeka Deep Water Convention, 147–48, 152; and western-states' lobbying effort, 141, 142, 143

Grinnan, J. B., 43

Grosvenor, Charles, 172

Gulf, Colorado and Santa Fe (GC&SF) Railway: Bragg's role in, 64; as commercial link to West, 45, 107–108, 111; expansion of, 106, 156; and federal lobbying effort, 100; Gould's relations with, 70–71, 72, 73; and Indian Territory

Jemison, Col. Elbert S., 89–90

jetties: best location for results with, 154; completion of, 185, 189–90; and deep water attempts, 56–60; Engineers' designs for, 117–18; Haupt's alternative design, 158–59, 160, 162–63; New Orleans' success with, 79; problems with, 63–65; progress by 1889, 146; proposals for Corpus Christi, 130; technical requirements for, 91

Jockusch, J. W., 24

John, Noah N., 45

Johnson, Andrew, 7

Johnson, Emory, 195

Johnson, S. R., 48, 49

Jones, James T., 92

Kansas, and Topeka Deep Water Convention, 147–49

Kansas City, Mo., 38–46, 53

Kansas City, St. Joseph and Council Bluffs Railroad, 47–48

Kansas City Journal of Commerce, 40, 44

Kansas City Times, 40

Kaufman, Julius, 75

Kelley, William D., 93

Kempner, Harris, 89–90, 104, 115, 117, 124

Kerr, Daniel, 172

Kerr, M., 49

Kervin, A. C., 138

Kessler, A. J., 125

Ketchum, Ed, 85

Kidd, George W., 45, 46, 146, 176, 179

Kilgore, Constantine, 126, 127, 149

Kimball, T. L., 48

King, Maj. W. R., 159

Kirby, John H., 157

Kopperl, Moritz: death of, 85; and federal lobbying effort, 33; and railroad expansion, 75; and railroad rates, 43, 49; return to Galveston, 7; support for Engineers, 52, 79

Kulp, W. O., 155

Labatt, Henry J., 12

labor system, post–Civil War, 6

Ladd, William F., 124, 187, 188, 189

Lake Charles, La., 151

Lanham, Samuel, 126

Lasker, Morris, 85, 89–90, 122, 129

Latin American trade, 19, 52, 71, 152, 185

Lea, Albert M., 10–11, 68, 190

Legate, James F., 151, 155

Levi, Leo N., 132, 187

Lindsay, J. M., 86

Longcope, C. S., 45

Lott, Uriah, 131, 132–33, 139, 157

Louisiana and Texas Railroad and Steamship Company, 76

Louisiana Western, 74

Louisville Commercial Convention of 1869, 20–21

Lowe, Richard G., 122, 124, 146, 187

Lubbock, Francis R., 20–21, 176–77, 181

Luckett, Alfred P., 45

Lutcher, William J., 157

Lydia Ann Channel, 130

Lykins, Johnston, 39

McAlester, Maj. Miles D., 11, 22, 190

McAlpine, William J., 30, 32–33

McAlpine, William K., 42–43, 66

McClellan, Lt. George B., 130, 190

McComb, David, 5, 35

McCook, Anson G., 152

McDonald, John, 176

McKee, James A., 15, 30

McKeen, Col. A. C., 16

Mackenzie, Ranald, 111

McKinley, William J., 169

McLemore, Marcus C., 132, 142, 177

McMahan, Thomas H., 7, 17

Madison, James, 23, 193

Magruder, Gen. John Bankhead, 7

Manderson, Charles F., 165

Mansfield, Maj. Samuel M.: criticism of private contract, 87–88, 88–89; doubts about competence of, 115–16; Engineers' defense of, 97; honoring of, 190; and renewed engineering commitment to Galveston, 79, 81–82; replacement of, 117

Mansure, C. H., 149

manufacturing, importance for South, 191–92

Marquand, Henry G., 71
Marsalis, T. L., 122
Marsh, Col. James E., 42
Marsh, W. W., 49
Marshall, C. K., 18
Marshall, S. S., 54
Martin, William, 126, 149
Mason, C. M., 187
Mason, William N., 141
Maxey, Samuel Bell: analysis of harbor improvements, 66–67; criticism of Engineers, 97; election defeat of, 118, 119; and federal lobbying effort, 98, 104; honoring of, 190; and Immigration Convention, 122
Mayhoff, Gustave, 75
Menard, Michel, 6
Merchants Club of Omaha, 48
Merchants' National Convention of 1868, 19
Merrill, Lt. Col. William E., 103–104, 190
Merriman, Frank H., 7
Mexico, importance of trade with, 71–72
Midwest, expansion of trade with, 37–50, 62, 107
Miles, Nelson, 111
Millard, Ezra, 49
Miller, Maj. Alexander Macomb, 190
Miller, Garland B., 45, 129
Miller, George L., 48
Miller, James F., 104
Mills, Roger Q., 60, 98, 149
Mississippi River, engineering project as competition for Galveston, 56
Missouri. *See* Kansas City, Mo.
Missouri, Kansas and Texas (MKT) Railroad: expansion of, 34, 44, 105; rate negotiations for, 44, 45, 47
Missouri Pacific Railroad, 70, 72, 105
Mitchell, F. D., 85
Moller, Jens, 100, 189
Montgomery, R. F., 49
Moody, William L.: and celebration of federal funding, 182–83; and Evans's visit to Galveston, 188; and Farmers Alliance, 125; and federal lobbying effort, 33, 85–86, 89–90, 92–93, 94, 95, 98, 104, 126–27; on federal regulation of

commerce, 118; on harbor improvement effort, 82–83, 120–21; at Immigration Convention, 121–24; and local deep water proposals, 115, 116–17; on press criticism of Galveston, 102–103; retirement from deep water committee leadership, 134
Moore, George, 25
Moore, Littleton, 126, 127, 142, 149
Moore, W. E., 125
Morgan, Charles, 76
Morgan, H. Wayne, 194–95
Morgan Company Railroad, 74
Morgan's Point, 178
Morrill, E. N., 180
Morris, D., 17
Morris and Cummings Cut, 130
Moses, Isaac, 12
Mott, Marcus F., 134, 142, 152, 176
Murphy, Jeremiah, 92
Murphy, Thomas, 49
Mustang Island, 130

narrow-gauge railroads, 40
National Bank of Texas, 8
National Grange, 166
nationalism, and Army Corps of Engineers, 69
National Republican, 103–104
National View, 96
natural advantages doctrine, 39, 40
natural forces, and deep water challenges, 30–33, 58–59, 67, 153, 199
Netherlands, The, dyke system of, 81
Newman, William H., 122–23
New Orleans, La.: advantages as harbor, 73, 74; commercial convention in, 17; as economic competition, 47, 82, 185; effect of Mississippi development on, 56
newspapers. *See* press, the
Newton, Gen. John: on Eads proposal, 59, 89, 90, 91; and federal lobbying effort, 65, 100; honoring of, 190; on Howell proposal, 98; mishandling of harbor improvements, 103–104
New West and Gulf Coast Association, 46
New York Times, 99
Nichols, W. H., 25

Nimmo, Joseph, 92, 93
Noel, P. G., 138
Norfolk trade convention of 1868, 19

O'Brien, G. W., 139, 155
Ochiltree, Thomas P., 86–87, 90, 94–95, 98
O'Connor, Laing and Smoot, 190
Oklahoma Territory. *See* Indian Territory
Olds, George, 47
Omaha, Nebr., 46–50
Onderdonk, Andrew, 114–15
Orth, G. S., 54
Osborn, Thomas A., 41
Outer Bar at Galveston, 28–30, 34, 52, 70
Overton, Richard C., 109, 110, 112
Owens, Joe A., 135

paddlewheel steamers, 3–4
Paddock, B. B., 138
Padre Island, 125, 130, 158, 161–62
Palmer, Gen. William J., 106, 109
Panic of 1873, 49–50, 60–61, 63, 67–68, 108–109
Parsons, Col. William H., 17
party politics: and slowness of legislative process, 169–70; and timing of debate, 170–71
Patten, N. B., 17, 25, 30
Peirce, Col. Thomas W., 74
Pelican Island, 11, 57, 160
Pelican Spit, 11, 58, 160
Penland, Samuel M., 115
Perkins, Bishop W., 149, 174, 180
Peters, Samuel R., 180
Philadelphia commercial convention of 1868, 19
Philadelphia Times, 96
Pierce, Franklin, 20
piers. *See* jetties
pile jetty design: construction of, 16–17; critique of, 31–32; vs. dredging alternative, 13–14; effectiveness of, 26–27; funding effort for, 25; improvements for, 30–32; plans for, 11, 21–22
Plumb, Preston B., 148, 151, 166, 180
Plumly, B. Rush, 15
pontoons, as tools for ship movement, 24

population trends. *See* demographics
Port Aransas. *See* Aransas Pass
Porter, George L., 45
Porter, L. B., 137, 156
Powell, Maj. John Wesley, 140
Powell, William H., 41
press, the: attacks on Galveston, 96, 99–101; in defense of Eads, 103–104; Galveston's courting of, 128–29; on Gov. Evans, 111; on intrastate deep water competition, 132–33, 165; on Midwest trade with Galveston, 38–39, 40, 44; Western States and deep water, 128, 136, 144, 149. *See also Galveston Daily News*
Price, William T., 99
private industry, federal government support of, 193–94

Quin, M., 43
Quinn, Lt. James B., 62–65, 66, 190

railroad development: costs of, 150; Denver to Texas, 107–13, 128; and eagerness for immigrants in west, 122–23; economic impact of, 3, 9, 10–11, 35, 51, 53, 68, 92, 119; federal role in, 27, 109–10, 194; Galveston connections, 4, 6, 8, 28, 34–36, 62, 70–78, 105–106, 185–86, 188, 191–92; and harbor improvements, 82, 84, 146; local development of, 121; promotion of, 21; rate competition and, 43–50; Southern need for, 19; state role in, 75; Western need for, 37–41, 151
Randall, Samuel J., 100
Rangel, Gustave, 43
Rankin, Joseph, 92
Ransom, Matt, 172
Rayne, Robert P., 12
Reagan, John H.: election victory of, 118–19; on Engineers' commitment to deep water, 79; and federal lobbying effort, 82–83, 87, 94–95, 98, 126, 142, 165; Jubilee activities, 181; and presidential visit, 186; and Topeka Deep Water Convention, 149
real estate investment, 135, 156–57, 192
Red Fish Bar, dredging of, 29

Shearn, John, 45
Shepard, Col. C. B., 20
Shepard, Seth, 104
Sherwood, G. H., 25
Sherwood, Lorenzo, 38
shoreline changes, and difficulties of deep water channel, 58
Shuegart, E. S., 49
Simpson, A. J., 48
Simpson, J. B., 122
Sinclair, William H., 179
Skinner, James D., 89–90, 115, 122, 146
Sledge, R. J., 125
Sloan, Samuel, 71
Smith, Lt. Col. Jared A., 145, 190
Smith, John Peter, 86, 124, 126
Smith, Williamson, 18
Somerville, Albert, 33
Sorley, James: commercial convention role, 17; and federal lobbying effort, 54, 89–90, 92; and Midwest trade, 45; and railroad rate negotiation, 43, 49
South, the: Galveston's withdrawal from customs of, 8; tariff opposition of, 23–24; trade as key to independence for, 19
Southern Commercial Convention of 1871, 17–18, 27
Southern Pacific Railroad, 73–78, 105, 185–86, 191–92
South Pass, 91
Southwest, the, economic future of, 71
Southwest Pass of the Mississippi, 56
Spalding, Charles C., 38–39
Speake, John, 17
Sprague, W. G., 135
Stanford, Leland, 73
Stanton, Lt. W. S., 11, 13
Stapp, R. B., 25
state government: Galveston development role, 26, 52–53; handling of immigration issue, 123; harbor improvement role, 23, 26–27, 114, 116–17, 134, 142; lobbying for support from, 51, 85–86; regulation of corporations, 72; regulation of railroads, 75
steamship line, proposal for, 71, 72
Stein, Albert, 18, 30–31

Stephenson, Isaac, 167
Stevens, Walter H., 190
Stewart, Charles: and celebration of federal funding, 177, 181; and federal lobbying effort, 104, 125, 126, 155, 166–67, 173–74; and Topeka Deep Water Convention, 149
Stone, D. C., 45
Stone, Eben F., 92, 98
Story, W. R., 138
Stover, E. B., 41
Street, Robert G.: attack on federal appropriations process, 83; and celebration of federal funding, 176; on Eads's death, 119; and federal lobbying effort, 85–86, 89–90, 94; and intrastate competition for port facilities, 132; and local aid for deep water, 114; on state aid for deep water, 116–17
Sumner, Charles A., 92
sundry civil appropriations: advantages of being in, 145; inclusion of Galveston in, 168–69, 173, 180
Swymmer, W. S., 25
Sydnor, Seybrook, 157

Talmadge, A. A., 71
tariffs, Southern opposition to, 23–24
technology, role in Western American economic development, 5
Terrell, Alexander W., 114
Terrell, Ben, 125
Texas, intrastate competition for deep water, 124–25, 129–33, 135–39, 144, 153–64
Texas and New Orleans Railroad, 74
Texas and Pacific Railroad, 70, 73, 74–75
Texas coast, natural workings of, 30–33, 58–59, 67, 153, 199
Texas congressional delegation, 86–88, 93, 121–24. See also federal government
Texas Harbor Improvement and Dock Co., 25
Texas Mexican Railway, 131
Texas Traffic Association, 73
Thayer, Gen. John M., 138
Thomas, C. S., 139

Thomas, John R., 98
Thompson, T. C., 95, 101, 104, 117
Thrasher, Col. John S., 54, 55
Throckmorton, James W., 27
Tiernan, Barney, 25
Topeka Daily Capital, 149
Topeka Deep Water Convention of 1889, 147–49, 150–51
Torrey, John F., 20
Tower, Zebulon B., 59, 65, 190
transportation development: costs of East Coast, 37; history of American development, 23; importance to regional economy, 19. *See also* deep water development; railroad development
Trezevant, J. T., 138
Tribune-Republican, 111
Trinity River, cotton-growing on, 4
Trueheart, Henry M., 122, 124
Tully, Pleasant B., 95
Turner, Frederick Jackson, 140

Union Pacific Railroad, 109–10
United States Military Academy, origins of, 68–69

Van Horn, Robert T., 39–40, 41, 42
Velasco port, 34
Virginia Point, 76, 77

Waldo, J., 45
Walker, A. J., 104, 146
Walker, Aldace F., 191, 192
Walker, Tipton, 11, 14
Wallis, John C., 24, 89–90, 104, 117, 124
Walter, Capt. J. C., 17
Walthew, J. M., 43, 49
Wanamaker, Gen. John A., 186
War of 1812, 23
water storage issue for the West, 139–40

Watts, S. P., 151
Waul, Gen. Thomas N., 54, 187
Webb, Walter Prescott, 5
Webster, Daniel, 23
Wells, Clinton G., 85–86, 89–90, 94
Wells, D. W., 20
West Bay, 57
Western States: cooperation of, 184; economic development of, 4–5, 42, 45; Galveston's desire to exploit, 8–9; Galveston's importance to, 52, 86, 133–41, 176, 186; increasing political power of, 163–64; political issues for, 150–52; railroads as connection to, 37–39; scarcity of population in, 36; support for Galveston port, 108, 113, 121–24, 128–29, 133–49, 166
West Point Academy, origins of, 68–69
Wharf Company, 96, 100, 132, 139
wheat production, 6, 43, 70
White, John D., 93
White, W., 122
Whitney, Charles, 76
Wilbur, Col. H. R., 48
Wilcox, W. P., 48
Willett, John, 161
Williams, Isaac, 12, 13
Willie, Asa H., 60, 61–63, 65–66
Willis, Albert S., 92, 93, 97, 98, 101
Willis, Richard S.: and federal lobbying effort, 89–90, 92, 105, 124; and immigration support, 123; on Topeka convention, 152
Wilson, James R., 54
Wright, Gen. Horatio G., 10–11, 59, 65, 79, 190

Yard, Nahor B., 12
yellow fever epidemics, 11, 22